Evelyn Wood, V.C.: The Ashanti, Gaika & Zulu Wars

Evelyn Wood, V.C.: The Ashanti, Gaika & Zulu Wars

The Campaigns in Africa 1873-1880

ILLUSTRATED

My Zululand Experiences

Evelyn Wood

Ashanti to the Zulu War

Charles Williams

LEONAUR

Evelyn Wood, V.C.: The Ashanti, Gaika & Zulu Wars
The Campaigns in Africa 1873-1880
My Zululand Experiences
by Evelyn Wood
Ashanti to the Zulu War
by Charles Williams

ILLUSTRATED

FIRST EDITION

Leonaur is an imprint of Oakpast Ltd

ISBN: 978-1-78282-776-4 (hardcover)
ISBN: 978-1-78282-777-1 (softcover)

http://www.leonaur.com

Publisher's Notes

Contents

Introduction 7

1873—Ashanti 11

1873-4—At the Head of the Road in Ashanti 25

1874-8—Aldershot: South Africa 46

1878—The Gaikas and Perie Bush 64

1878—From King William's Town to Utrecht 84

1878—Preparations for War 96

Christmas 1878.—The Invasion of Zululand 105

1879—In Zululand 122

1879—The Inhlobane, 28th March 134

1879—Kambula, 29th March 145

1879—The Prince Imperial 159

1879—Ulundi 168

1879—Complimentary Honours 178

1880—H.I.M. The Empress Eugénie 186

Ashanti to the Zulu War 193

Sir Evelyn Wood V.C.

Introduction

The British Empire was undeniably a unique military and political achievement in world history. Britannia in the form of the Royal Navy 'ruled the waves' and the British Army almost continually fought colonial wars until the map of world 'turned red'. Yet the Victorian era's influence, for all its successes and innovations, has ultimately become defined in the public imagination by its jingoisms from the 'bull-dog breed' to the 'stiff upper lip'.

Of course, there actually were 'stirring deeds that won the Empire' including pitched battles against exotic enemies across the globe in which every soldier dressed in red fell or where 'the Gatling was jammed and the colonel was dead' or where resolute bands of British or colonial troops led by able and resolute officers through courage and tenacity prevailed against the odds to keep the Union flag flying so that civilisation as the Victorians saw fit to mould and enforce it marched forward.

The British Empire created some truly remarkable and dedicated officers who believed in the empire and all it stood for; personifying its principles and values in every fibre of their beings and prepared to shed their blood in its maintenance. In the pantheon of the British Empire appear the names those officers who could genuinely be said to have significantly contributed to making the British Empire 'great'.

These military men were once as famous as the most renowned modern celebrities, familiar to those who study the period today, but largely forgotten by everyone else. Many have been dignified in stone in the towns and cities of the British Isles and internationally and it is probably fair to speculate that most of the people who pass by their statues have no idea who they were or what contribution they made in the service of their nation. In fact, it would not be unfair to suggest that most people have little inclination to discover who these people were to the extent of reading the inscriptions on the plinths of these memorials. Time moves quickly on making yesterday's men irrelevant and notions of imperialism or colonialism are not as popular as they once were.

This introduction is not the place to present a list of these now largely neglected men and women. It is assumed that any potential reader of this book has some knowledge of the subject and will know who most of them were. It is sufficient to acknowledge that, without much expectation of dissent from the informed reader, the subject of this book, Henry Evelyn Wood may be counted among their number as an example of the most outstanding kind.

Wood was one of those remarkable men whose life as a soldier was so full of incident in many countries and conflicts that his career could almost be the subject of fiction. George Macdonald Fraser's wonderful fictional rogue and unabashed coward, Harry Flashman comes to mind as a character who invariably (though reluctantly) found his way to places where the soldiers of the Queen Empress were covering themselves in blood and glory and that implicitly implausible coincidence is an essential part of the entertainment and humour of the Flashman series.

Evelyn Wood, of course, was as far from Harry Flashman's personality as it is possible to imagine for no one has the letters V.C. appended to their names for inconsequential reasons. Nevertheless, in reality, wars came Wood's way (or he put himself in their way) with a frequency to rival those of the fictional Flashman throughout the Victorian era. Indeed, during his long career he served in the Crimean War, the Indian Mutiny (where he won his Victoria Cross), The Third Anglo-Ashanti War, against the Kaffirs, The Anglo-Zulu War, The First Boer War and the Mahdist War in the Sudan. Seniority eventually removed him from campaigning and he became in due course acting Commander in Chief of the Forces and a Field-Marshal.

It would be astonishing if Wood's career (which began incidentally in the Royal Navy as a young midshipman, but which he had to quit because he suffered from vertigo) had not attracted the attentions of a biographer and that book is as lengthy as Wood's long career would ensure it would be. Furthermore, Wood wrote a substantial and entertaining autobiography. There can be little doubt that those readers who are interested in the man rather than the campaigns in which he took part will be well rewarded by reading both these books in their entirety since they inevitably reveal different perspectives of their common theme.

However, this book has been created based on a different set of criteria. Firstly, students of military history often focus their studies on those particular periods, campaigns and wars which are their particular interest irrespective of the personalities who served in them and pulling those details from a larger, more expansive work can be something of a chore. It is also the case that details of a long career where an officer has become senior in rank can be rather dry reading in the later stages of that career as the subject's role becomes increasingly administrative. Similarly, long passages about family background and life, school days and periods of peacetime soldiering and sporting and travel activities are rarely what the modern reader of military history finds most interesting. These soldiers are most interesting at the peak of their powers as soldiers when they were at a rank which ensured they would have some influence on events, but that they would still be in the heart of the action on the field of conflict. In the case of Evelyn Wood this period was arguably during the 1870's when the British Army was engaged in sub-Saharan Africa. Finally, this consideration is particularly relevant to the many students especially interested in the wars against the Ashanti, Gaika (Kaffir) and Zulu tribal peoples.

The publishers are aware that the Anglo–Zulu War is particularly fascinating to many aficionados of the history of the British Army and Evelyn Wood's actions in that conflict on Hlobane Mountain and at the battle at Kambula are particularly interesting and, of course, covered in considerable detail in these pages. The action at Kambula is particularly noteworthy in contrast to the debacle at Isandlwana as a demonstration of the successful defence of a fortified British camp in the face of overwhelming Zulu numerical superiority when that action was commanded by a talented and determined officer.

Ultimately, this book, concentrating on Evelyn Wood's western and southern African campaigns is designed to present an entirely focused view of the man and his campaigns during this period by combining biographical and autobiographical content within a single manageable volume. Additionally, maps and illustrations appear in the proper places which were absent from any of the original editions. Although this book has been edited from two much larger works nothing from either of them is absent from this book which is pertinent to its intended subject material.

Leonaur Editors, 2018

SIR EVELYN WOOD V.C.

CHAPTER 1

1873—Ashanti

In the month of August, 1873, I was sent to Rugeley, in Staffordshire, as the staff officer of General Sir Daniel Lysons, who taught me more of the details of camp life than anyone else under whom I have served. In the month of May I had chanced to go into Sir Garnet Wolseley's office in London and found him poring over a Dutch map of Ashanti, and he told me, in reply to my question, that there was a king there who required a lesson to bring him to a sense of the power of England. I said laughingly, "There is a river halfway—the Prah—I will steer your boat up;" and he turned round sharply, saying, "So you shall, if we go." It was while going up that river many months later that Sir John Commerell was wounded.

I had been only a few days at Cannock Chase when I received a letter from Arthur Eyre saying it was known at Aldershot that an Expedition was about to start for the West Coast (of Africa) and asking me to interest myself in his behalf. I did so readily, from the following circumstance. When riding one afternoon with my wife in the previous autumn, I noticed Eyre trying five hunters in succession over the practice-jumps under Tweezledown Hill.

The horses had been bought by brother-officers at Tattersall's two days before, and their owners preferred that their capabilities as hunters should be tested by some person other than the purchasers. Marking the look of determination with which Eyre rode, fixing his eyeglass by contracting the muscles of his brow, I observed to my wife, "If I go on service again, that boy shall come with me." So, on receiving Eyre's note, I endorsed it with the curt remark, "The son of a good soldier, his mother is a lady;" and he was selected.

It was the end of the month when I received a telegram from Sir Garnet Wolseley:

We go out on the 12th September. You go with me on Special Service.

Sir Garnet's original intention had been to take two battalions, each about 1300 strong, made up of picked men from the most efficient battalions in the army at home, each of which was to furnish a company under its officers, and I was to have commanded one of these battalions. The commander-in-chief, however, vetoed this principle, which has, nevertheless, since been accepted in the organisation of Mounted Infantry Regiments, and Sir Garnet was told he was to try and do the work with what natives he could enlist, and that if he failed he might have the three battalions first on the roster for Service. This sound principle where large numbers are concerned was very unsatisfactory when every man, whether an officer or in the ranks, was of value.

My soldier-servant. Private Rawson, begged leave to be allowed to go with me, but the Secretary of State refused his permission in a letter the wording of which, considering that 25 officers were embarking, is peculiar:

Mr. Secretary Cardwell considers that the climate is particularly fatal to the constitutions of Europeans.

On receipt of this quaintly worded refusal, I wrote to the Army Purchase Commissioners—I having been a purchase officer up to the rank of Major—to ask what I was worth that day, in other words, how much the country would give me if I retired and received for answer the sum of £4500.

I had declined to join in the petition to Mr. Cardwell, which was originated and put forward by two of my friends who are still happily alive. One of them, however, having been an Artilleryman, had paid nothing for his steps. The claim in the petition to have the purchase-money returned at once was not only illogical, but if granted would have been grossly unfair; for if A had purchased over B, B would undoubtedly have resented A getting his money back and retaining the seniority that he had purchased with the money.

It was stated, and I believe with accuracy, that if the petitioners had confined their request to the Secretary of State that the money should be payable to their heirs on their decease, Mr. Cardwell would have supported the application. But as the matter stood, on accepting promotion to the rank of general, I, like my brother purchase officers, helped the Consolidated Fund of the Nation.

The steamer in which Sir Garnet and his staff left Liverpool on the 12th had been newly painted, which added to our discomfort She rolled so heavily as to throw a watch out of the waistcoat pocket of one of the staff overboard as he leant over the ship's side, and on more than one occasion we thought she had turned turtle as we were all tossed out of our berths. We reached Cape Coast Castle on the morning of the 2nd October. I was sent to Elmina, a Dutch fort, about 12 miles off, to the west of the chief village of the settlement.

★★★★★★

The fort, St. George della Mina, named from the gold mines in the vicinity, is said to have been built by French merchant in 1383, though the Portuguese allege that they built the first fort. The Dutch held it from 1637 to 1872, when England took it over. St George stands on a rock close to the sea, just above high water, and St. Iago, a fort inland, 100 feet higher, commands both St George and the town built on either side of the Beyah backwater.

★★★★★★

There were six officers in the fort, of whom three had fever, and the other two startled us by the offer of "Square-face" (trade gin) instead of five-o'clock tea, and one of them still more so by drinking the glass poured out for but declined by Arthur Eyre, after he had drunk his own. It was, perhaps, more remarkable that they were alive than that they were not well, but the climate at that season was, it must be admitted, intensely depressing.

Amongst my instructions was an order impressing upon me the necessity of exercising great care over the scanty supply of rain water, there being no springs. All the potable water was collected from off the roof of the castle into iron tanks, so before daylight the next morning I went to the issue place, and after a few West India soldiers had been supplied, I was astonished by the approach of a long line of elderly black women, each with a large earthen jar on her shoulder.

"Who are these people?" I asked the interpreter, "and why should they consume our water?"

To which he replied glibly, "Please, sir, all ex-governors' wives have liberty take water." (The English Government took over the fort in 1872.)

I allowed it for the morning, but had the women informed that I could not recognise their claim for the future.

The state of Elmina was peculiar. The Ashantis had attacked the loyal part of the town, which was separated from that inhabited by Ashantis and their friends by the Beyah backwater from the sea, and had been repulsed by Colonel Festing, Royal Marines. The main body

SIR EVELYN WOOD IN CAMPAIGN UNIFORM

of the Ashantis remained at villages about 15 miles from the Coast undisturbed by us until after Sir Garnet Wolseley's arrival

I was instructed to summon the chiefs of the villages who were supplying the Ashantis. Those in the hamlets so close to us as to feel insecure, obeyed my summons; but the Chief of Essaman wrote back, "Come and fetch me if you dare;" the Chief of Ampeene, a village on the coast, sent no answer, but cut off the head of a loyal native, and exposed it to our view. The strangest answer came from another head-man, who was evidently of a vacillating mind; for he wrote, "I have got smallpox today, but will come tomorrow."

I was ordered to punish these men, and without telling any of my officers what I was about to do, collected sufficient natives in the loyal part of Elmina to carry our ammunition, and hammocks for wounded men, into the castle at sunset, and having had the gates locked, spent the night in telling them off as carriers for their respective duties. When Sir Garnet Wolseley and the Headquarter Staff, with some white and black troops, landed at daylight just under the castle, we were able to start within an hour—180 white men and 330 black soldiers.

A small party of Haussas under Lieutenant Richmond led the advance, and then came a section of the West India Regiment under Lieutenant Eyre, followed by sailors and marine artillery, and two companies of marines. For an hour we marched across a marshy plain, often through water, and in one place up to our knees for 100 yards. On each side, as we passed away from the marsh, were wooded undulations, with shrubs bordering the path, which was about a foot wide. Beautiful creepers, purple, red, mauve coloured sweet -peas, and bright yellow *convolvuli* met the eye at every moment

Farther on, the bush, which was in patches only close to the plain, became denser, and occasionally we passed through defiles which, if held by an enemy, must have cost us many lives. We were near the village of Essaman at 7 a.m., when the advance guard received a volley fired at 100 yards distance; occasionally some brave men awaited our approach until we were so close up that the slugs did not spread in the body of the first of our men killed. The enemy stood around the clearing on a hill upon which we formed up, and the 2nd West India Regiment, with the hammocks, became enfolded in dense smoke.

The Special Service officers were serving under the eye of Sir Garnet Wolseley, and apparently wishing to justify his choice in selecting them, adventured their lives freely. Colonel M'Neill, Chief of the

Staff, led the advance. The command of the column was entrusted to me, and Sir Garnet, who was carried in a chair, had no definite duties, which was also the case with his staff, so that they were free to enjoy themselves, which they did by leading the advance with a lively audacity which, whilst it excited my admiration, caused me some uneasiness when I reflected on what might happen if they fell. Led by these staff officers, the column pressed on, and we never again during the campaign advanced so rapidly on our foes.

The enemy left the village of Essaman as Captain Brackenbury, (now General Sir Henry Brackenbury, G.C.B.), and Lieutenant Charteris, (son of Lord Elcho—died of fever), reached it. The surprise of our foes was complete, and we found the place stored with provisions and powder. Having rested for an hour, we marched on to Ampeene, about 5 miles off, situated on the beach. Its chief fled with most of his people, after firing a few shots. It was 12 noon, and the heat was intense as we started, as it had been for the last four hours whenever the Bush was clear enough for us to see the sun. All the Europeans had suffered considerably, and Sir Garnet proposed that we should rest content with what we had done; but I had undertaken to visit the Chief of Ampeene, who had beheaded the loyal native, and expressed my desire to fulfil my promise

Sir Garnet, in the first instance, said I might go on with the native troops only, but the sailors, with whom my relations were always happy, wished to accompany me with their 7-pounder guns; then the marines were unwilling to be outdone by the bluejackets, and thus at two o'clock the whole party went on to the village, a toilsome march of 5½ miles along the edge of the sea, through deep sand. We had no casualties at Ampeene, where Sir Garnet and his staff embarked in a launch for the commodore's ship, returning to Cape Coast Castle, while after destroying the village I turned back towards Elmina, which was reached at 10 p.m. Some of the officers never recovered their health during the campaign after this march. We covered 22 miles, most of the time under a burning sun.

★★★★★★

Sir Garnet Wolseley wrote:—

Cape Coast Castle, 5.38 a.m., October 15th. What hour did you get back last night? I watched you through a glass till you got close to the marines we left on the beach. . . . . . . I have to congratulate you on the very able manner in which you did everything yesterday. I am very much obliged to you. The operations were well carried out, and all your previous arrangements were admirable.

★★★★★★

This action, though not of much importance in itself, was the first successful Bush fight in West Africa, and therefore not only the experience but its result was valuable. All previous attempts had ended disastrously from 1823 downwards. A few white men under the Governor then sold their lives so dearly that the Ashantis quarrelled for his heart, hoping they might assimilate with it his undaunted courage. The details of this fifty-years-old story were remembered, and thus the effect of the fight on the Ashantis, who had hitherto been the attacking party, was great; but the effect on the Coast tribes was even greater.

We had left them, although they were supposed to be under our protection, to defend themselves, until they had ceased to believe in our power or courage to oppose the foe. The orders issued before Sir Garnet Wolseley's arrival were in themselves demoralising; for instance, an officer sent to Dunquah was directed to give "every moral aid" to the Fantis, but he was "on no account to endanger the safe concentration of the Haussas under his command."

The Chiefs of the Fantis gave the same sort of order, for we learnt after the campaign that a king who furnished a contingent of fighting men for our service strictly enjoined his brother, who commanded them, not to venture under fire on any account, whatever the white officers might say.

Sir Garnet Wolseley in his despatch dwelt on the moral effect of the expedition into the bush, and two months later received the approval of Her Majesty.

★★★★★★

I have Her Majesty's commands to convey to you and Lieutenant-Colonel Wood, who under your general direction was in immediate command, Her Majesty's approbation. . . . I observe with great satisfaction the terms in which you speak of the services rendered by Lieutenant-Colonel Wood, V.C.

★★★★★★

On the 26th October, leaving Elmina in charge of Captain Blake, and bluejackets of H.M.S. *Druid*, I marched at daybreak to Simio, which I reached about eleven o'clock. I had with me half a company of the 2nd West India Regiment, and 35 Elminas of No. 2 Company, and was joined by a large party of Fantis from the neighbourhood of Abbaye. The latter showed great disinclination to move farther north, and ab-

17

Skirmishing in the 3rd Ashanti War

solutely refused to stop at Simio for the evening. They returned, therefore, to Abbaye, but their chiefs remained with me. I proposed to attack the Ashantis at Mampon next morning and sent to Captain Blake to ask him to come up and help me; but I was not able to carry out my intention, for I was ordered back to Elmina by the general, which, considering what we learnt later of our black allies, was fortunate.

It was some weeks before I raised my (Wood's) regiment of four companies, to something over 500 strong. The 1st Company was composed of Fantis, enlisted near Cape Coast Castle, and it would be difficult to imagine a more cowardly, useless lot of men. The 2nd Company, which was the only one of fighting value, and which did practically all the scouting work, started on a modest footing of 17 men, enlisted generally in the disloyal part of Elmina, or that part sympathising with the Ashantis, and some few Ashanti Haussa slaves that we took in one of our first reconnaissance expeditions.

The 3rd Company, Haussas, had been brought from Lagos, and were described as the sweepings of that Settlement, all the best men available having been previously enlisted. They were first put under the command of Lieutenant Gordon, who had been the moving spirit at Elmina before we landed, but he being sent to the Hospital ship, they were commanded by Lieutenant Richmond, until he in turn succumbed to the effects of the climate.

I was then in some difficulty, but martial law having been proclaimed, the Civil prison was under my jurisdiction, in which there was a fine stalwart black, whom I asked for what he had been imprisoned. He said for attempted murder.

"What made you do it?"

"I was drunk."

"Well, if I let you out, and enlist you, will you undertake not to murder me, drunk or sober?" He promised cheerfully, and I got the advantage of that promise on Christmas Day, which we spent at Prahsu. The sergeant had been of great use, and maintained an iron discipline, in a way of which I could not approve; for he kicked and cuffed every black whom he could reach, and who was not as brave and active as himself. The men therefore hated him. He had remained quite sober until Christmas Day, when I was sent for by one of the officers, who said the sergeant had got a loaded rifle, and had cleared the camp of No. 2 Company. When I reached the spot he was dancing, and mad drunk, defying all and sundry. I told off a dozen men to stalk him, and then approached him unarmed. He recognised me and did not offer to resist.

I walked straight up to the man, saying, "Stop this nonsense, and give me that gun;" and he handed it over. It was no sooner out of his hands than three or four of his men, who had doubtless suffered at his hands, jumped on him from behind, and knocking him down, tied him. This was apparently a sufficient lesson, for he gave no further trouble for the next three months we spent in the country. The Haussa company was later withdrawn, being replaced by 160 men from the Bonny and Opobo Rivers, under command of Prince Charles of Bonny, who had been educated in Liverpool. The men were small, beautifully made, very clever at all basketwork, but with no special aptitude for war.

The 4th Company enlisted in the Interior, east of Sierra Leone, were Kossoos, (wild pigs). They came with a great reputation for courage, saying they preferred to fight with swords, and we gave them naval cutlasses; but their only marked characteristic was intense cruelty. It is said that they did charge on the 31st December under Lieutenant Clowes, who was an excellent leader, after I had been wounded; but although I credit them with the intention, the fighting could not have been serious, as they had few or no casualties. Later on, in the campaign, I personally took an Ashanti prisoner, while scouting at the head of the road, and knowing that he would not be safe away from me, had him put outside my living hut, where he was fed for three days.

I was out of camp for half an hour, superintending the bridging of a stream, when Arthur Eyre ran to me, crying, "Pray bring your pistol; I want you to shoot one or two of these brutes of Kossoos. They have got the Ashanti prisoner away and are practising cutting him in two at one blow."

I hastened to the spot, but the man was beyond human aid, his body having been cut three parts through. I had the Haussa sentry who stood over him brought before me as a prisoner and called upon him to recognise the Kossoos who had taken him away; but the man said he could not tell one Kossoo from another, adding he took no notice, as several men having come with a non-commissioned officer, he understood I wanted the man killed. The Kossoos realised that Englishmen would disapprove of their conduct, for when they were paraded within a few minutes of my arrival, they had anticipated that I should inspect their swords, and every cutlass was bright, and without a sign of the bloody use to which it had been put I learnt afterwards that they had told the Ashanti to stand up, as they wanted to practise cutting him in two at a stroke, and, with the stoicism of his race, the man made no difficulty.

A peculiarity of the battalion was that while the 1st or Cape Coast Castle company could talk to those raised at Elmina, but never would do so, as they were deadly foes, neither company could talk to the Kossoos, or the Haussas, or indeed understand them. There was, however, one advantage in this diversity of language and interests; for whereas corporal punishment was our only deterring power, except execution, and neither company would flog its own men, I made the Kossoos flog the Haussas, and the Haussas flog the Kossoos, and so on all round.

During the month of December, Chiefs Quamina Essevie and Quacoe Andoo came to offer me assistance. I had had a great deal to do with Essevie when I first landed. Andoo was such a fluent orator that we nicknamed him "Demosthenes"; and Essevie, though he said but little, was evidently a man of determination. They both accompanied me on our first expedition to Essaman and Ampeene, twelve days after we landed, with the carriers. Andoo had brought carriers in for me, and when I told him I was going out, he begged to be allowed to go home and do fetish.

I was somewhat inclined to refuse but reflecting that the man had come in on the understanding that he was a free agent, I assented, and he returned at 1 a.m., four hours before we started, and we are still on friendly terms. Essevie joined me early in December with twenty-two sons of his own body begotten, all between the ages of twenty and twenty-three, he himself being a man of about forty years of age, and the finest of the family. He brought also about twenty of his relations, but all his men were engaged on the following terms, which were approved by Sir Garnet, "that we be discharged on the day upon which Lieutenant-Colonel Wood, from any cause whatsoever, ceases to command the regiment."

On the 6th November, in obedience to an urgent order from the general, I made a long march, which lasted from 8 a.m. till 10 o'clock at night, to join him at Abrakampa, which village, held by Major Baker Russell, had been invested by the Ashantis, but whose attack was, however, limited to a heavy expenditure of ammunition.

The morning after I arrived, 1000 Cape Coast Castle men, who had been sent by Sir Garnet to fight under my command, joined me at Abrakampa, and were paraded in the clearing facing the Bush. The order of battle was extraordinary. In the British Army, officers and their men quarrel for the post of honour, but here each company struggled, and edged away to the west, where it was supposed there were fewer Ashantis than in the front (north). The Fantis were fine men in stature, bigger than the Ashantis, and all armed with Enfield rifles. Behind them stood their chiefs, handling whips, and yet again behind the chiefs were Kossoos with drawn swords.

My warriors being ordered to advance, moved forward a dozen paces, while their chiefs belaboured all within reach, and in time drove all the men into the Bush, remaining themselves, however, in the clearing until some of Sir Garnet's Staff assisted me by using "more than verbal persuasion." One gifted officer used so much persuasion to a chief as to break a strong umbrella!

With much shouting and firing the warriors slowly advanced, followed closely by the menacing Kossoos; but once in the bush the Fantis got beyond control, for 100 Kossoos could not drive on 1000 Fantis, and nothing more was done, the Ashantis falling back until a party of Haussas and Cape Coast Castle men cut off their retreat at the village of Ainsa, when a few of them, taking the offensive, put the Cape Coast Castle men into such a panic that they fired into each other, killing 20 of their own men, and coming on the Haussas, who were in the act of crossing a stream, ran over them so hastily as to drown one of the company. They ran on till they reached Cape Coast Castle, 20 miles away, and there dispersed. The general, writing of them, said:

Their duplicity and cowardice surpasses all description.

While the King of Akim told us frankly that their hearts were not big enough to fight in the way the white men desired, yet individuals behaved well enough to satisfy even exacting Englishmen. The personal servants of the staff officers as a rule showed courage in action when accompanying their masters, and the two Elmina chiefs while with me never showed signs of fear—Essevie, the father of many children, being remarkably courageous.

It should be recorded also that the Fantis, when deserting, never stole their loads. Although they dropped them under the influence of fear when fighting was going on, they took the opportunity as a rule of leaving them close to a guard before they ran home.

The women had most of the qualities which are lacking in the men. They were bright, cheerful, and hard-working, and even under a hot fire never offered to leave the spot in which we placed them and are very strong. As I paid over £130 to women for carrying loads up to Prahsu, I had many opportunities of observing their strength and trustworthy character; for to my knowledge no load was ever broken open or lost They carried 50 or 60 lbs. from Cape Coast Castle to Prahsu, a distance of 74 miles, for 10s.; and the greater number of them carried a baby astride of what London milliners used to call a "dress improver."

When I moved into the bush with the few men I had enlisted, although I was immune from fever I suffered considerably from exhaustion. In my *Diary* for the 12th November is written:

> When I got into the clearing where we halted, I could only lie down and gasp.

My head, eyes, and forehead ached, and I remained speechless until I was conscious of being severely bitten, when I struggled up, and obtaining a lantern, found my stretcher was placed on an ant-heap. All the officers, in carrying out work which would only be that of an ordinary day in Europe, were affected by tbs exhausting nature of the climate. Our men behaved badly; but then, as I have explained, we could not talk to them, and the command of the companies constantly changed hands, from officers falling sick. The Haussa company commanded by Lieutenant Gordon, after ten days was put under Lieutenant Richmond, who in his turn became sick, and although he tried determinedly to remain at duty, he never really recovered the exhausting march of the 14th October, except for one week at the end of November, in which he rendered us great assistance by his stoical demeanour under fire.

Another lieutenant spent nearly all the campaign on board the *Simoom*, a Hospital ship lying off Cape Coast Castle. He landed for duty eight times, but only did one march, when he was obliged to return. The climate affected our tempers, too, and most of the officers preceded their words with blows. Eventually, after issuing several orders forbidding the practice of striking or kicking our soldiers, I wrote a memorandum, which I passed round to the officers, to the effect that I would send back to Cape Coast Castle for passage to England the next officer who struck a soldier in Wood's Regiment.

Three days later a man came with a bleeding shin and babbled out a complaint of which I understood nothing but the words "Massa ———."

Calling for the doctor, whose courage in action was only equalled by his more than human kindness to all under his charge, for he never took food or lay down to rest till he had seen all the officers, I said, "Surgeon-Major, examine No. —— and report on his injury, and how he came by it." (As every black man was apparently called Quashi or Quamina, we knew them only by the numbers suspended from their necks.) I did not venture to ask the company commander, for being as straightforward as he was brave, he would at once have answered, "I kicked him," and indeed there could be no doubt that he had done so, for the man's shin was marred with hobnails and mud. The doctor reported in writing:

> I have examined No. ——, and, his statement to the contrary notwithstanding, am of opinion he injured his shin by tumbling over a fallen tree.

I called the officer concerned and read the two memoranda to him, observing, "If another man in your company injures his shins in that way, you will go back to England."

He saluted, and went back to his bivouac, when I said to my friend the doctor, "How could you write such an untruth?"

> To save you from a great folly. I knew if I told the truth you would have sent him home. You have not got a braver officer here, nor one more devoted to you, and you will never be killed in this expedition if he can save your life; that is the reason I told a lie.

I was really very glad, for the occurrence had the desired effect: although I do not pretend to say that no officer struck another black, yet they all realised that I was in earnest in endeavouring to suppress the practice. I sympathised fully with those who lost their temper I Our officers were brimming over with energy, and had to deal with races naturally indolent, and the climate was, as I have said, very trying.

Ten days before I left Elmina, Captain Redvers Buller (General the Right Honourable Sir Redvers Buller, V.C, G.C.B.) came over from Cape Coast Castle, carried in a hammock, and the moment he reached the castle, taking out his note-book, said, "Please order me a cup of tea, and give me some information as quickly as you can."

I asked, "Why this hurry?"

"Because I feel I have got fever coming on, and I am not certain how long my head will last"

He wrote down carefully all I had to tell, and then, having drunk a cup of tea, started back. He soon became delirious and imagined that the Fanti carriers were Ashantis surrounding him. Seizing his revolver, he fired three shots, but fortunately in the air.

The general also suffered considerably, and when I went on board the *Simoom* to see him, I felt doubtful if he would ever get to Coomassie.

We lost touch with the Ashantis for three weeks in November. They were moving back towards the Prah, and avoiding the main track running from south to north until they got clear of our advanced post, which was then near Sutah. I was now ordered to take charge here, the general writing to me:

> There has been a terrible want of energy lately at the head of the road, so I want you to go up there, for I expect very different from you. I will send you some more officers when the next mail comes in. Have the enemy's position constantly under your scout's supervision, so that I may hear when he begins to cross the Prah, as I may possibly come up with 500 sailors and marines and attack him.

CHAPTER 2

1873-4—At the Head of the Road in Ashanti

The day after we occupied Sutah, which the Ashantis had quitted the previous morning, I went out with 6 European officers and 300 men to advance to Faisowah, and left No. 1 Company (the Fantis) at Sutah, to bring up our baggage as soon as some carriers were obtained from the Fanti camps in the neighbourhood. The enemy's rear guard of 4000 men under Amanquatsia had been reinforced two days earlier by 5000 (slaves) fresh troops from Coomassie, and the commander had orders to retake the offensive.

The country in which we were operating was a dense forest of gigantic trees, many 150 feet high, laced together with creepers supporting foliage so thick as to shut out the sun, which we never saw except in the villages; indeed, the light was so dim that I could not read my English letters until we came to a clearing, and the dreary monotony of endless green was oppressive beyond description. There were scarcely any birds or animal life except small deer the size of a terrier, and rats and venomous insects; few flowers, except round the villages, where the undergrowth was not so thick as near the coast

On the other hand, it was close to the villages that most of the fighting, such as it was, occurred, where the system of African cultivation offered good cover to our enemies. They clear the ground by

FOREST SKIRMISHING

fire, then sow, in the ashes of the trees, and when the soil is exhausted abandon the spot, and build another village. This is easy, as four men can make a hut, the walls formed of palm leaves, within an hour. On the sites of these deserted villages there rose lofty vegetation, impenetrable except to naked savages crawling on their hands and knees.

Our track ran almost due north, passing occasionally through swampy ground, there being water up to our knees in one place for over 900 yards.

At 2 p.m. the advanced guard under Captain Furse, 42nd Highlanders, who was acting as second in command of Wood's Regiment, was fired on half a mile south of Faisoo, but drove the Ashanti rear guard back across the river, and from the open ground of Faisowah. He took a prisoner, who, seeing our numbers, advised us not to go on, stating that as it was *Adai*—that is, the Ashanti Sunday—they would not retire. Furze under these circumstances asked for orders. Now, I had been ordered to "harass the enemy, hang on his rear, and attack him without ceasing," so I gave the order "Advance."

When we came under heavy fire in the clearing of Faisowah, I extended Woodgate's Kossoos to the east of the track, and Richmond on the west side with the Elmina company, in which there were 25 Haussa Ashanti slaves, whom we had taken in previous reconnaissances. The Haussas I extended in line behind, intending to pass through them if I were obliged to retire. Sergeant Silver and two white marine artillerymen were with me, using a rocket tube, and their cool, courageous bearing was an object lesson to the blacks who could see them.

There was a heavy expenditure of ammunition for half an hour, when, as I had no reserve of it, and the Ashantis were extending round both flanks, I said to Arthur Eyre, the adjutant:

Now, neither of the men in front of us will come away as soon as they are told, but Woodgate will be the slower, so go to him first, and order him to retire at once; and then come back to me, and you shall go to Richmond.

This he did; and my forecast was correct, for after I had got Richmond and his Elminos safely back through the extended Haussa line, I had to wait for Woodgate. For a mile our retreat was carried out in perfect order, but just south of Faisoo some carriers came up with my Fanti company, which I had left to bring up the baggage, and who, though not actually under fire, fled panic-stricken. They threw their loads down on the ground, unsteadying the greater part of the Kos-

British Infantryman

soo company, and all the Haussas, who rushed along the narrow path on a frontage of 11 men—a path which only accommodated two men abreast in the advance. The Elmina company only kept its ranks; the officers of other companies, Gordon, Richmond, Woodgate, and Lieutenant Pollard, R.N., by holding a few men together, kept back the Ashantis, who followed us up 4 miles.

Our casualties were slight—one killed and eight wounded, while four men who fled into the bush, reappeared, one a month later. The bush on either side was so thick that the Ashantis could only crawl slowly through it, and did not dare come down the path, as they were shot by the European officers. I feared at one time that Sergeant Silver, marine artillery, would be trampled upon till he was insensible, and drew my revolver to keep back the crowd from him. I was just about to fire, when a black man seeing my face knocked down the nearest Haussa who was pressing on Silver and kept back the fugitives until the sergeant recovered his breath. I halted at nightfall, when we had retreated 7 miles, intending to stand; but the Ashantis, imagining I had been reinforced, became panic-stricken, and fled northwards—recrossing the Prah three days later.

Sir Garnet reported:

This attack caused the whole of the Ashanti Army to retreat in the utmost haste and confusion, leaving their dead and dying everywhere along the path.

The effect on the European officers of their exertions on the 27th was marked. Next morning, I was the only effective officer, and spent the day in instructing three companies in aiming drill. I had been on my back on the 16th, after two very long marches extending over twelve hours, although the progress made was comparatively small; but possibly on this occasion the excitement of the fight kept me up, and I did not suffer at all. Lieutenant Richmond was never again effective during the expedition, and the health of his predecessor Gordon was seriously broken; but he had been for months on the Coast prior to Sir Garnet's arrival.

Lieutenant Woodgate struggled on, but some days afterwards I found him lying insensible on the track; and some conception of our duties may be formed when I state he had £132 on him, mostly in silver, for we were all paying carriers as they put down their loads. Arthur Eyre, also, whose irrepressible energy always led him to overtax his strength, had to go on board ship sick, and came back to me only when we reached Prahsu.

The energy of the Commanding Royal Engineer of the Expedition, Major Home, was inexhaustible. I was warned by our surgeon-major that my friend, who was living with me, must break down unless he tried his system less. At the doctor's suggestion, I issued a circular memorandum that:

> Officers under medical treatment were not to go out in the sun without the doctor's sanction.

Home resented this order and told me that he did not intend to obey it A few hours after, on returning from visiting parties cutting a path towards the Ashantis, he intimated his intention of going southwards, and, instigated by the doctor, I begged him to lie down instead. He absolutely refused to do so and told his hammock-bearers—for he was being carried—to proceed. I shouted to the rear guard, composed of men from the Bonny River, to stand to their arms, and then explained to Home that he would suffer the indignity of being stopped and brought back by the little black men, unless he obeyed my order. He did so, and lying down on my bed, desired me to get a messenger to go back to Cape Coast Castle with a letter, reporting me to Sir Garnet. This I did; and he, being too weak to write the letter, dictated it to me, and I steadied his hand while he signed it, for he was in a high state of fever.

I wrote on the outside, "The poor fellow is off his head," and agreeably to my promise sent the messenger off at once. We duly received an official answer to his question whether he was to be considered as under the orders of anyone but Sir Garnet Wolseley. It was to the effect that as Commanding Royal Engineer he received his orders from the Leader of the Expedition, but as an officer he was under the Senior in whose camp he might be on duty.

The Ashantis having recrossed the Prah, I asked that I should have a fortnight in which to teach my men to shoot They, under Major Home's directions, had built barracks for Europeans at every halting-place up to Prahsu, and I suggested that the work at the head of the road should be taken by Major Baker Russell, whose regiment had been at Abrakampa, or some other clearing, for six weeks; but on the day the order was issued the whole of the carriers deserted, and the general was obliged to order Russell's and Wood's Regiments, as well as the men of the 2nd West India Regiment, to carry loads for a fortnight, for without this help the rations for the Europeans could not

The Third Ashanti War

have been got up to the front.

I spent Christmas Day at Prahsu, helping Major Home to build a trestle bridge across the river. The King of Coomassie sent down ambassadors to arrange terms of peace. They were somewhat alarmed on first crossing the river but became reassured when in the camp of Wood's Regiment, where they were kindly treated. Unfortunately, in the afternoon they were shown the action of a Gatling gun, and the sight of the bullets playing on the water in a reach of the river (which is broad at Prahsu) so alarmed one of them, that, by a complicated arrangement of a creeper fastened to his toe and to the trigger of a long blunderbuss, he blew off his head that night. We duly held an inquiry, much to the astonishment of the most important ambassador, who, after listening to the evidence, showed some impatience at our endeavouring to record the facts accurately, and observed, "The man being a coward was afraid to live, that's all."

I was ordered to take the body over the river, that the man might be buried in Ashanti, and the Bonnys being clever at all basket-work, in a very short time made a perfect Hayden's coffin. (So called from the gentleman who proposed in the early seventies openwork coffins for burial in England.) When we were standing round the grave, I was astonished by two of the Ashantis throwing earth on the coffin, in precisely the same reverential way we see at our burial services, and on our return to camp asked the ambassador what was the meaning of it? He said briefly, "For luck," adding a widow always did it at her husband's funeral, hoping that she would thus get another spouse by whom she would have children. Imagining that the custom must have been adopted from seeing our missionaries bury their dead, I asked if the practice had originated since white men came to the country, but he replied that it had been in use hundreds of years earlier.

Before we advanced from the Prah, I received the following original letter from Major W. Butler, (Now General Sir William Butler, G.C.B.):—

Akim Swaidroo,
January 2nd, 1874.

My Dear Colonel—The King of Accassi's queen has been carried off by the Haussas, and her chastity is in danger. Express messengers have arrived to announce her detention at Prahsu when tending plantains. Please do what you can to save Her Majesty's honour—or the plantains—for I cannot make out

32

which is rated at the highest figure by the king. I am *en route* to Iribee—Yours in haste,

W. Butler.

The messenger brought a slip of paper also, with the significant words:

Please send me some quinine.

I had to send Her Majesty back under escort, as she preferred the society of a Haussa to that of the king. Major Butler had expended much energy, and all the ready eloquence for which he is distinguished, in endeavouring to induce the kings to the east of the Cape Coast Castle-Prahsu road, to march with him across the Prah. His reports were a series of buoyant hopes due to the man's indomitable nature, alternating with despair at the successive disappointments which he had to undergo. We heard that he finally crossed the Prah with 3 Fanti policemen, but he was followed a few days later by 400 Akims, who could not be persuaded even by my courageous and persuasive friend to incur any risk from the enemy's bullets.

On the morning of the 30th January, a few minutes after we reached the clearing south of Egginassie, where Wood's Regiment was to bivouac as Advanced guard, Home asked me for a Covering party for the Fanti road-cutters. I walked round and looked at the faces of my seven officers, who were asleep; all had fever. I thought Woodgate looked the brightest, so I awoke him, though he had been on Piquet all night.

"Covering party? Yes, sir; I'll start at once."

"Have some breakfast first."

"Oh no; I've got some biscuit, and there's plenty of water about the track."

That evening Russell's and Wood's Regiments had cut a pathway that would take three men abreast, up to the outpost of the Ashanti Army, which was holding the clearing, and village of Egginassie, the southern end of Amoaful, which gave the name to the fight of the next day.

The general's plan was to advance, with one European battalion, by the pathway which ran from south to north, while a column under Colonel McLeod, 42nd Highlanders, consisting of 100 sailors and marines, and Russell's Regiment, with two guns and rockets, cut a path in a north-westerly direction. A similar column under my command was to cut a path to the north-east

33

The brunt of the fighting was borne by the 42nd under Major Cluny Macpherson, which advanced with great determination, pressing back and breaking through the front line of the Ashantis. As the bush was very dense, this fact was not known to the Ashantis on the east and west, and they continued to work round our flanks, penetrating between them and the 42nd Highlanders on both flanks.

The right column before I was wounded had cut 200 yards of track, the procedure being as follows: two workmen each wielding two cutlasses, slashed at the bush, being protected on either side by sailors or marines. We had been working an hour or two, when besides slugs which rattled round us, fired generally by Ashantis lying prone on the ground, there came several bullets over our heads, fired rather behind us, where I was superintending the advance. I called to the men behind me to go into the bush and see who was firing, and shouted, "42nd, don't fire this way."

At first nobody moved, and with an angry exclamation I ran back, and was parting the thick bush with my hands, when Arthur Eyre, pulling me by the skirt of my Norfolk jacket, protested, "It is really not your place," and pushed in before me.

There was immediately an explosion of a heavy Dane gun, and when the smoke had cleared away, I saw Eyre was unhurt, and he exclaimed, "There are no 42nd men there; the fellow who fired at us is black, and quite naked."

Two or three volleys cleared that part of the bush, but between nine and ten o'clock, as I turned round to speak to a staff officer who was bringing me a message from the general, an Ashanti lying close to me shot the head of a nail into my chest immediately over the region of the heart. Sticks were flying freely all the morning, and when I recovered from the stunning effect of the blow, I asked Arthur Eyre, who was bending over me, "Who hit me on the head?"

"No one hit you, sir."

"Yes, somebody did, and knocked me down."

"No, I'm afraid you are wounded."

"Nonsense! It is only my head is buzzing, I think from a blow."

He pointed to my shirt, through which trickled some blood, and said, "No, you have been wounded there" He helped me up, and said, "Let me carry you back," but asserting I was perfectly able to walk alone, I asked him to stop and ensure the advance was continued I walked unconsciously in a circle round and round the clearing we had made, and so had to submit to being supported back to Egginassie, where the ammunition-carriers and hospital stretcher-bearers had been placed. As most of the enemy were firing slugs, my body could only have been seriously hurt in the spot in which the slug struck; for Woodgate had stuffed my pockets with the War Office note-books, which he asked me to carry, and when I protested, said, "Well, as you are sure to be in front, I should like to save your chest."

My friend the surgeon-major, who had been taken away from Wood's Regiment a fortnight previously, to serve on Headquarters Staff, came to see me, and put a probe into the hole through which the head of the nail had passed. The first doctor who examined me had expressed an unfavourable opinion, based on his diagnosis of the very weak action of the heart.

Noticing my friend's face was unusually grave, I said, "I believe you know I am not afraid to die, so tell me frankly what my chances are."

He replied, "There is some foreign substance just over your heart; I cannot feel it with the probe, and do not like to try any farther, but as you are alive now, I can see no reason why you shouldn't live;" and this satisfied me I was not to die that day.

It, however, was not the opinion of the other medical officers, and the Principal Medical officer of the Expedition, afterwards Sir William Mackinnon, Director-General of the Army Medical Department, a friend of mine, went to Sir Garnet, who was on the west side of the clearing, to ask him to say goodbye to me before I was carried back to a clearing at Quarman, three-quarters of a mile farther south, where it was intended to establish a hospital. Sir Garnet Wolseley has an optimistic temperament, which has carried him onward through his remarkable career, and he absolutely declined to say "goodbye" to me, alleging that he would see me again at the Head of the road within a week, as indeed he did; but Mackinnon said, "No, sir, you never yet saw a man live with a shot in his pericardium."

******

From Sir Garnet Wolseley to Secretary of State for War:—

Amoaful, 1st February 1871.

The officer commanding the columns performed their difficult task most excellently. . . . Lieutenant-Colonel Evelyn Wood, V.C, was wounded, while at the head of his troops."

******

The stretcher-bearers put me down in the clearing, and a man of the Army Hospital Corps dosed me with Brand's Essence of Beef, and brandy, until I somewhat petulantly asked him to leave me alone and attend to somebody who required assistance more.

"But you are very bad, sir," he said.

Ten minutes later the Ashantis attacked the clearing. My Sierra Leone servant, putting my rifle between my feet, and revolver on the stretcher, sat down tranquilly alongside with his Snider. However, the measures for defence taken first by Captain C. Burnett, (now Lieutenant-General C. Burnett, C.B.), and somewhat later by Colonel Colley, (later, Sir George Colley), who managed to be present at every fight or skirmish from the time of his landing, repulsed the attack, which was never serious. Next day there was a skirmish, after which the sailors paid me the compliment of asking Commodore W. N. W. Hewett, (died as Admiral Sir W. N. W. Hewett, K.C.B.), my friend of the Crimea, to get them placed under my command, as they were not happy under a military officer who did not understand them.

The force moved slowly on, and on the evening of the 3rd of February was only 16 miles north of Amoaful. That morning I received a note from Arthur Eyre, lamenting my absence, both for my sake and for that of his comrades, who had worked so hard since early in October. Eyre wrote that Sir Garnet and his staff had forgotten the promise made after our very hard work, that, come what might. Wood's Regiment should be represented when the troops entered Coomassie. Eyre ended his letter:

> Our last company has now been left to garrison a post, and we shall never see Coomassie till it falls.

After reading the pathetic appeal twice over, I sent for the doctor, and in order not to give him any chance, assured him that I was perfectly well. This was not absolutely accurate, for I had been lying on my back since noon on the 31st; but I showed him Eyre's letter, and in accordance with my assurances he sympathetically replied that I might try and overtake the general.

I started half an hour afterwards, and sent a runner to the chief staff officer, Colonel W. G. Greaves, (now General Sir George Greaves, K.C.B.), with a message that I was coming up and intended to carry forward the most advanced company in accordance with the general's promise. I was detained for 5 hours by the *commandant* of a post, who declined to allow me to take on the company until a strong patrol he had sent out returned; but eventually moving at a quarter to six, we marched all night, Furze, Woodgate, and Arthur Eyre. Rain fell in torrents, and it seemed that every step we took forward on the greasy path brought us at least half a pace backwards, but finally at four o'clock we came up with the Headquarters. Colonel T. D. Baker, (later, General Sir Thomas Durand Baker), warmly congratulated me on my arrival, saying:

> The chief is asleep, but he told me to give you his love, and say he is delighted you have come up, and wishes you to take the advanced section of the advanced guard, when we move at daylight.

I took over the duty from my friend Major Baker Russell, who grumbled good-humouredly at my luck in getting up in time to replace him in the forefront of the fight He had enough, however, for we were together all the morning. He observed,:

> As you are here, I must tell you that there is an Ashanti about 60 yards in front of us with a heavy blunderbuss; I hope you won't let him put its contents into you.

We had been ordered to do everything we could to save the lives of the Ashantis, and I took over from Baker Russell a wretched interpreter, himself an Ashanti, whose duty it was to advance with me, calling out in the vernacular, "It is peace, it is peace. Don't fire." This man knew his countryman's position behind the tree, and showed the greatest disinclination to accompany me when, about six o'clock, we advanced; but the ambushed Ashanti fired over our heads.

We were three-quarters of a mile from Ordasu, a village on the River Ordah, which the Ashantis had anticipated holding; for when eventually we drove them out of it, their food was still boiling in the cooking vessels. I spent four hours trying to get the Bonny men to advance. They had never been taught to fire, and their idea was to lie prone on the ground, and, elevating the muzzle of the Snider in the air, fire it as quickly as possible. My friend Essevie, who was there, with a few of the Elmina company, showed the courage which he had always displayed, and kicked and buffeted all black men, including his sons, with the greatest impartiality, to drive them on; but we made little progress.

I think it was a mistake to allow the blacks to head the advance. They had built barracks, they had made bedsteads, they had taken every outpost, no European soldier being disturbed at night, and we should have got on faster if Europeans had been placed at once at the head of the track. There were few casualties—in fact, nearly all were confined to the weak company of Wood's Regiment, which lost 1 officer and 3 men killed and 10 wounded, while the European Regiment supporting us with a strength of 450 men had only 17 men wounded, most of them slightly.

The density of the bush may be realised by this fact: while I was teaching a Bonny man to fire, an Ashanti in the bush discharged his gun so close to the Bonny man's head that the slugs did not spread, and the force of the charge threw the man's body from west to east across the path. While Baker Russell and I were talking, he standing up with the complete indifference to danger he always apparently felt, I ordered Arthur Eyre to kneel down, like the other Europeans, but he had scarcely done so when he was shot through the body, and from the look in his face I saw that his last hours had come. He held up his hand for me to remove his rings, saying, "Goodbye; please give them to my mother."

The bullet had pierced the bladder, and he suffered so terribly, in spite of the doctor giving him all the morphia that his system would accept, that I felt relieved when he died two hours afterwards, (the only surviving child of a widow.) He had accompanied me, except when in hospital, in every patrol and skirmish I undertook, and whenever he foresaw danger invented some excuse to get between me and the enemy. He had inherited his father's impulsive temperament and all his determined courage and was moreover a delightful companion.

When we got into the clearing at Ordasu we halted for an hour, and the 42nd Highlanders coming up with heads erect and shoulders back, moved on into the bush on either side of the track. Colonel McLeod was old-fashioned in his ideas. I never saw him willingly deploy to the right, or outwards. When at Aldershot he was accustomed to deploy to the left and would move his battalion from the left up to the right to deploy back again; but there was certainly no more stoical man in the army when bullets were flying. When he had extended a company, half on each side of the track, he called for the Pipe-Major, and saying, "Follow me," walked down the path, followed by another company. The resistance soon died away, and the column moved on in single file towards Coomassie.

Just before it started. Major T. D. Baker, (later, General Sir Thomas Durand Baker, K.C.B.), came to me and said, "The chief says you are to take over the rear guard." A wounded marine had just been decapitated by Ashantis, who had crossed the path immediately behind the headquarters staff. I protested that I had been walking since 10 a.m. on

COMASSIE, 4th FEBRUARY, 1874

GENERAL SIR GARNET WOLSELEY, TO SECRETARY OF STATE FOR WAR. "IT IS WITH THE GREATEST REGRET I HAVE TO REPORT THE DEATH OF LIEUTENANT EYRE, 90TH LIGHT INFANTRY, WHO WAS MORTALLY WOUNDED IN ACTION. I CANNOT REFRAIN FROM STATING WHAT A GREAT LOSS THE ARMY HAS EXPERIENCED IN THE DEATH OF THIS GALLANT OFFICER."

the 3rd, and to put me on rear guard would result in my not reaching Coomassie till after dark. I mentioned the name of an officer senior to me for the duty, but Baker said, "No, I suggested that, but Sir Garnet wishes you to do it."

Shortly after we left the clearing we came on the body of a chief, who had been shot by the 42nd Highlanders, while near him were three slaves who had been decapitated by one of the chief's relations, for the Ashantis have a theory that when a great man dies he should be accompanied into the next world by slaves as body-servants.

At the southern entrance of Coomassie Lieutenant Maurice, (now General Sir Frederick Maurice, K.C.B.), Sir Garnet's secretary, met me at 9 p.m., and said, "The chief says you are to take up a line of outposts covering the town."

As the night was pitchy dark, I observed, "Where is the chief, and where is the enemy supposed to be, and where am I to go?"

Maurice replied, "I asked him that, and he observed, 'Evelyn Wood is sure to know, leave it to him.'"

I went away a few hundred yards from where I understood the Headquarters Staff was lying, and, halting close to some huts, sent an Ashanti for clean water; for the stream we had just crossed had been polluted by the bodies of human sacrifices. I had barely fallen asleep when a staff officer came to me and told me to fall in my men, and proceed to the palace, which was on fire. I went at once, but the fire was nearly out when we arrived, and I slept till daylight, when I was again summoned, and ordered down to the coast, with a convoy of sick and wounded.

I left Coomassie on the morning of the 5th February, with the remnants of Russell's and Wood's Regiments, and a company of the Rifle Brigade, escorting some 70 wounded and sick Europeans, nearly all the former belonging to the 42nd Highlanders.

Although no serious attack was probable, my charge occasioned me some anxiety. All the wounded who were unable to march were in cots slung on long bamboo poles, carried by eight men, and so in single file, which was the only arrangement of which the path admitted, our line of march extended over nearly two miles.

When Sir Garnet went forward to the Ordah River, the troops accepted cheerfully four days' rations for six, and thus it came about that on the evening we arrived at Ordasu, where Arthur Eyre was buried, except a small bit of biscuit, the wounded had no rations of any kind. Just as we had lifted the cots of the wounded off the ground and placed them on tripods of bamboos, an impending storm broke, the heavens opening, rain fell as it does only in the tropics, and within ten minutes there were 10 inches of water on the ground.

I had ½ lb. of tea and some sugar, which my servant carried in a haversack, and, assisted by Furse of the 42nd, after infinite trouble, I made a fire over a projecting root of a big Banyan tree. In turn we held an umbrella to shelter our fire from the rain, and finally had the satisfaction of raising the water to boiling-point, and into it I put all my tea and sugar. When we had handed round the last pannikin, I said I would have given a sovereign for a tin of tea, and Furse remarked, "I would have gladly given two." Next day we moved onwards, and met a convoy of supplies, so there was no further scarcity. I received orders to halt, send the convoy on with the Rifle Brigade, and remain behind, following the Europeans as rear guard.

The strength of the white soldiers was husbanded, and wisely so, in every respect. They were never put on outposts. Up to the Prah—74 miles, just halfway to Coomassie—they slept in large bamboo huts which accommodated 50 men, provided with comfortable beds, filtered water, washing-places, latrines, cooking-places, sentry boxes, commissariat stores. A hospital and surgical ward was erected every 8 or 10 miles. Everything, in fact, was so arranged that the Europeans had nothing to do except cook their food and lie down on their arrival in camp. All these arrangements were carried out by Major Home, to whom Sir Garnet expressed his warmest thanks.

They were deserved. During the expedition, Home and his officers had cut a fairly smooth track, about 8 feet wide. He bridged 237 streams, laid down corduroy over innumerable swamps, some of which required three layers of fascines, and in one place alone, between Sutah and Faisowah, stretched over 800 yards.

When the Ashantis in their retirement approached the main path, near Mansu, Home was there with 43 natives, and had just built a fort. His men—Fantis—were untrained, and he had only 40 rounds of ammunition. The general ordered him to fall back towards the coast, but Home held his fort, and the enemy, not being able to pass him, moved farther northwards in the bush before they regained the track.

When we were coming down country, some of the worst traits of the Bonny men became evident. They absolutely refused to carry their own sick and wounded, and after I personally coerced 8 men into carrying a Bonny who was very ill, when I had gone back to look for another sick man on the line of march, they deliberately carried their comrade into the bush 50 yards off the track, and there left him to die. The exertion of walking from front to rear of the column was great, and thus it was that, when coming along slowly—for I was suffering from intestinal complaints and could walk only by resorting frequently to laudanum and chlorodine—I heard a noise in the bush which attracted my attention. My servant told me he thought it was nothing, but I persisted in looking, and there found the Bonny man whom I had put into a hammock an hour earlier.

I had him carried to the next encampment by some of Baker Russell's men, and upbraided Prince Charles, the captain of the company, who spoke and wrote perfect English, for the conduct of his men. They, however, received my reproaches with apparent unconcern. Next morning, I arranged that the Bonny company should march behind the sick; but when moving off. Prince Charles informed me that his men absolutely refused to carry, saying that they never regarded a sick and wounded man in their own country, and always left him to die.

I halted the Kossoo company, and directing them to cut some stout bamboos, told the Bonnys that I should begin with the right-hand man, and unless they picked up their sick comrade they would suffer severely until they obeyed orders. They refused, so I had the right-hand man thrown down and flogged until I was nearly sick from the sight. Then I had the next man treated in a similar manner, but he received only 25 lashes when, turning his head, he said, "I will carry." The company then gave in, and undertook to carry their comrade down to the coast

Two marches farther on, from the carelessness of an interpreter, and the peculiar reticence of the native character, I nearly had a man flogged unjustly, the remembrance of which would have been very painful to me. The native soldiers for choice carried everything on their heads, blanket, ammunition, rifles and cooking-pots, and thus when a shot was fired in the bush, or a man moved unexpectedly, everything came down with a crash, and as we had several false alarms, I was obliged to provide against this trouble.

This I did by issuing two cross belts for each black soldier. For two successive mornings I noticed that one man in the Elmina company was still carrying loads on his head. I fined him a day's pay, and when I saw him disobeying orders the third morning I had him made a prisoner. He still refused to carry his kit except on his head, so I sent for the doctor, and said to the Elmina, "When the men have eaten, I shall flog you."

While I was having a cup of cocoa, a deputation came to the tree under which I was sitting, to beg their comrade off, saying, "You have put us in front on every occasion; when you, or your white officers went out, whether they belonged to our company or not, we have always escorted them, and we beg you will not flog this man"

I explained that he must obey orders. They still gave me no indication of why the man had refused to obey orders, but when I saw him and asked for a reason, he replied simply, "The belts hurt me;" and on my further questioning him, he opened the front of his shirt, and showed a deep hole in his body, which he had received from a slug in action at Ordasu, and into which, without troubling a doctor, he had stuffed a lump of grass! I rejoiced in my persistence in questioning the man, which was the means of saving me from doing a great injustice.

I spent some anxious days at Elmina on my return, for Arthur Eyre had kept all such public accounts as we had, as well as my private accounts, and I provided the food and liquor for all the officers of Wood's Regiment, charging them the actual cost, and although my friend had kept accurate accounts up till his death, it was difficult for me to arrange satisfactorily with the officers, who seldom messed with me four or five days at a time. Finally, I embarked on board the *Manitoban*, and came home with our general, to whom the success of the Expedition was due. When he went out there was a cloud of evil auguries; advisers differed, and the causes of anticipated disasters varied, but nearly all predicted failure.

The successful result was due primarily to Sir Garnet Wolseley. His mind it was that animated all, for to his other great qualities he added that fire, that spirit, that courage, which gave vigour and direction to his subordinates, bearing down all resistance. Everyone acknowledged his superior military genius, and when, on coming home, I was asked by the adjutant-general and the military secretary what my brother-officers and I thought of Sir Garnet, I replied, "If he had gone down, I doubt whether there was any man big enough to have entered Coomassie with only one day's rations."

As I was leaving Elmina, I said to my friend Essevie, "You have done very well throughout the four months you have served with me, and I should like to send you a present from England. Have you any preference?"

After a moment's reflection, (he wore only a small loin-cloth on his gigantic body), he replied, "Well, I should like a tall black hat" Before the ship sailed, however, he wrote me a letter, asking if I would sell him one of my umbrellas.

I sent him both as a present; but the request put another idea into my head, and on reaching London, having ordered him a 23*s*. Lincoln & Bennett black hat of the largest size ever made, I called on Mr. Lawson, Secretary of the Army and Navy Co-operative Society, and said I wanted him to make the biggest umbrella ever seen—the sort of thing which would take two men to carry—and with a different and startling colour between every rib. "Do you know that will cost you over twenty guineas?"

"Possibly; but I should like to send a black man something of which he may be proud." And he booked the order. A few days later he wrote to me that, as I probably knew, my idea was not original, and he had found in the City an umbrella such as I desired, which had been ordered by the Colonial Office for a chief on the Gambia River three years previously; but the sable potentate having misbehaved, the umbrella was still on sale, for, as Mr. Lawson quaintly wrote, "There is no demand." He bought it for me for £12, and also made for me a ten-guinea walking-stick, ornamented with gold bosses, and the hat, umbrella, and stick, on receipt at Cape Coast Castle, were handed over to Essevie and Andoo, on a full-dress parade of the garrison, which marched past these somewhat unusual emblems of honour.

Twenty-two years afterwards, my eldest son took part in the next expedition to Ashanti and was sitting one day in the market-place of Coomassie, when he saw a native carrying a handsome gold stick. He, like most Englishmen, thinking that money would buy anything that a black man possessed, called to him, "Hey, sell me that stick."

The man replied, "I cannot; it belongs to my chief."

"Oh, he will take £5 for it"

"No," said the man, "he would not take any money for it;" and somewhat unwillingly he handed it over for closer inspection.

My son read on it, "Presented to Chief Andoo by Colonel Evelyn Wood, 1874." Essevie was dead, but Andoo still lives, (1906), and was in Coomassie with the Expedition of 1895-96.

My mother was staying at Belhus, the seat of Sir Thomas Barrett Lennard, when I arrived home, and the tenantry and local friends gave me a great reception, as did, a week later, the 90th Light Infantry; for when I went down to stay with the officers at Dover, the regiment turned out and carried me up the heights to the barracks in which the regiment was quartered.

A MAP
TO ILLUSTRATE THE
ASHANTI CAMPAIGN
1873-4.

CHAPTER 3

1874-8—Aldershot: South Africa

Soon after our return from the West Coast we were honoured by a command to Windsor, officers of the rank of lieutenant-colonel and upwards only being invited to dine at the royal table and to remain the night at the castle.

I had intended to postpone being called to the bar, but my friend and tutor Captain Blake, Royal Marines, thinking I might be too busy later to read further, advised me to apply at once, and I was called during the Easter term.

At a dinner given by the lord mayor to Sir Garnet and the Ashanti warriors, I sat near the prime warden of the Fishmongers' Company, and in the course of conversation he learnt I was a grandson of Sir Matthew Wood, which resulted in my being invited to join the livery of that company, which I did a few weeks later.

At another civic feast I sat next to a retired rear admiral, who was annoyed at Sir John Glover's name being noted to return thanks for the navy. This was a mistake; for Glover, one of the most indomitable of men, had left the navy as a lieutenant, with the honorary rank of captain, and the admiral had reason, therefore, for his vexation, which he showed throughout the dinner. He presumably must have seen my name on the plan of the table, which he studied from time to time. In an interval between two speeches he expressed to me an opinion shown by the following conversation:—

"A great deal of unnecessary fuss is being made over these men who have been to Ashanti."

"Yes, sir"

"They have done just nothing at all to what I did when I was there."

"Pray, when was that, sir?"

"In 1823."

"Oh, that was when Sir Charles Macarthy was killed?"

"Why, were you there?"

"No, sir, I wasn't there,"

"Oh, but you must have been—you know about it."

"No, I wasn't there, but it has been my business to read about what took place before we went there."

"Well, I will tell you a remarkable story of what happened to me that year. We were going up the Niger to attack a village at daybreak,

WOOD AND HIS STAFF AT ALDERSHOT

and although the days were hot, the nights were cold, and I was wearing two pairs of trousers. We were fired on before we reached the village, and a ball from a *jingal* nearly as big as my fist went in at my hip, wrapping round it bits of both pairs of trousers."

"Really, sir, I am thankful you are alive here tonight to tell the tale."

"Yes, but more wonderful still, that ball went through my body and came out the other side."

I had been sipping wine for three hours, and perhaps being nettled by the admiral's disparaging remarks on my friends, observed quickly, "What, sir, and both pairs of trousers wrapped round it?"

The moment I had spoken I reflected that he had distinguished himself in trying to reach the North Pole, that he was old, and I had been disrespectful; but I was immediately relieved by his cheerful answer, "Yes, and that's the most extraordinary part of my story—the bits of both pairs of trousers came out with the ball!"

I received three months' leave for the recovery of my health, at the end of which I had hoped to join the Headquarters of my battalion at Dover, but the lieutenant-colonel then in command did not wish to have a full colonel with him, who would often, in field operations, have command of the brigade, and persuaded my brother-officer and junior. Major Rogers, to come from the Depot to Headquarters.

I joined at Hamilton on the 1st July, and the officer in command of the depot, when I called on him, said to me politely, "Now, Colonel, there is only enough work for one of us here, and I am fond of work."

I said, "May I assume, then, that it is a matter of indifference to you where I live, or how often I come into barracks?"

"Quite so," he assured me. "Come when it suits your convenience, no oftener."

So, I lived pleasantly for two months in the Manse at Dalserf, immediately over Mauldslie Castle, at which my wife and I spent half of each week.

The miners, who lived all around, were then earning high wages, and I had great difficulty in obtaining milk for my family, until I called on a farmer and asked him as a favour to let me have some, I sending for it. He assented, though not graciously, observing, "Every man should keep his ain coo."

Early in September I was ordered to Aldershot as Superintending officer of Garrison Instruction, with my office at that camp. Some years previously there had been a serious outbreak of scarlatina at Sandhurst, and the cadets had necessarily been removed, the college not being re-opened for a considerable time. To educate the cadets, whose studies had been interrupted, as well as with the average intake of candidates through Sandhurst—about 300 *per annum*—classes were formed in the principal garrisons of the United Kingdom, as far east as Colchester, south as Shorncliffe and Cork, and in the north at Edinburgh. The young gentlemen were gazetted to regiments on probation and taught the Sandhurst course as far as possible by Staff College graduates, in classes of from 15 to 25.

My duty was to visit them as often as I thought necessary, and see the Syllabus was duly followed, and that Instructors and pupils were doing their best for the service. I learnt a good deal about schools in England, for as a rule I talked to all the young men in the class, and they, with the feeling that they were in the army, gave me valuable information as to our public schools, the general tone of which was, according to the information I received, undoubtedly very high.

The difficulties at some stations in the way of regular teaching and progress were serious, where the temptations for asking leave of absence were unceasing. One instructor complained bitterly to me.

"Although I have got," he said, "as gentlemanlike a set of young men under instruction as it is possible to find in the whole world, it has been heart-breaking to try and keep them together for concerted work. First of all, their mammas and their sisters wanted them to dance all night, while by day they were constantly away at Epsom, Ascot, and Goodwood. Then I hoped, the Season being over, I should get them to work, but with the middle of August came requests for leave for grouse-shooting, followed in September by applications for a few days' partridge-shooting, and early in October out-lying pheasants demanded attention. Now one of the best young fellows in my class wants leave for cub-hunting."

"Oh," I said, "you should put your foot down; tell him to cub-hunt at daylight and get here at ten o'clock."

"He would do that cheerfully," was the answer, "but he is Master of the Hounds, and his kennels are 200 miles from London!"

I enjoyed my life, doing most of the travelling in the summer and early autumn, and enjoying a considerable amount of hunting. I took a house near the Staff College, and after doing a day's work in the office at Aldershot often got a ride in the afternoon with the college drag hounds.

After riding with the drag, about tea-time one evening, my friend Lieutenant E. R. P. Woodgate (later, General Woodgate, mortally wounded at Spion Kop, in the Boer War), walked up from Blackwater Station, carrying his bag, and in his abrupt, decided way said, "Can you put me up for the night? I want to talk to you."

"Yes, certainly."

After dinner, he observed, "I want to go to the Staff College."

"Well, what do you know?"

"I was well taught at Sandhurst, but I have not read much since."

Next morning, I gave him after breakfast a complete set of examination papers, and observed, "Do as much of these as you can, and I will look over them tonight after dinner."

As the result, I said, "With two months' instruction you would probably succeed in the competition for entrance to the college, but it may take you three."

"What will it cost me?"

"About 20 guineas a month."

"Then I must abandon the idea, for I have only got £14 available."

I thought of my friend's case in the night, and next day wrote to a tutor who had been successful in teaching me, and whom I had obliged with a small loan of money some years before. I made no allusion to the loan, but asked him if he would, as a personal favour to me, teach my friend as much as he could for £14. This he did, and so successfully that Woodgate had no difficulty in getting into the college. He reappears farther on in my story.

The Council of Military Education were troubled by the irregularities of Boards of Examination on officers for promotion, for neither candidates nor boards realised the discredit of "obtaining aid from books or other sources," and I was invited to become Examiner for all Boards in Great Britain. Although the suggested salary was tempting, I declined, explaining officers would, if trusted, come in time to see their duty in its true light, while their hands would always be against an individual, whose questions would moreover become stereotyped.

In order to have a little money for my favourite sport of hunting, I accepted the office of Examiner in Tactics, but it was monotonous work reading 100 answers to the same questions.

My friend Major General Arthur Herbert got me appointed to his division for the autumn manoeuvres in the following year, and, on the 23rd April, 1876, I was appointed Assistant Quartermaster-General at Aldershot, where I served with a pleasant, but one of the most determined men I ever met in my career. Colonel George Harman, later Military Secretary. He was a fine horseman, slight in build, but with a handsome, aristocratic face, and never afraid of saying the most unpleasant truths to his superior officers if he thought it was his duty to do so. Not having been to the Staff College, he liked me to arrange the tactical schemes, and to the best of my recollection I framed, and got permission for, the first example of Minor Tactics, in June 1877, to be carried out by field officers. The idea was so popular that the system took root and has been continued to this day. Previously to this drill season no officer under the rank of a general had had, as a rule, the opportunity of handling the three arms of the service in tactical operations.

In the spring of that year, towards the close of the hunting season, I was at my brother-in-law's, going through the accounts of his Irish property, when I received a telegram saying that my eldest son, a child of six years old, was ill, and Surgeon Alcock telegraphed to me to buy some salicylate of soda, which was not then a drug supplied in army hospitals. When my wife and I reached the North Camp, I was warned by my friend Alcock that the child was very ill, with a temperature of 104°, and that unless the salicylate of soda brought his temperature down, he could not live. Alcock explained that the drug, although often given in America, was not in common use in England, and its effect was uncertain, so I watched with intense anxiety the effects of three doses, given in close succession.

We found the boy wrapped in cotton-wool, with his knees drawn up to his chin, and he screamed with the apprehension of being touched before I got to the bedside. Within an hour the painful look in his face relaxed, and after the third dose had been swallowed his knees gradually resumed a natural position, and the child slept, being able the same evening to look at the picture-books we had purchased for him as we passed through London. He recovered, but eight years later had a second, though less severe attack, which obliged me to re-move him from Wellington College, and I was compelled to have him watched with great care for two years, allowing him to do but very little work. I was advised by three of the leading physicians in London, who examined him, that it was hopeless to expect he would be able to do anything but sedentary work.

Six years later, when the lad wished to enter the army, I took him to one of the doctors who had given the unfavourable opinion and asked him to re-examine him, as I should not feel justified as a general in allowing him to go up, unless I were satisfied he was sound, what-ever the Medical Board might decide. After a severe test the opinion

COLONEL WOOD'S QUARTERS, ALDERSHOT, 1876-77

was favourable, and four years later he hunted successfully the regimental pack of foot beagles.

I had what I always consider was a flattering offer about this time from Mr. T. White the outfitter (a miniature Whiteley), who supplied most of the officers and non-commissioned officers of the Aldershot Division. When he was a young man, working in his father's small shop at Hartley Row, on the Bagshot-Basingstoke Road, His Royal Highness the Prince Consort, having induced the Treasury to purchase 10,000 acres, initiated the Aldershot Camp. Mr. White came to Aldershot, which was then only a hamlet, and prospered with the rising town. He was not only my provider, but a friend for many years; indeed, our business relations commencing in 1866 have continued without intermission with the firm until this date, and every time I have gone on service my telegraphic requisition has been, "Send me what you think is necessary."

This confidence has always been justified. When Sir Daniel Lysons commanded the 1st Brigade, he and I worked a good deal with Mr. White, inventing and improving camp equipment for officers, whose amount of baggage was then closely limited; and later the general and I went through Mr. White's books on a proposition being made to start a local ready-money establishment, similar to the Army and Navy Stores.

Mr. White coming to me one day, asked for a private interview, in which the following dialogue occurred:—"Colonel, you have been of great use to me about camp equipment and with your advice generally, and I have been thinking for some time that I should like to make you a proposition, but I hope if it displeases you you will forgive me."

I said, "What is it?"

"Can I induce you to leave the Service, and join me in business?"

"Yes, the subject would require thought as to terms, but if they were sufficiently good I would consider it for the sake of my children."

"Well, may I ask what terms you would require?"

After ten minutes' calculation, I replied, "£3000 a year taken out of your business, and invested in any security approved by me, payable to me as long as I wish to retain it, irrespective of the time and attention I give to the business, or to our agreeing or disagreeing on any points."

Mr. White jumped, nearly falling off his chair, and observed, "£3000 a year is a large sum: pray may I ask what your pay is now, sir?"

"£664, including allowances."

"The difference, you will allow me to say, is very great."

"It is, yet not so great as the difference in serving Her Majesty Queen Victoria and Thomas White."

"Oh, sir, I am afraid I have vexed you."

"No; on the contrary, you have paid me a greater compliment as to my capacity for business than I am likely to receive from anyone else."

In August, my friend General W. Napier, the Governor of the Military College, Sandhurst, offered me the post of *commandant* there, under him. All my relations with him and with his family had been of the happiest description, but I did not like the idea of settling down at Sandhurst before I commanded a battalion; this feeling influenced me again when I was informed I might be considered for the Staff College. Moreover, I thought Colonel Colley, (Maior-General Sir George Colley, killed in action 1881), then Military Secretary to Lord Lytton, Viceroy of India, would make a far better *commandant* of the Staff College in every respect (except in personally encouraging the drag hounds), and I asked a common friend to write and urge him to become a candidate.

Colley replied that he was engaged in too important work, and I hesitated for some time as to whether I should ask for the post. My regiment was amongst the first upon the roster for the Colonies, and the prospect of serving as a major on 16s. a day was not attractive when balanced against the advantages of the Staff College—£1000 a year, a good house, and the immediate proximity of Wellington College, where I intended to send my sons.

When the offer was definitely made, I consulted Sir Alfred Horsford, who had been one of my kindest friends ever since I served with him in the North Camp at Aldershot. I pointed out the pecuniary and other advantages, and when I had ceased speaking, he said, "Do you want my frank opinion?"

"Certainly, sir, please."

"Well," he answered, "accept it; and if your regiment goes on service you will be a miserable man for the rest of your days."

This settled the question in my mind.

Early in November, when coming from Belhus, where Sir Garnet Wolseley (Field-Marshal Lord Wolseley), and Colonel W. Butler (General Sir William Butler, G.C.B.), had been shooting, Butler mentioned in the course of conversation that if worse news came from the Cape, the 90th would be put under orders. Sir Garnet condoled with me, for although he was in the War Office at the time he was not aware of the state of the Roster for Foreign Service. He told me in confidence then, what I had suspected for some time, that we were on the brink of a war with Russia. Indeed, at Aldershot, not long before, I had given a lecture on "The Passages of the Danube and the Passes of the Balkans."

The Ministry had intended to employ another general officer in command, but he having stipulated for a larger number of men than the Government was willing to employ, at all events in the first instance, Lord Beaconsfield's choice fell on Sir Garnet, and he told me how much he regretted that I should not be with him.

I said, "Perhaps Cetewayo will give us a fight," but he replied, "No, Shepstone will keep him quiet until we are ready."

Colonel Butler said, "When we fight Zulus, we shall want 10,000 men, and I shall go out on the second wave of Special Service officers." And so, he did.

The officer commanding my regiment was then, and may possibly have been all his life, a "Glassite," but had latterly accepted the idea that it was immoral to fight. All the time I was at Aldershot I performed his duties on courts martial, as he was unwilling to take an oath. At the end of December, at his request, I accompanied him to London, when he asked that he might be allowed to remain in England, on leave, till the 1st April 1878, when his command would expire, and that I should take out the battalion. (Later he asked to remain on till November 1878, in order to complete thirty years' service, and thus get the full pension of 20s. *per diem*.)

He endeavoured to convey his wishes to the adjutant-general and military secretary, but entirely failed to make them understand his position; indeed, I believe they imagined he was suffering under some physical ailment, for the words he frequently used were, that he "had the strongest reasons for not wishing to go into camp."

He embarked on the 11th January, and on the 27th I followed the battalion, having indeed been very unhappy since I saw them off at Southampton with the band playing "Far away."

The battalion had its complement of lieutenant-colonel and two majors, I (the senior), being on the staff, was supernumerary, so when a month later I was sent out, it was "On Special Service," with the promise given to me verbally by the commander-in-chief, the adjutant-general, and the military secretary, confirmed in a memorandum which was handed to General Thesiger, that I should succeed to the command on the 1st April. But this understanding was not fulfilled

The battalion on arriving at Cape Town was divided; five companies were sent to Fort Beaufort, where the Gaikas were restless, and three companies to Utrecht, in the Transvaal.

When I got to the Amatola Mountains, six weeks later, the five companies were gradually withdrawn from the colonel commanding, and he remained in charge of some Hottentots at Fort Beaufort until June, when he returned home, being retained in nominal command of the Regiment till November, when he completed his thirty years' service.

My fellow-passengers on board ship were General the Honourable F. Thesiger, who was going out to command at the Cape, Major Redvers Buller, and other staff officers. We arrived at East London, British Kaffraria, on the 4th March, and a more uninviting spot than it was then, it would be difficult to imagine. It consisted of corrugated iron huts, surrounded by broken glass bottles and empty jam tins, dotted about on bleak, bare sand-hills, through which the muddy Buffalo River cut an opening 250 yards wide to the sea, depositing a barrier of sand, which up to that time had presented insuperable difficulties to forming a satisfactory harbour, although the problem had engaged the attention of the most eminent of our British Marine Engineers. There were no roads; the so-called hotel provided shelter and food, but while there were bath towels there were no baths, and the one closet was common to whites of both sexes and Kafir servants.

A few days before our arrival, two boatmen had been washed off a lighter in crossing the bar and drowned, as capsizing in a heavy roller it remained upside down. This fact, and the prospect of being battened down in a chamber with my horses, and tossed about in the rolling waves, added considerably to the interest of the arrangements for passing through the breakers, which all of my companions preferred to undertake in a lifeboat. This alternative was not open to me, as I felt bound to accompany the groom and my horses; but nothing occurred, except that in two successive heavy waves as we crossed the bar the horses were knocked off their feet

The general and his staff were going to King William's Town, 50 miles distant, to which place there was a railway. I had no difficulty about a horse I bought from a Dutchman at Cape Town, but a well-bred, weight-carrying hunter named "War-Game," standing 16.2, could not be fitted in any horse box or truck available, and I handed it over to a Kafir with orders to lead it up to "King," the familiar local abbreviation of the chief town of the eastern provinces. Later, hearing of a larger truck up the line, I succeeded in getting the horse safely to the settlement, and it falsified all the predictions of those who advised me that an English horse would be useless for service in South Africa. "War-Game" was knee-haltered and turned loose with the horses of my companions, although in the Transvaal, on account of horse-sickness, I stabled him in wet weather wherever shelter was available. The animal kept his condition and was brought home at the end of the Zulu War, carrying me well to hounds for many seasons. He was very troublesome onboard ship, for in the rough weather we experienced near Madeira he got his foot over the front of the box, which was on deck, and at another time had both hind feet over the side of the ship at one moment.

The general relieved by Lieutenant-General the Honourable F. Thesiger had reported that the war was over. This was accurate as regards the outbreak in the Transkei. In that open country the Galekas in attacking our fortified posts had been easily defeated, without inflicting any loss on our people; but coincident with the general's arrival at King William's Town, the Gaikas under Sandilli broke out in rebellion, and moved westward towards the Buffalo Range, a lower feature of the Amatola Mountains.

Sandilli, born in 1822, had fought against us in the wars of 1846, 1848, and in 1850-53, and commanded a devotion from his followers which he did not deserve. He had, so far as I know, no redeeming trait in his character. When he was twenty years of age, he assented to his mother (she was rescued by a missionary), being put to death by torture, by the advice of witch doctors, a profession which might easily, and should have been suppressed in 1857, when one of these pests persuaded the Kafirs on the Kei River to destroy everything edible, with the result that 67,000 died of starvation. Sandilli was born with a withered foot, so could not lead his men in action, who nevertheless, such is the tribal spirit, would accept death to save him. In all the previous wars from 1835, in the time of General Sir Harry Smith, to that of General the Honourable Sir George Cathcart, 1851-52, Sandilli had always managed to evade capture.

One of his sons, Edmund, had been in a Government office, and his apparent object in joining his father's rash attempt to regain Kafirland for the natives was the fear of his younger brother, Guonyama, a real savage, being elected to the headship of the Gaikas. All through 1877 the witchdoctors were urging the important chiefs to rise; Sandilli hesitated until the Galekas under Kreli had been defeated, and then it was an accidental beer-drinking quarrel between Galekas and Fingoes which precipitated the outbreak.

The Fingoes, a remnant of eight tribes originally in the south-east of Africa, flying from the Zulus, became slaves to the Galekas, and their first cousins the Gaikas, to whom they acted as hewers of wood and drawers of water, the Kafirs despising every sort of work, except that of herding cattle, their fields being cultivated by the women. In 1835 the Fingoes were taken under British protection. They accepted missionaries, and many were in 1877 more prosperous than their former masters, having more wives and more cattle, and thus an antagonistic feeling arose between the Gaikas and their former slaves.

When General Thesiger and his Staff reached King William's Town on the 4th March, the farmers alarmed by Sandilli's rebellion had crowded into the towns, abandoning their farms even within one mile of the Settlement. There were near Fort Beaufort, 45 miles to the west of King William's Town, two or three hundred Gaikas under Tini Macomo, who however were not anxious to fight; but on the 9th March news was brought in of Sandilli's being near Grey Town, and of his men having murdered three Europeans at Stutterheim, on the eastern edge of the Buffalo Range. The position was curious; for while Sandilli's men were attacking a village, they sent their women to sit down near it, so as to be out of danger.

When the news was received, I was dining at the mess of the 24th Regiment and had asked to sit next to a man whose name was already well known in the colony, Captain Brabant, a member of the Legislative Council. He had served as adjutant of the Cape Mounted Rifles, and when the corps was disbanded took to farming near King William's Town, and had been successful. He was a man of middle age, somewhat impetuous, with great personal courage, an iron constitution, and for his age very active habits; these qualities, combined with some military knowledge, marked him out as a Colonial leader of men. I found him socially as a soldier an agreeable comrade.

The general told me next day he intended me to proceed to Keiskamma Hoek, 25 miles to the north of King William's Town, where I was to endeavour to command harmoniously some Colonial farmers. There had been considerable friction between Colonists and Imperial officers in the Transkei Campaign. That afternoon Captain Brabant had a warning letter written by a friend in Keiskamma Hoek, stating that Mr. Lonsdale, the magistrate, had been repulsed by Sandilli's men, and that an attack on the village was expected at daylight.

MUSICIANS OF THE 24TH

Brabant urged me to start at once, and I agreed to go after dinner, which would in any case bring us in before daylight; but the general would not sanction it, as I was to take out two companies of the 24th Regiment next day, leaving one about halfway, at Bailie's Grave.

★★★★★★

The name given to a little post from the fact that in 1836 a Colonist of that name with 24 Hottentots had been surprised there by Gaikas, and after a brave resistance killed without one man escaping. It was not known for many months what had become of the party, in spite of a protracted search ordered by Sir Harry Smith. Eventually a belt worn by Macomo was recognised as having belonged to the deceased Hottentot leader, and later his Bible was repurchased from the Gaikas, with a pathetic note on the fly-leaf that the detachment was surrounded, their ammunition nearly exhausted, and they must soon be killed.

★★★★★★

The Buffalo Range and its adjoining hills, over and above which our operations were carried out for the next three months, is about 12 miles north of King William's Town, which settlement lies in a hollow of a plateau bounded on either side by parallel ranges of mountains. The track from King William's Town to Keiskamma Hoek runs generally for 12 miles in a north-westerly direction, passing over an undulating country nearly bare of trees, when the traveller sees in front of and above him a wall-like mountain, covered for miles with lofty trees and dense underwood.

The southern side is precipitous, and, under the term "Perie Bush," extends for 6 miles from the Buffalo River on the east to the King William's Town—Bailie's Grave Keiskamma Hoek road, on the west Bailie's Grave post is a small square earthwork, 12 inches high, a relic of the war of 1851, on a neck, which runs generally from east to west, and connects this wall-like side of the Buffalo Range with a mountain 2 miles south-west of Bailie's Grave, called the Intaba Indoda, to the west of which there is also a precipitous fall to the southward, bounded by the Debe Flats.

The track north of Bailie's Grave post, bending northwards, passes under, in succession, Goza Heights and the Gwili-Gwili Mountains, which tower 2000 feet above Keiskamma Hoek, the original "great place" of Sandilli's father, well known in the war of 1851-52. The scenery in the valley is beautiful beyond description. The basin, in which Germans had formed the most fertile farms I saw in the colony, is surrounded by fantastic hills. It possessed seven churches—each, it is true, only the size of an Aldershot hut—six being Lutheran, and one Church of England.

★★★★★★

When the German Legion, enlisted towards the conclusion of the Crimean War, was about to be disbanded, all who cared to go to South Africa were sent out, to the great advantage of the colony. They were industrious, hard-working, and successful gardeners, giving their old country names to prosperous villages, such as Wiesbaden, Hanover.

★★★★★★

The main feature in the range is the so-called Buffalo Poort, at the head of which the river rises in a ravine (locally called a *kloof*), which extends 5 miles in a southerly direction, being at its mouth 2½ miles wide from east to west. At its head, where the spring rises, the slopes are comparatively gentle, the gorge being about 50 feet deep; but it falls away rapidly, and at the mouth of the valley a man standing on the rocks above may throw a stone which, according to where it alights, will travel 600 or 800 feet below him. All this valley is clothed with magnificent forest trees, and most of it with thick undergrowth, and is so rugged that within one pace there is often a drop of 20 or 30 feet; and in one of our skirmishes two Gaikas being pressed by us fell nearly 100 feet and were killed.

To the eastward of the *poort*, or valley, there is another hollow, the stream of which joins the Buffalo River under a bold granite precipice, called Sandilli's Krantz, and again farther east a valley called the Cwengwe forms the boundary of the tangled mass of forest-clad rocks in which the Gaikas hid for three months. Sandilli's Krantz covers 30 acres of rocks, formed by a portion of the cliff having broken away, and unless one has lived in the cave it is nearly impossible to find an individual in it, and throughout the war of 1851-52 it was undiscovered by Europeans.

The whole Buffalo Range extends 12 miles from north to south, and 8 miles from east to west, the highest points being on the northern and eastern sides. These are in themselves considerably above the edge of the valley called the Buffalo Poort, and from the western side of the *poort* the ground slopes gradually, covered with bush, but interspersed with open glades. In these glades the Gaikas fed their cattle and basked, for the warm sun is as necessary to the red Kafir as is his food.

61

When my party, one company of the 24th, Lieutenant Rawlings, and 10 mounted men of the 90th Light Infantry, reached Keiskamma Hoek, we found the magistrate, Mr. Rupert Lonsdale, preparing for another reconnaissance. He was reticent as to the previous day's proceedings, in which he had lost two men, but I learned later that he had led in the advance and had covered the retreat. He had reconnoitred up on the mountain and was passing under one of its highest points, Mount Kempt, with 60 white residents of Keiskamma Hoek, and about the same number of Fingoes, when they were fired on by Kafirs in ambush, and had to retire.

For the next three months Lonsdale dined with me at least twice every week, and had many other meals with me, and thus I got to know him very well. He had served in the 74th Regiment, until insufficient means forced him out of the army, and he chanced to go to the Cape to nurse a sick brother. He told me many amusing stories of his short army life; one instance, which occurred at Colchester Camp, I repeat.

Lonsdale was fond of playing cards, and one summer morning, when his party broke up about 3 a.m., he saw, to his astonishment, an officer of his acquaintance walking up and down between the huts, carrying a lighted candle, and humming Handel's "Dead March."

Startled, Lonsdale said, "What are you doing here in your nightshirt?"

"Don't you know," the man replied, "I am dead, and they're burying me? Just listen to the band;" and he again started his mournful dirge.

Lonsdale, seeing his state, humoured him for a few minutes, and taking his arm, they walked up and down to this dismal music Finally, when passing the door of the man's hut, which stood open, my friend said, "Here we are at the cemetery," and leading him into the hut, put him into bed. Then, blowing out the candle, he said, "There you are, 'dust to dust, ashes to ashes,'" and covering him over with the bedclothes, added, "We will fire the three volleys in the morning." Next day the man was ill and did not remain long in the Service. (I wrote to the Military Secretary of Rupert Lonsdale, in the following December: " Brave as a lion, agile as a deer, and inflexible as iron, he is the best leader of natives I have seen.")

Lonsdale was about thirty years of age, of slight but strong build, and he strode along at the head of his Fingoes, setting a pace which even they, who when paid will run 6 or 7 miles for hours in suc-

24th Foot in South Africa

cession, found severe. The Fingoes themselves were nearly always led by certain men of character, not necessarily Heads of Locations who controlled them in camp, but other men, who became self-constituted leaders in action. These were Gaikas married into Fingoe families, and though this fact was not in itself sufficient to render such men loyal, yet if, as in some cases, their fathers were not "Out" in the 1851-52 war, they had come to consider themselves Government men. Four were to my knowledge shot leading their Fingoe fellow-villagers against the Gaikas.

About six months previously, Lonsdale had raised 250 Fingoes, and sent them to the Transkei to serve under Mr. Frank Streatfield, a Kentish gentleman, who at the time of Kreli's rebellion had broken up an ostrich farm in Albany, preparatory to his return to England. Offered the command of native levies, he cheerfully accepted the duty, and did excellent work, living with me generally when we were on the Buffalo Mountain. He was unknown to his men prior to the last six months, and so had not the great advantage of Lonsdale, who had known for two years all the 900 Fingoes he raised in his district.

The magistrate is in the mind of the Fingoe, or of the Kafir, of far more importance than the governor, or any general, inasmuch as the magistrate not only rewards, but he punishes. Thus, Lonsdale had the unstinted devotion of his men, actuated not only by respect, but by self-interest. They were absurdly overpaid, receiving 2s. *per diem* and free rations, being able to live on 2d. a day, and at a time when the British soldier got 1s.

CHAPTER 4

1878—The Gaikas and Perie Bush

The general's intention was to drive the Gaikas from the Gwili-Gwili Mountain, the north-west end of the range, where most of them were, towards the south of the Buffalo Poort, where a line of our people awaited them. The Keiskamma Hoek column, composed of 300 whites (85 being soldiers) and 300 Fingoes, was to climb the rugged western face of the mountain, begin and direct the attack, while Commandant Frost with 500 mounted men was to ascend from the direction of St. Matthew's, north-east of the Hoek, and join hands with me. Streatfield with 250 Fingoes was to ascend the Rabula Height, and Captain Brabant with about 200 whites was to go up from Bailie's Grave and follow in support of the right of Wood's column. Troops were placed east of the mountain to prevent the Gaikas

SKETCH MAP

to illustrate the

GAIKA REBELLION

Scale of Miles

going towards the Kei.

On the afternoon of the 16th, when riding towards Kabousie Nek to concert measures with Commandant Frost, I met him riding with Major Buller to call on me. He lived near Queenstown, whence he had brought 500 *burghers*, many Dutchmen. He was for a South African farmer wealthy, and in addition to great moral courage his personal cool bravery was remarkable even amongst daring spirits. I saw him watch unmoved his eldest boy, serving as a *burgher*, fired on at close quarters by a Kafir. The lad escaped, though the stock of the carbine he was aiming was cut in twain by the Kafir's bullet. Frost later, from his place in the Legislative Assembly, criticised in strongly worded adverse terms the *burgher* system of using untrained levies without discipline.

Having arranged our concentration for daylight on the 18th, I rode southward to Bailie's Grave to impress on Captain Brabant the part he was to play in the drive, as to ensure success he must wait until we passed him. At sunset on the 17th, Mr. Bowker and his troop of Grahamstown farmers had not arrived. Mr. Barber with 50 Cradock men, many being Dutchmen, had been for some days at the Hoek. Their leader was over six feet high, strongly built, with a fine handsome face, and such frank manners as to render all duties with him a pleasure.

At 9 p.m. I paraded my little force, Mr. Bowker having arrived. Above the Hoek our Fingoe scouts had counted over 1000 Gaikas on the Gwili-Gwili Mountain, and I had seen enough of the climb, 2000 feet above us, to have made me uneasy, but that our Fingoes were within 300 feet of the crest, which I hoped to reach at daylight, while the Gaikas were still chilled by cold. Although the entire distance was only 8 miles from the Hoek, the actual ascent was severe, and would in daylight, if opposed, have been costly in lives. Leaving at 10 p.m., we marched in single file through thick bush up a path so steep and rugged as to oblige us to dismount at 1 a.m. Messrs. Lonsdale, Barber, and I led, and without having halted we reached the crest only at daylight, climbing the last 300 yards through boulders of rock which a dozen determined men might have held for hours.

Fourteen days of very hard work combined with little sleep had brought a return of my neuralgic pains, which, although not severe, obliged me to take doses of chloral and bismuth, and foreseeing that I might be on the mountain for three days, I took the precaution of getting a large bottle from a doctor in King William's Town, who enjoined me on no account to finish it until the third day. When we started my pain was worse, and it increased as I climbed, with the result that when we reached the top of the mountain and I sat down on a stone to rest, I had finished the bottle, and was tormented with acute thirst I asked each *burgher* as he came up for a drink, but there was not one of them who had put any water in his bottle of "Cape Smoke," and so I had to endure the thirst until, the day having broken, we moved on, and came to a stream.

The Gaikas retired from the clear plateau of the Gwili-Gwili Mountain, and after breakfast Barber's and Bowker's Colonials and Streatfield's Fingoes descended into a deep ravine which intervenes between Gwili-Gwili and Rabula Heights, whence the *burghers* emerged late in the afternoon, exhausted by their climb.

Captain Brabant had an easier ascent, up which, indeed, we took waggons two months later. When he gained the crest at daylight, he saw two miles below him, to the eastward, some Kafirs and cattle in an open glade, and advanced till he had dense bush on either hand. (The Colonial papers attributed Brabant's reverse to Colonel Wood having for some reason failed to support him. Our *burghers* only laughed at the local papers, but it was republished in the *Times*.) The Kafirs opened fire, and Brabant fell back with some slight loss, Streatfield, who went to help Brabant out, having an officer killed.

This impatient disregard of orders spoilt the general's plan. Late that evening a path across the intervening ravine was found, which Frost's men and the Hoek columns crossed next day. The night was cold; most of the men had a blanket, but as we were carrying three days' food, the officers had left their blankets below. I personally did not suffer, for Mr. Lonsdale emerged from the bush at sundown, near Brabant's bivouac, too tired to attempt to return, so Captain Nixon, Royal Engineers, and I sheltered under the magistrate's waterproof sheet.

When we were having our coffee before advancing next morning. Captain Nixon, who had given me much aid as a staff officer, warned me that he had overheard the *burghers* say that they intended to refuse to enter the bush. I took no notice until the men were falling in at daylight, when the two leaders came to me, saying that the men declined to go into the bush, as it was not a fit place for Europeans, and they suggested that the driving of the main valley should be done by Fingoes.

I replied, "I do not agree with you; we have got our orders, and you are to take your men through the bush."

A KAFIR WARRIOR

"But the men will not go, they are all determined."

"Well, gentlemen, I shall write to the general that you refuse to obey orders and having sent off my letter I shall go in with this company of the 24th Regiment We shall probably not do the work as well as you can, but if I become a casualty I do not envy your position."

I said no more, and in a quarter of an hour the *burghers* entered the bush, from which they did not emerge till late in the afternoon, when some of them, hearing I was going through the ravine to the south end of the range, where Captain Brabant had been repulsed, formed a guard round me so that I could not be hit except through the bodies of my escort. Until they went home, we never had another difference, and they endeavoured to anticipate my wishes.

★★★★★★

The high commissioner, writing on the 15th August 1879, writing out the important hearing which the position of the Flying Column in Zululand had on the safety of Natal and the Transvaal from January to July, said: "I would beg to call attention to the excellent political effects of the dealings of these two officers with the colonial forces, and with the colonists in general. Up to 1878 there had always been amongst the colonists something of a dread of the strict discipline which was, as they thought, likely to be enforced by a military officer were they to serve under him, and a great distrust of Her Majesty's officers generally to conduct operations against the Kafirs. This feeling has now, I believe, disappeared amongst all who served under General Wood and Colonel Buller."

★★★★★★

Next morning Commandant Frost and his men followed the Hoek column across the ravine and bivouacked in the glade whence Captain Brabant was driven on the 18th of March; Brabant moving a mile farther south on the mountain range. As we advanced the Kafirs disappeared in the bush, followed by Mr. Lonsdale and his Fingoes. Neither Kafirs nor Zulus fight on two successive days, unless compelled to do so.

When Lonsdale's Fingoes went down the Buffalo Poort, 500 women and children came out of the bush as the Fingoes advancing came near them. The poor creatures had nothing on except a blanket, and this we were obliged to remove to search for powder and lead, which many of them carried. When the operations ceased for the day, I was willing to let them return to their husbands, as I could not feed them;

but they refused to go back, not knowing where they would find their men, and moreover fearing ill-treatment at the hands of the Fingoes.

The starving women sat on a hill which rose from the plateau on the mountain for twenty-six hours and suffered severely from cold and want of food. I was called to them, as one wished to complain to me of a Dutchman who she said had taken away her child. The Dutchman, who was in Commandant Frost's Contingent, admitted he had the boy, but added that he had given its mother a shin bone of beef for the child; this the mother acknowledged, but she was unwilling to give back the beef even to obtain her boy. I compromised the matter to the satisfaction of both parties, by giving the man five shillings for his beef and restoring the child to its mother.

There was another woman with a baby apparently on the point of death, and I gave its mother a small bag of biscuits. When we carried out the same operation on the 8th May, about half the number of women came out of the Bush, and on seeing them I said to the interpreter, "Why, Paliso, here are some of the same women."

"Oh no, master; these are Seyolo's, and the others were Sandilli's women."

"I can see identically the same women," I replied, and accosting a young woman with fine eyes, I talked to her through the interpreter for a few minutes, and then asked her if she was up in the same place last moon.

"Yes," she replied. '

"Is the woman here who had the sick baby?"

"Yes, she is eight or ten farther down."

"Well, I recognise you—do you recognise me?"

She looked steadily at me, and replied, "No; all white men's faces are exactly alike." Which is the reproach we level at the Kafirs.

On the 20th a thick fog prevented our seeing more than 40 yards, so movements of troops became impossible, and many of the Gaikas passed out of the Perie Bush unseen by us on the mountain or by the troops who were guarding the roads 2000 feet below us. Frost and I went to Brabant's bivouac, and arranged a drive for the 21st March. The Hoek column was to line the path which led to Haynes' Mill; Frost was to remain on the crest near Brabant's bivouac, to prevent Kafirs breaking back towards Gwili-Gwili; while Brabant, who knew more of the Perie Bush than any other Colonial present, was to descend the other precipitous side and work eastwards towards the path lined by the Hoek column.

Brabant had greatly underrated the difficulties of his task. He entered the bush at 8 a.m., and almost immediately came on a precipice, down which his men swung themselves on monkey ropes. (The growers which hang from and interlace the forest trees.) He failed to move eastwards, and after a determined effort emerged at 5 p.m. on the plain almost due south of where he entered the bush, consequently neither Frost's men nor the Hoek column saw a Kafir, and at sunset I sent the troops down the mountain, having there no food for men or horses.

The apparent result of our three days' operations, and four days' residence on the mountain, was not commensurate with the discomfort we underwent. We killed an unknown number of Gaikas, took several horses and some cattle, with 17 casualties, whites and blacks, but on the other hand the Gaikas had never before been harassed in the Buffalo Poort.

When the troops descended, I rode down the mountain and round by Bailie's Grave to General Thesiger's camp at Haynes' Mill. About 6 miles from the camp I came on a small draft recently landed, consisting of a young officer and a dozen men, on their way to join the Headquarters of the battalion. Their waggon had broken down, and they were in a state of excitement, having just killed a Kafir. After a few minutes' conversation, I went on to the general's camp, but missed him, he having gone round by the eastern side of the mountain to see me.

I dined with the general's staff officer, and at half-past nine, with a bright full moon, started back on a well-worn waggon track. When we got about 80 yards from the wagon, four shots rang out sharply, striking the ground at my horse's feet. The two orderlies Frontier Light Horse unslung their rifles to fire back, but I stopped them, and on riding up found the small draft, which apparently had not yet recovered from their excitement, had mistaken us for a party of Kafirs coming to attack them.

The musketry instructor of the battalion was living with me as a guest and had told us the day before we went up the mountain of the great improvement he had effected in the shooting of the men. He was consequently much chaffed when it became known that the regimental armourer and three first-class shots had missed four horsemen at 80 yards distance, I had been in the saddle several days from 4 a.m. till 7 p.m. and rode throughout the night of the 21st-22nd March, when my horse died of exhaustion. The work told on me, and I had to go to bed for three days, having a high temperature. I was at duty again, however, on the 27th, when we received orders for another drive. The general went up the Cwengwe Valley to Mount Kempt, leaving the direction of the operations in my hands, regarding which the Staff officer. Captain F. Grenfell, (now Lieutenant-General Lord Grenfell, G.C.B.), wrote:

> The Lieutenant-General gives Colonel Evelyn Wood the greatest latitude for these operations.

Commandant Frost having joined the general's column, which consisted of two companies of the 24th Regiment, with two guns, at Mount Kempt, was sent round from the northeast to ascend the Gwili-Gwili Mountain. Captain Brabant, placed under my orders, was to ascend the Rabula Heights. On this occasion the orders were executed, but the result of the operations was meagre, for the Gaikas evaded us; we now pitched our camp on the mountain plateau, and our presence annoying the Gaikas even more than the drives, as they could not emerge from the bush to bask in the sun and graze their cattle.

The next week we saw but little of the Kafirs, for all the white men were employed in cutting broad paths in the bush, while the Fingoes were carrying our tents and baggage up the mountain. When we had got enough food up, we tried another drive, but the result was unsatisfactory; the paths, however, annoyed the Gaikas, as they could not drive their cattle across the glades without being seen, and thus some fell into our hands immediately.

Nearly all the *burghers* had now gone home: they disliked being on the mountain, where their horses suffered from cold. They had enlisted for three months, a month of which was to be allowed for the return journey, and although in deference to the general's wish they had stayed on for another drive, their patience had now become exhausted. Like all amateur soldiers, they varied greatly in quality. Many were landowners, well off, and serving for the love of their country; others were men attracted by the pay of 5*s. per diem*, which was more than they could earn in the towns and villages or on farms. To the reproach that they were leaving before the fighting was over, they replied, "We got leave from our employers for three months; if we stay on, will the Government guarantee us work, if our employers refuse it?" And to this reasonable question no answer was obtainable.

On the 5th April, 700 Fingoes having arrived from the Transkei District, the General arranged another drive, to start from Mount Kempt, where he took up his position, straight down the Buffalo

Poort to Haynes' Mill. The Fingoes were, however, undisciplined, and fired away twenty rounds a man, without any adequate results. It is only fair to state that they had no such leader as had the Hoek Fingoes in Mr. Lonsdale, whose men were not given more than five rounds for a days' operations. We moved that morning at 4 a.m., and were in our assigned positions at six, and after eleven hours, in which 1500 Fingoes searched the bush while the soldiers lined the paths, the result was indeed incommensurate: 3 Gaikas killed.

When I returned to the Hoek late at night, I heard that Captain Warren, (now Lieutenant-General Sir Charles Warren, K.C.B.) Royal Engineers, with a troop of the Diamond Field Horse, had been surrounded by 1500 Kafirs, and arranged to start at 3.30 next morning to his relief. Sleep was impossible, for Mr. Streatfield arrived at midnight, and Mr. Lonsdale at 2 a.m., and it was necessary to concert with these gentlemen the movements of the Fingoes westwards.

I heard at daylight, when at Bailie's Grave Post, the correct story of Captain Warren's skirmish the previous day; he had skilfully ambushed Seyolo, whose men fled.

★★★★★★

The Gaika was the legitimate head of his section of the tribe, but was deposed by General Sir George Cathcart in 1852, and imprisoned for a time, his younger brother, Siwani, being made chief.

★★★★★★

On the 4th April, Seyolo induced the tribe to rise, and with 500 men was seen crossing the Debe Flats early on the 5th April, making for the Tutu Bush. Captain Warren concealed about 50 men in a hollow, from which they fired with effect. Seyolo charged bravely, but 20 of his men fell, and the tribe scattered in the bush, leaving many of their wives behind.

I anticipated the general would come down from Mount Kempt, and so waited for a couple of hours, when he appeared, and approved of my suggestion that I should go westward and prevent the Kafirs breaking out north-west to the Amatola Basin. At Burns Hill I found a company of the 90th Light Infantry, and two miles farther off I heard of another. Ordering the men of both companies to eat, and parade as soon as possible in shirt sleeves, they marched off within an hour, going up the Makabalekile Ridge. I preceded them with 8 men, my personal escort, and picked up near Burns Hill 80 Fingoes and 80 Hottentots. I carried them on with me, leaving orders for two squadrons of the Frontier Light Horse, coming from Bailie's Grave, to follow me. The bush on the Makabalekile Ridge extends for about 1500 yards, then there is an undulating plateau, named Tutu, extending a mile from east to west, and a mile and a half from north to south, the plateau being bounded on its east side by a deep ravine running practically north and south, called the Zanyorkwe.

Just as my 8 men arrived, riding in extended order, a body of Kafirs ran out of the ravine, but were driven back by my escort, and the Fingoes coming up, I extended them at intervals along the edge of the bush. When two hours later the Frontier Light Horse and a company of 90th Light Infantry arrived, I sent them down into the bush, and was superintending these movements when I saw the Fingoes, whom I had left fairly steady, running rapidly. Cantering up to them, I soon perceived the reason: bullets were striking all around them, the line battalion on the high ground to the east of the Intaba Indoda Ravine having mistaken the Fingoes for Kafirs.

As I led the former back to the edge of the bush, hoping that the regiment, which was only 1400 yards off, would recognise I was a European officer, the artillery dropped a shell 40 yards from us; I noticed the Fingoes, like myself, had not the same fear of shells that they had of the bullets, and after three or four minutes the firing ceased, except for an occasional over-shot fired at Seyolo's men, who were in the bush close underneath us. We learned next day that the Transkei Fingoes had disappointed the general, for they were driven back three times, and for several hours left the body of two of their white officers in the hands of Seyolo's men.

I lost four horses, which was provoking, but in a manner, which made me admire the audacity of the Kafirs. After I had re-established my line of Fingoes, some 20 Gaikas ran out in the open, from a spot where the Fingoe line was weak. The position was awkward, because I had nobody with me except my personal escort of 8 men and the horse-holders of the Frontier Light Horse, the other men being all below in the Bush. When we fired, the horses broke away from the horse-holders and careered over the plateau, four of them running northwards in a narrow glade where the bush closes in on either hand. The horses chased by my orderly ran close to the trees, from which Gaikas darting out pulled them into bush so dense that our men who were in the ravine, and later emerged close to the place, saw neither Kafirs nor horses.

At nightfall we marched back to Burns Hill, where I had to provide food and shelter for the hungry, coatless companies, 90th Light Infantry. They sheltered in the Mission Church, and as there were sheep close at hand, lumps of mutton were soon broiled on the fires. Next day Lonsdale's and Streatfield's Fingoes moving from the Rabula Valley through the Tutu Bush, killed 20 of Seyolo's men with but few casualties, while with the 90th companies and Frontier Light Horse I held the plateau. On the following day the Fingoes advancing from the Rabula, with two companies of the 90th and Frontier Light Horse, again went through the Tutu Bush and drove out some of Seyolo's men, who, after a skirmish with the general's small force, then encamped at Bailie's Grave, succeeded in getting across to the Buffalo Range. Next day I heard that another small tribe had broken out and were making for the Tutu, and I followed them with a few mounted men, but only overtook their women, the men escaping into the Zanyorkwe Ravine.

Now for about three weeks the rebels remained unmolested, and Seyolo appreciating the situation, coming down from the Intaba Indoda Bush, destroyed all the Fingoe huts within two miles, carrying off large supplies of food and cattle. On the 23rd April he attacked Streatfield's Fingoes, but was beaten back, although they were obliged to shift their camp, as it was too close into the bush.

Captain Bowker, whose men had all gone home, came to me as a staff officer, and was very useful in many ways, as I was new to the country.

★★★★★★

Bowker was one of eleven children not one of whom was under 6 feet, and three of his brothers were 6 feet 3 inches. Like many others of those serving with us, he had seen his cattle driven off, and had known his relations and friends murdered by Kafirs; but he had a high type of mind, as is indicated by the following story. In a petty skirmish in 1864 he was fired on by a Basuto, who missed him but killed his horse. Bowker fired on the Basuto as he ran and broke his arm. The man fell, but when Bowker approached stood up stoically to meet the death he anticipated. Bowker bound up his arm and let him go, thinking no more of the matter.

Many years after, when Bowker was travelling with his wife in a waggon in Basutoland, buying cattle, he halted at a *kraal* at sundown, and as usual the Basutos crowded round him. He noticed one man who stared at him closely and then disappeared, but came back within an hour, with all his family, bearing on his head a bundle of firewood, a sheep, and some milk and vegetables, saying, "I offer these gifts to the man who broke and mended my arm." The firewood could not have been worth less than half a crown, as the country is treeless, and the only fuel is the manure of cattle.

★★★★★★

He told me a great deal that was interesting and was one of those who agreed with me as to our obligations in sparing Kafirs who no longer resisted. Many of the Colonists with whom I had talked had disagreed with me on this subject, alleging that as the Kafirs never spared us we should treat them in a similar manner. Several said to me on the Buffalo Mountains, "You don't understand; the women you want to feed would gladly inflict nameless tortures on you if you were their prisoner."

The volunteers having gone home, the general was now left with only one battalion and two guns, for the Transkei Fingoes being untrustworthy had been disarmed. We could not satisfactorily clear the Intaba Indoda Range with Lonsdale's men, and so for three weeks the Gaikas were unmolested. The broken country in the valley of the Zanyorkwe River, about 6 miles from north to south, and 10 miles from east to west of the ravine, is clothed with thick bush, the densest part of which gives its name. Tutu, to all the adjoining woods. The neck of land connecting the Kafirs' stronghold with the Buffalo Range, 4 miles farther east, is generally speaking covered with bush, with an opening of a mile near Bailie's Grave; thus, our difficulties were greatly increased by the vicinity of these two natural strongholds of the Gaikas.

The general had urged the Colonial Government to collect more volunteers, and I was instructed to raise all the Fingoes I could in the district to the north-west of King William's Town, Tini Macomo, son of Sandilli, and Chief of the Fort Beaufort District Gaikas, being then in the Tutu Bush. General Thesiger took me to Fort Beaufort and being satisfied there were no armed rebels in the district, ordered the 90th Light Infantry to Burns Hill, to work under my command, the lieutenant-colonel remaining at Fort Beaufort, in command of some Hottentots.

I was glad to see the Water Kloof, of which I had read a good deal. It appeared to our forefathers very difficult, but they never penetrated the Perie Bush, with which it cannot compare as a natural stronghold for the black man. The Water Kloof ravines are not nearly so deep or rugged as are those in the Perie, and the bush is broken up by intervening patches of cultivation.

At the end of April, the general's preparations for driving the Tutu Bush were complete. He was to direct the operations on the eastern, and I on the western side; he kept under his own command the 2nd 24th Regiment, some Fingoes, 4 guns and white volunteers under Von Linsingen, who had raised also 600 loyal Kafirs. Generally speaking, Bowker's Rovers were to hold the mouth of the Zanyorkwe Ravine, Lonsdale and Streatfield were to move from it, with the two companies of the 90th Light Infantry under Major Hackett up through the bush, while Von Linsingen was to advance from Debe Flats, and join me on the Tutu Plateau, which I was to gain by passing up Makabalekile Ridge, with three companies of my Regiment, and about 100 men of the Diamond Field Light Horse, and a company of Hottentots.

On the evening of the 29th April, Seyolo, who was aware of our operations, undertook to hold the ridge himself against me, and boasted that he would capture the guns if they were taken up the bush path. He commanded on the Tutu Plateau, while Tini Macomo was to hold the Tutu Bush itself.

At daylight on the 30th, the General having got into position on the eastern crest of the Zanyorkwe Ravine, shelled the rebel bivouac. Tini Macomo at once dispersed into the Tutu Ravine, while all Seyolo's men hastened westwards to support their piquets, who were already ambushed on the Makabalekile Ridge. It was covered with bush from 150 to 200 yards wide, from north to south, and extended for 1500 yards, through which the attacking force had to pass before it reached the open plateau.

The general had written to me on the 29th, saying he expected to see me on the plateau half an hour after daylight, to which I replied, "I will start in good time, but I shall not be there so early if Seyolo knows what to do."

One of the best companies in the battalion was commanded by Captain Stevens, who was fortunate in having an excellent coloursergeant. It was the last company to come in from Fort Beaufort, and I invited Stevens and his subaltern, Lieutenant Saltmarshe, to mess with me. I gave them a good dinner at seven o'clock on the 29th, and awoke them soon after midnight, when they, being young, consumed a 2 lb. tin of Cambridge sausages and a couple of chops. Saltmarshe seeing that I took nothing but a cup of cocoa, said to me chaffingly,

"You don't eat, sir; are you nervous?"

I said, "Yes; but even at your age I could not breakfast heartily at 1.15 a.m., having dined at 7 p.m. the previous evening."

At dinner-time, Stevens, who had been intimate with me at Aldershot, had asked whether he might lead the attack, and I replied that such was my intention. I was somewhat later in getting into position than I had intended, for after extending a company on either side of the timber-waggon track, which was about 6 feet in breadth, I was obliged to post personally a company and two guns which I intended to fire along the southern crest of the Tutu Plateau, on which I knew that any Kafirs reinforcing those already on the Makabalekile Ridge would pass.

The officer commanding the company was short-sighted, and so unfortunately was the lieutenant in command of the two guns, and although later several bodies of Kafirs passed within short range not a round was fired at them. When I cantered up, after placing the guns, Stevens said, "You promised we should lead, and you have left us behind."

"Yes," I said, "but now come on." Riding in front of the company, I led it on the track into the bush. We had scarcely got 100 yards when a fine stalwart Kafir advanced as if to shake hands; he had apparently heard the guns moving on the flank and did not see us until I told one of the men to shoot him. Fire was now opened on either side of the path, on which the company was advancing in file, and I told Stevens, who was in front, to press on. As he did so, Mr. Saltmarshe ran after him, but catching him by the collar as he passed, for I was still mounted, I said, "Go back to the rear."

"Why?" he asked, somewhat impatiently.

"Because I order you;" then seeing from the lad's face he felt the rebuke, I added, "I do not want, my boy, all my eggs in one basket." Ten minutes later, when we had advanced 400 or 500 yards, or one-third of the distance to the plateau, the firing increased in intensity, especially on the northern side, although nearly all the bullets cut the trees, and at one time my pony's back was covered with leaves, which fell like snow in a winter scene at a theatre. The Gaikas approached closer and closer, till a Kafir, almost touching Stevens, fired, and knocked a big hole in his face.

I was sitting in the centre of the company, and beckoning to Saltmarshe, as his captain was carried away, said, "Now it is your turn."

I noticed that, although his face was set, and he was still eager to fight, yet the fall of his friend had sobered him, for he asked in a quiet voice, "What am I to do, sir?"

"Go to the head of the company, fire two or three rounds, then advance 50 yards and drop again."

He had made one advance only, when a Gaika fired so close to him that his chest was knocked away by the charge. The rebels now made a rush, and the Hottentots, who were on the southern side of the path, whence there came but little fire, ran down the path, carrying with them half a dozen of my men, who had been near Saltmarshe. Colour-Sergeant Smith, a little man, so short that I often wondered who could have enlisted him, had a heart entirely out of proportion to the size of his body, using most opprobrious language to the men, led them forward again.

I sent back for Major Cherry, who was in command of the detachment, as the company was now without officers. At that moment Captain Stuart Smith, Royal Artillery, asked if he might bring up a gun, and on my saying I was afraid we should not get the horses clear of the muzzles, he observed cheerfully, "Oh, it does not matter if we shoot them;" and in a couple of minutes he had two guns unlimbered, and firing case into the Bush close on the ground from whence most of the fatal shots had come. Major Cherry now led on the company, and in a few minutes the Gaikas drew off, and we got on to the plateau with but little further loss. I then reaped the advantage of my ride the previous day to Alice (Fort Hare), where I had bought several yards of calico, for with a strange want of forethought the signalling equipment had been left at Cape Town.

I was now able to report to General Thesiger across the ravine, for we were standing only 1600 yards apart, and the Gaikas had been driven below the plateau into the ravine. This fight ended disastrously for Seyolo's men; our columns converging at the common centre, met them as they tried each avenue of escape, and after nightfall, crossing the King William's Town-Keiskamma Hoek road, they took refuge in the Perie Bush.

When we were on the mountain plateau in March, we felt the want of guns, to prevent the Kafirs coming out to bask in the sun without taking the trouble to attack them, so I was anxious, now we had to follow Seyolo's men, to take the 7-pounders up, although I had been told it was utterly impossible to get anything on wheels up the face of the Rabula Mountain, which looks at a distance precipitous. Captain Stuart Smith, under the orders of Major Harness, Royal Artillery, accomplished the feat. He hooked in 48 oxen, and then, putting a pair of staunch wheelers in front, attached them to the horns of the leading pair of oxen.

The horses, although often on their knees, kept the oxen in a straight line, and the whole team, urged by some twenty Africanders with long whips, eventually got both guns up to within 100 feet of the crest, whence they were hauled up by a company 90th Light Infantry. We began work after nightfall on the 7th, and by daylight on the 8th were on the mountain: with 4 companies 90th Light Infantry, 2 guns, the Frontier Light Horse, and 1500 Fingoes. Sandilli and Seyolo had been warned of our attack by the so-called loyal Kafirs, and the actual number of Gaikas killed was less than in other drives; but a determined attack led by Major Redvers Buller so demoralised the rebels that they never again attempted to resist white men.

Buller, with a squadron Frontier Light Horse, following some straggling Kafirs on the wooded precipice overlooking Haynes' Mill, was fired on, and though he drove the enemy from the edge of the bush, they held some rocks 50 feet down, and a few men sat in high trees, which enabled them to fire on the plateau.

Just as I arrived from another part of the elevated plateau, which consisted of a series of terraces, Captain McNaghten, Frontier Light Horse, fell mortally wounded. Major Buller reported that there were only 30 Kafirs immediately below him, the man who shot McNaghten being in a tree farther westward along the precipice. He explained that most of the enemy were behind a big rock, 40 feet down, a place so steep that you could not go down without holding on, or sliding, so it was difficult to turn them out as I wished, and he demurred to the inevitable loss of men in the operation. I suggested that it was only the first man down who was likely to be shot, and signalling to Captain Laye, (now Major-General Laye, C.B.), who was on a terrace, 200 feet below me, he brought up his company.

While he was climbing up, I told Commandant Lonsdale to take his men into the bush and extend them higher up the valley, and Commandant Maclean to do the same farther westwards, with orders to work round the spot where the Kafirs were lying concealed. I explained the operation and its dangers to Captain Laye, telling him he was to sit and slide down the rock, ordering one of his most trustworthy men to keep close to him. Just as the company, which had extended while in "dead" ground, approached the edge of the precipice, Buller jumping up, shouted, "Frontier Light Horse, you will never let

80

those redcoats beat you," and forming himself into a toboggan, he slid down, under fire, which fortunately passed over his head, and most of the Kafirs disappeared before he regained his footing.

Coincident with Buller's slide, some of Lonsdale's Fingoes arrived at the rocks, and getting below the Gaikas, they were caught as in a trap, but selling their lives dearly, killed two of our men. The Fingoes lost a few men, and an old woman came to me with a large hole in her face, a bit of the jaw-bone having been shot away. She was unconcerned, however, and when I proposed to hand her over for medical aid, declared she would much sooner have a plug of tobacco to chew. A young Fingoe had an altercation with our doctor, a Colonial, and I was appealed to to settle the dispute. Two of the Fingoe's fingers had been shot off by slugs from a Gaika's gun, and the hand was in such a mash that the doctor wished to amputate the fingers at the second joint

My coloured soldier objected strenuously and said that if he might have six weeks' leave he would come back again. And so, he did. His cure, which was that ordinarily adopted by the natives in such cases, was peculiar. Returning to his village, he was pegged down on the ground, the maimed hand being buried in the earth, without any bandage or dressing upon it, and the man was not allowed up until it had healed over.

It was, however, an unpleasant sight, for all the ragged bits of skin remained, and the man would have had a more useful hand if he had submitted to the doctor's operation.

From this time till the end of May, the object of the Gaikas was to evade our men. Forty or fifty Fingoes worked through bush which required 500 men on the 18th March, and daily the small parties killed a score of rebels.

In the third week of May, Major Buller nearly caught Sandilli in his cave, where he lived unmolested throughout the war of 1851-52; there was, however, a back exit, to us then unknown, by which the old man escaped. Major Buller, with two companies 24th Regiment, the Frontier Light Horse, and Lonsdale's Fingoes, remained near the cave for forty hours, which prolonged visit caused Sandilli to move northwards.

From the 12th March, when I left King William's Town, I scarcely ever slept for two nights in succession on the same spot. Constant work, shortness of sleep, and the great alternations of temperature, often over 40° between midnight and noon, and the want of nourishing food, told on me. I was unwell on the 10th May, but the general being 80 miles away, visiting the Transkei, the 3000 white and black soldiers on and around the Buffalo Range were under my command, so I stayed on the mountains until a high temperature and pulse 104° obliged me to go down.

For a fortnight the glands in my groin, armpits, and neck had swollen; my skin peeled off like a mummy, and chilblain-like openings appeared on my hands. I gave four Hottentots, who are more intelligent than Kafirs, £2 to carry me down to the Rabula Valley, where Dr. Alcock, my Aldershot Doctor, thus diagnosed my case: "Overwork, want of sleep and of nutritious food." Milk and eggs every four hours, with "All night in," soon restored me, and on the 27th I accomplished a long ride, involving many hours in the saddle.

The Gaika Rebellion was now over: Tini Macomo in the Water Kloof, Seyolo in the Fish River Bush, and Sandilli in the Perie, were hiding in caves. On the 29th May a patrol of Lonsdale's men skirmished with a few Kafirs near Mount Kempt, and were startled at the resistance, until they recognised amongst the slain Dukwana, an elder of the Emgwali Mission, who had shot several of our officers, and was now killed in protecting the flight of Sandilli. He fell mortally wounded, and with his death the rebellion ended. He had fought in 1835, '46, '48, '51-52, and had always previously escaped. A fortnight after his death ladies were riding about unescorted where no small armed party could have ventured since March, and in three months what we may hope was the last Gaika revolt had been suppressed.

The number of regular troops employed by General Thesiger in suppressing this outbreak was far less than those engaged in 1851-52, but we never had the same number of Gaikas under arms against us, and the area was smaller; and we had the great advantage of telegraphic communication, the wire having been carried through Kaffraria by the Director of Telegraphs, Mr. J. Sivewright, with considerable danger to himself and Staff.

In the wars of 1847-48, 1851-52, the Kafirs always got their news before our troops; now the position was reversed, and Mr. Sivewright's daily bulletins, posted at all telegraph stations, checked nearly all disaffected chiefs. The Galekas, after a defeat, sent to the Gaikas announcing a victory, and calling on their cousins to rise, but the messengers were disconcerted by the Gaikas describing the Galekas' defeat Moreover, tactics had undergone a change. When the 90th Light Infantry came under my command, the battalion had received an order, emanating from Headquarters, Cape Town, that it was never to be employed in the bush.

In 1851-52, Colonel Eyre, with the 73rd Regiment, broke this established rule, to the immense disgust of Kreli, who in the quaint words of the interpreter excused a defeat by saying, "No two men stop one bush; one man come, other man go." To enter the bush boldly in the face of Kafirs is not only the most efficacious, but the safest method. I can only recall one out of the many white leaders shot in 1878 who was killed in the dense bush. In nearly every case our loss occurred just outside the bush, or in paths from unseen foes.

By the middle of June, the Regular Troops were concentrated, and the Volunteers recently collected were sent home. I was ordered to prepare the 90th Light Infantry for a march to Maritzburg, in Natal. I was offered at this time the command of the Colonial Forces, to be organised into three battalions, with a salary of £1200 and £300 travelling expenses; I considered the offer until I learnt the Colonial Government did not intend to let the *commandant* nominate the battalion commanders. I had been tempted by the pay, but on the other hand wished to command the 90th Light Infantry, and not being allowed to suggest my own choice of subordinates settled the question.

General Thesiger was generous in his praise. In his despatch, dated King William's Town, 26th June 1878, he wrote:—

From the 9th to the 29th May the troops under Colonel Evelyn Wood gave the rebels no rest.

Para. 62. Colonel Evelyn Wood, V.C., C.B., 90th Light Infantry, on Special Service in South Africa, has had command of a separate column of Imperial and Colonial troops, from the time that I assumed the direction of military operations in the field. I cannot speak too highly of the good service rendered by this officer. He has exercised his command with marked ability and great tact. I am of opinion that his indefatigable exertions and personal influence have been mainly instrumental in bringing the war to a speedy close.

I would beg to draw attention to those officers who are especially brought to notice by Colonel E. Wood.

(Signed)   F. Thesiger.

He wrote to me on the 21st June:

I have written to His Royal Highness I could never have succeeded if it had not been for your active and energetic aid.

CHAPTER 5

1878—From King William's Town to Utrecht

On the 26th June, my new command, the Natal Column, con-sisting of 4 guns, 5 companies 90th Light Infantry (in which I was still a supernumerary major), and a company Mounted Infantry, left Kei Road, Major Buller with 200 Frontier Light staying behind for a week to enlist men, was to overtake us. Up to Kokstadt we marched over treeless rolling plains, and in spite of the fact that we crossed 122 (unbridged) rivers, it frequently happened there was not sufficient wa-ter for the Column. I rode, therefore, every march three times. Leav-ing my excellent staff officer. Captain F. Grenfell, (now General Lord Grenfell, G.C.B.), K.R.R. Corps, to encamp the column, I went on to the next camping ground, as local information was unreliable.

It was generally offered by storekeepers, whose estimate of the quantity required was often based on the assumption that all Euro-peans would consume bottled beer. This, indeed, many of our men did, at 2s. a bottle. Our canteen President bought at Mount Frere £40 worth of stores from Mr. McGregor, (ex-private soldier, 73rd Regi-ment). who had become a prosperous colonist. He interested me by extolling Colonel Eyre, though he was present in the march from the Perie to the Döhne, when Eyre burned the blankets and food of the stragglers. Two other former 73rd men rode 40 miles to see "A friend of Master Arthur Eyre, their own colonel's boy." (Killed in Ashanti.)

The arrangements for equipping the battalion which now came more closely under my command left much to be desired, and I doubt whether the officers realised more clearly than those in authority at home the necessity of good boots and flannel shirts in order to main-tain soldiers efficient. I was obliged to buy flannel shirts for the rank and file which cost the men 12s. each, as they had been allowed to go on service wearing cotton, and some with only one of that nature. This accounted for many having fever on the Amatolas, as the tem-perature varied from 75° at noon to 30° at night.

Nor was the administration more creditable to our military rulers. In order to economise passage money, no non-commissioned offi-cer or soldier with less than eighteen months to complete twenty-one years, was allowed to embark, while all the recruits were sent out. Thus, the sergeants and old soldiers left at home had nothing to do, while the officers had insufficient non-commissioned officers to help in training the recruits. Incomplete and unsatisfactory, however,

MAP OF THE PERIE BUSH

Scale of Miles

NOTE. The hill slopes are covered with thick bush and forest trees as were the regimental arrangements, they were virtually all that existed in South Africa, the departments being represented by very few officers; and thus, no sooner was I ordered to march, than I received a requisition for 5 non-commissioned officers, and selected men to form a hospital, and 5 to form a commissariat department. In the result this left but 7 duty sergeants with the 5 companies of rather more than 500 men.

The difficulties of crossing the numerous rivers in the journey of 500 miles exercised our patience. When the team of 16 or 18 oxen failed to pull the waggon and its load out of a river, another team of similar strength was hooked in, often with the result that one of the wheels was wrenched off by a boulder of rock which stopped the progress of the vehicle. This procedure was suitable, moreover, only when the "pull out" was fairly straight; if, as frequently happened, the gravel forming the ford was deposited on a curved line, every waggon had to be hauled out by one team assisted by manual labour, and to lift or extricate a waggon with its load equal to 6000 lbs, dead weight involved much labour. Even with comparatively easy fords the crossing of a river—for example, the Kei, between 80 and 90 yards wide, only 4 feet 6 inches deep—took five hours; the first waggon entering the water at 7.30, and the last pulling out at 3.30, the waggons taking on an average forty-five minutes to cross; and although I had arranged for a short march, we did not encamp till nearly 11 p.m. the day we crossed the river.

At Colossa, a village which Captain Grenfell and I visited in advance of the column, I asked him to go into a *kraal* to ask where was the nearest drinking-water. He observed that there was not much chance of ascertaining, as he had no interpreter; but I replied that I thought he would find the mother of some children whom we saw playing could speak English, as I noticed they were playing like English children a "dolls' dinner party," with white berries to represent food, on little bits of tin representing plates, and none but the children of a Fingoe, or one who had been about white people, would be so advanced in their amusements. The result proved that my surmise was correct.

When we were travelling through Bacaland to the north of Pondoland, I was riding with an interpreter and 2 white soldiers two hours' march in advance of the column, and near Tchungwassa, a valley under Mount Frere, came on a native who had the head of another between his knees, and was engaged in curling every separate bit of wool on the man's thickly covered skull. The Bacas and neighbouring tribes spend hours in order to produce results which seem to us funny. I have seen the wool on a man's head twisted up to represent the head of a castle in a set of chess men, and a bird's nest is a favourite device. Sitting down, I asked the hairdresser why he was taking such pains, and he explained because there was a wedding feast in the next village.

"How much are you going to charge him for the job?"

"Oh, nothing; he is a friend of mine."

"Well, how much would you charge him for what you are doing if it was a matter of business?"

"I always charge a shilling when I am doing it as I am now."

"Do you know who I am?"

"Yes, you are the general of the army coming here today."

"Well, what will you charge to dress my head?"

I fully expected the man would say 5s., but looking at my scanty hair, with a merry twinkle in his eye he exclaimed, "Oh, I will do you for three pence!"

I had a visit from Macaula, Chief of the Bacas, when I entered his territory, a fine big savage, 6 feet 3 inches in height, and broad in proportion. He was the happy owner of 22 wives and informed me that he had 59 children. I said laughingly, "Why not make it 60?"

He observed, with great gravity, "I had forgotten one; I heard this morning as I was coming here that I had another, and so it is 60." He was very anxious to buy my weight-carrying hunter "War-Game," as, weighing 15 stone, it was difficult to find a pony to carry him, and asked if I would sell the horse. He was startled by my statement that he cost 24 oxen as a four-year-old, a trek ox there being reckoned at £10.

The object of our long march was to impress the Pondos with a sense of British power, and I had been warned on leaving King William's Town that I might have to coerce Umquikela, one of the chiefs of Pondoland. He and his relative Umquiliso had given the Colonial authorities much trouble, for there was continual warfare between the tribes, with the result that those who got beaten invariably fled into the land set aside for tribes under our protection, and, moreover, Umquikela had recently misbehaved.

The governor, Sir Bartle Frere, informed General Thesiger that while he was confident I should not fight if it was possible to attain our end without bloodshed, yet it had been determined that Umquikela should be deposed from the position of chief unless he behaved better. This black potentate was under the influence of traders, to whose advantage it was that he should retain his independence. He received much good advice from a widow, Mrs. Jenkins, who lived at Umfundisweeni, (the place of teaching), about 40 miles to the south of Kokstadt. Mr. Jenkins had lived amongst the Pondos for many years, and was deservedly held in high esteem by them, so much so that his widow stayed on, being known by the name of the "Pondo Queen." She was embittered against the high commissioner, and the Colonial Government, and, like other advocates for the rights of the "black man," was under the impression that the government could do nothing right, and her favourites could do nothing wrong.

Prolonged correspondence by telegraph, and indecision on the part of the Colonial Government, caused the column to be halted for over a month at Kokstadt, an uninviting, treeless, barren waste, to the great vexation of all ranks. To me it was less irksome, as I had the interest of the political situation, the two resident magistrates being ordered to work with me, and, moreover, I had a delightful companion not only in Captain Grenfell, whom I have mentioned, but in Lieutenant Arthur Bigge, (Colonel Sir Arthur Bigge, K.C.B., K.C.S.I.), Royal Artillery. He came to me with a good reputation, and I saw a great deal of him in camp, although on the lines of march but little, having chosen him to make a road sketch from King William's Town to Maritzburg, which he did very well. He and Grenfell accompanied me to Umfundisweeni, where I was sent by the High Commissioner to interview Umquikela.

I went down on the 17th of August with an escort of 20 mounted infantry, and Mrs. Jenkins, outside whose garden I pitched my tent, did her best to induce Umquikela to meet me. She was an interesting old lady but had lived so long amongst the Pondos as to lose the sense of justice where they were concerned. She was very angry with Macaula, Chief of the Bacas, because he had just killed a number of Pondos, and she inveighed against his conceit in having 22 wives, as he was too small a chief to have that number. I asked whether that was her only objection? She said, Yes; she thought it was presumptuous of him.

She told me in the course of conversation it was difficult to explain, how earnestly she prayed for the Pondos when they invaded Bacaland. I asked, was not that rather hard on the Bacas, because they had done nothing wrong? I got no reply to this, and politeness as a guest prevented my saying that her prayers did not seem to have influenced the result, for although at first the Pondos, owing to their great numerical superiority, carried all before them, yet for some unaccountable reason they became panic-stricken, fled, and were slaughtered in great numbers by the pursuing Bacas.

Umquikela at first agreed to meet me on the 17th, but I had assented to it being altered to 8 a.m. on the 18th, explaining that I could not wait longer, as I was due at the Ixopo, 50 miles to the north-east of Kokstadt, on the 19th. At nine o'clock on the 18th I received a message asking me to wait till 2 p.m., and shortly after that hour Mrs. Jenkins, who was playing the part of "Sister Anne" in *Blue Beard*, triumphantly pointed out to me a crowd of natives coming over the hill about three-quarters of a mile distant. There, however, Umquikela remained, and nothing would induce him to come nearer.

Mrs. Jenkins, his adopted mother, sent him many messages, and at five o'clock in the evening told me she fully admitted I had given him every chance, and said she thought it was of no use for me to remain; so, I started on my 40-mile ride back to Kokstadt, which I reached before daylight, and at three o'clock that day was on the Ixopo, where General Thesiger came to dine and sleep, in the little inn. With the kind thought which he always had for others, he, although a teetotaller, brought down a couple of bottles of Perrier Jouet champagne.

We stayed up most of the night talking of the Pondos, about whom, and also the magistrates in the neighbourhood, the general wished to report to the high commissioner. Before we parted it was nearly morning, and to my great pleasure he told me the column might move on by easy marches towards Maritzburg, leaving behind two companies of the Buffs, which were in the neighbourhood.

I brought to the attention of the general the fact that the Imperial Government was paying 30s. *per diem* for every waggon throughout the month we remained at Kokstadt and urged that sufficient waggons and oxen should be purchased to complete with regimental transport any force which might be sent into Zululand. This the general undertook to consider, and when on the 31st of August I rode into Maritzburg a few hours in advance of the column, he told me the principle was approved, and I was to report to him the cost.

I left Maritzburg on the 7th September, having spent a week in formulating a scheme for Regimental transport, and on my way up country with my staff officer, Captain E. R. P. Woodgate received authority to purchase sufficient to equip the 90th Light Infantry, at a cost of £60,000. (General Woodgate was mortally wounded at Spion Kop, Natal, January 1900.)

On reaching Utrecht on the 17th, I inspected the left wing of the battalion, and found that the men were as badly provided with kit as were their comrades with whom I had been serving in the Amatola Mountains, insufficient regimental necessaries had been brought out with the battalion—as previously stated. I had hoped that the left wing, which had been stationary, would be better equipped, but the regimental reserve store of necessaries landed with the companies consisted of four flannel shirts, and four mess tins, and no steps had been taken prior to my arrival to complete the men with equipment.

The district *commandant*, writing from Pieter-Maritzburg, at first resented my strong representations on the subject, but it was time that somebody spoke out, because 5 soldiers had just been sent up from the base, not only unarmed, but unclothed. I was supported, however, by General Thesiger, and from that date until the end of the Zulu Campaign, my suggestion that no soldier should leave the Base without being properly equipped was carried out.

When I returned to Natal in 1881, I found the battalions had slipped back to the old state of unreadiness, for when I inspected two at Lang's Neck I found many of the men had only one, partly worn, pair of boots. There can be no doubt that the regimental system of that time, which practically left all supplies in the hands of the quartermaster and induced the company officers to regard him as a store holder who might be expected to produce anywhere, and at the shortest notice, anything required, was faulty.

The War Office arrangements left much to be desired. When the battalion was ordered out in consequence of the Gaikas having revolted, it might have been reasonably expected that the men would have to encamp, and possibly to fight. They were generally very young, for all recruits were embarked, and although there was an excellent system amongst the non-commissioned officers, yet many of the older ones were not allowed to go out. Thus, the battalion was deprived of some of its most experienced old soldiers in order to save their passage money, which at the time might be taken as £12.

Such maladministration was comparatively of little importance when fighting Gaikas, but it would have been serious if the battalion had to meet the Zulu army in the field soon after it disembarked. This our young soldiers did successfully twelve months later, but it was after marching 1000 miles, and living in what was, after we left the Perie Bush, a healthy climate, for, with proper sanitary arrangements and the absence of public-houses, the young soldiers improved out of recognition.

When I had looked round the little village of Utrecht, which possessed a *laager*, or square walled enclosure, 10 feet high,—without loop-holes or platform from which men could fire over its walls; a magazine standing on an ironstone soil, with no lightning conductor,—and had taken the necessary and obvious steps to improve the situation, I rode on the 19th to Luneberg, a German Lutheran Mission Station 36 miles to the north-east.

The pastor, the Reverend Mr. Filter, spoke English, but neither his family nor his flock spoke aught but German, so I had considerable colloquial practice for the next four days, during which I bought oxen, waggons, and Indian corn, at a cost of £2500. The average price of new waggons, with all their equipment, and a team of 18 oxen, varied from £260 to £300. I liked the straightforward ways of the German settlers, for, three days after I gave one of them a cheque for £270, he returned it to me, saying one of his cows had "lung sickness" and he feared that his oxen might be contaminated already, so he did not venture to send my purchase to Utrecht.

After some conversation with Mr. Filter and his family, I went to see Faku, the chief sent by Cetewayo to frighten the Dutch settlers away from the border, which he had done effectually. I was curious to see the so-called military *kraal* about which I had read while still in England. It was made of wattles, 6 feet in height, and 22 yards in diameter.

He asked me, "Are you going to invade our country?"

"No, not without orders; and so far as I know such orders are not contemplated."

He was impressed by my being unarmed, carrying only a riding-whip, while he sat surrounded by twenty of his warriors. The result of my visit was that he sent to Cetewayo, saying he was satisfied that no immediate invasion of the country would be made from the Luneberg-Utrecht side, and the Maqulusi tribe, which had been assembled in the Inhlobane Mountains, was sent home.

Next day I started with my interpreter, Paliso, who had accompanied me from the Amatola district, Kaffraria, to ride southwards, and then along the Yagpad (hunting road). I intended to stop the night at Potter's store, 35 miles distant, on the Pemvane River, which, as I was told at Luneberg, the owner, from his friendship with the Maqulusi, had been able to keep open, although the district had been abandoned by the Dutchmen. When I reached it, however, I found it was practically empty, and its owner had left.

The Zulus were in a state of excitement: four regiments had recently gone to Ulundi on the king's summons, and four more were then moving down. The men to whom we spoke were so truculent in their behaviour, asking when the Germans were going to obey Cetewayo's orders and leave Luneberg, and showing, moreover, so strong a desire to take my kit, that I decided to go on another 35 miles until I got out of the disputed territory. In my 70-mile ride that day the result of Cetewayo's message was apparent, for there was only one farmhouse with a roof on it, and most of the gardens and fields were being cultivated by Zulus. The mules pulling the Cape cart with my luggage were quite fresh at nightfall when I crossed the Blood River, but my three horses all showed signs of fatigue, and after I halted, the horse I bought at Cape Town, which had gone gaily up to that time, died after ten minutes' pain.

I spent the next ten days purchasing and organising transport, in obtaining which and some mealies I expended £10,000, which rose to over £50,000 by the 1st June 1879. I was obliged to employ my one Staff officer in examining roads, and thus I had to do more than I was really able to carry out to my satisfaction.

On the 1st October, General Thesiger wrote to me that the high commissioner wished to encourage the Luneberg settlers to remain on their farms, in spite of Cetewayo's notice to quit, and asking me if I could raise a Volunteer force. I replied that this was impossible; and on the 16th, the general being away, his chief staff officer, reiterating Sir Bartle Frere's wishes, directed me to be prepared to take the Utrecht garrison to Luneberg, and suggested that I should tell the Germans I was coming.

Next day the high commissioner writing to me in the same strain, as had the general on the 1st October, explained his anxiety to prevent the Germans moving, and his hope that I would do all I could to help them, adding that, of course, he did not intend me to take any military steps without the general's approval. He ended his letter by expressing his gratitude for the work I had done in Pondoland, and for my successful dealings with the chiefs there. To the chief staff officer I wrote that the main risk of the movement would lie in its being known in advance, and that if the troops arrived at Luneberg before the Zulus got warning, in my opinion nothing would happen; and in this view I was supported by the *landdrost* of Utrecht, Mr. Rudolph, who knew the Zulus well.

During the first week in October, Witchdoctors went round the *kraals* on the border, "doctoring" with charms the males who did not belong to the regiments summoned to Ulundi; and on the 14th, Mr. Rudolph warned me that unless I supported the Luneberg settlers at once they would leave, as the friendly Zulus in the neighbourhood, apprehensive of being massacred, had slept out of their *kraals* for several nights.

On the 15th I forwarded the *landdrost's* official letter to the chief staff officer, explaining that, owing to the importance of keeping the Germans at Luneberg, which was our line of communication with Derby, and because of the number of friendly Zulus around the settlement whose service I wished to engage, I had decided to take two companies there to support the Germans. I was urged to do so by a Dutchman named Piet Uys, whose acquaintance I made at this time, and whose father had been killed by Zulus at Weenen in 1838.

I wrote privately to the general the same day, saying I had considered the responsibility I incurred in leaving Utrecht for a day or two with only one company (until the company I had called up from Newcastle could arrive), and had come to the conclusion that if he were present he would approve of my action. I continued:

"I believe many people will consider two companies too few for Luneberg. I think we ought to have more; but if the Zulus come there, I hope our men will not fight less well than their predecessors did at Lucknow. It is possible you may not approve at Maritzburg of my action but believing you would do so if you could see and hear all I see and hear, I feel I should be unworthy of the confidence you put in me if I hesitated to do what I thought was right."

My general, with the generosity with which he always treated me, replied:

"You have taken a serious responsibility upon yourself, and I doubt very much if you have acted wisely. However, you may depend upon my backing you up, as of course, in your position, you are bound to act in whatever way you consider necessary under what, I presume, are very pressing circumstances."

The high commissioner, regarding my action in the political point of view, wrote:

I think Colonel Evelyn Wood deserves our gratitude and acknowledgments for taking the responsibility and saving us from the disgrace of leaving the Germans without protection.

Later, the Governor of Natal, who did not generally agree with Sir Bartle Frere's views, wrote to the same effect, saying that my action

PIET UYS

had effectually stopped any further raid.

I wrote to the general on the 22nd October:

I am sorry I have not your full approval of the course I have adopted, though with your usual kindness you support me. I thought it over for twenty-four hours. On the one hand, I incurred certain Military risks incidental to all warfare, and especially when engaged with such small forces as are usually employed against savages; on the other hand, I risked the almost certain abandonment of the Pongola Valley, involving the loss of the assistance of the farm Kafirs and separation from the Swazies. . . . Though I fully appreciate your generous kindness in endorsing my action, I am anxious, if ill results come from what I think was my duty, it should be known I acted after receiving a copy of your letter to Sir Bartle Frere, (this letter refuses the assistance on account of military risks), I suppose you hardly realise how anxious your unvaried support makes me to act in accordance with your wishes. A 'safe man' would not have run the risk, but I did what I believe you would have told me to do if you had been here.

When Parliament met in February 1879, the Secretary of State for the Colonies, in answering a question put by a member of the Opposition, explained Luneberg was outside the district on which there had been an arbitration, adding:

Colonel Wood could not have taken any other course consistently with his duty.

I started two companies on the 16th October for Luneberg, but the next morning they had only got 7 miles on their journey, being stopped by the difficulties of a mountain-track over the Elandsberg— and it became necessary for me to join them, in order to ensure their progress, as I was anxious to get the companies intrenched at Luneberg before the Border Zulus knew of the movement. By dint of considerable exertion, they reached the Mission Station on the afternoon of the 18th.

I had ridden into Luneberg on the 17th, when I had to undertake a distasteful task. I had purchased from Mr. Filter an ox, for the men's rations; but on my asking him to be good enough to have it killed, he said that was impossible, and that I must kill it myself.

I asked, "Surely some of your farm Zulus will kill it?"

"Yes, certainly," he assented; "but they will kill it as slowly as possible, inflicting as much pain as they can before the animal dies, transfixing it with *assegais* in non-vital places."

I then tried to make my Fingoe interpreter, Paliso, slaughter the ox, but he absolutely declined, saying that he had never done such a thing; so, finally, I had to go in the *kraal*, and shoot it.

When I had settled the companies in their camp, I sent to tell Manyoba (whose *kraal* was 5 miles from Luneberg, and who, in the absence of Faku, was Cetewayo's representative) that I wished to see him but received no answer; and after waiting two hours I rode out to his *kraal*, accompanied by Paliso.

In the *kraal* there were women only, and they informed me that the chief was away on a hill. About 2 miles off I saw a crowd of men, and suspecting it was Manyoba and his kindred, I went on. On riding up I found about 100 men sitting down, most of them with guns, and the remainder with *assegais*. I asked for Manyoba but was assured that he was away.

I knew that he had been seized by the Boers some years before and imprisoned for a considerable time on account of cattle thefts, and believed he feared the same sort of treatment. One or two men came out of the crowd, and said they wanted to know why I wished to see their chief I explained that I had brought soldiers to Luneberg, not to attack the Zulus, or, indeed, to cross the border, but because Faku and, indeed, Manyoba had threatened to kill the Germans unless they left the settlement.

The Zulus wished to argue as to our rights, but this I declined, saying that as the chief was not there, they could give him my message, and I should go back. I was riding away, when there came a shout of "Stop!" and Manyoba, surrounded by a guard of a dozen men, came forward. Two of the younger men caught up their guns, which were on the ground, but the chief told them to put them down, saying, "They are only two." I stayed twenty minutes, and I think reassured Manyoba; but he must have had a strange idea of our power, to be nervous of one white and one black man, when he was surrounded by 100 of his tribe.

CHAPTER 6

1878—Preparations for War

The general having desired me to go to Wesselstroom and ascertain whether it was possible to get any Dutchmen to come out in that district, in the event of a Zulu War, I went up on the 8th November, and was told by the *landdrost* that the feeling was so hostile to the Imperial Government that he doubted any Dutchman coming out. He said if I could persuade Swart Dirks Uys and Andries Pretorius to join us, they would bring over many others. Piet Uys told me that the feeling of his countrymen was so intensely bitter that he doubted whether any of them would come out, but he would do his best to help, not because he loved us, but because he realised the importance of the Border question.

I left Captain Maude with Mr. Swart Dirks Uys to buy ponies, while I returned to Wesselstroom to purchase waggons. Mr. Henderson, the Field Cornet, accompanied me. He was riding a mare whose foal, only twelve days old, cantered along in front of us. I should have preferred to have traveller faster than the baby colt was able to go, but as Mr. Henderson had remained sixteen hours in Wesselstroom to show me his farm, I could not easily shake him off, though I foresaw that he would cost me the loss of valuable time, which indeed was the case. He had a beautiful farm, utilising the sources of the Pongolo River, and he detained us till a herd of 100 horses could be driven past for me to admire. Eventually, after losing three hours of valuable daylight, we left, and mounting a steep hill to the south of his farm we had a glorious view, overlooking 40 miles towards Ulundi. There Mr. Henderson said "Good evening" to us, after pointing out the direction of his brother's house.

We quickened our pace, for a storm threatened to break every minute. Coming to a very bad place on the side of a steep hill, I made Paliso and two 90th orderlies, Walkinshaw and Stringer, dismount and walk, holding back the mule cart, while I led the horses, and at 5.30 we reached a plateau where a streamlet crossed the track. Here I decided to halt, instead of making for Mr. Henderson's house, for rain was falling heavily, and lightning played vividly around us, attracted by the iron-stone which cropped out on the surface of the ground. We soon had a tent up, off-saddled, and unharnessed the mules, when we saw that the mule waggon was stuck on the spot where I had had the cart handled down. Maude walked up to see what was wrong, as a boy came in, saying, "Please, Sare, him waggon turn over." I sent up my servant Fox and two men, keeping one mule driver to catch the horses and mules, which we tied in a circle.

It was now quite dark, and rain was falling in torrents. I sent a Zulu for water and put the men's rifles inside the tent. Taking one of

T. White's lanterns, (Messrs. T. White & Co., Outfitters, Aldershot), I started soon after seven o'clock, with matches in my pocket, and one hand held carefully over a cracked pane of the lantern, but I found that not even a whole pane would keep the candle alight in the furious gusts that swept over me. I trudged on, but got off the track, and was even grateful to the lightning, which helped me to regain it. I found the men breathless from exertion.

The waggon driver had lost his nerve and fearing to drive against the scarped side of the hill, went over the edge of the road, and when Maude got up, the waggon was 30 feet down the slope, all four wheels in the air, and the mules entangled in a heap. When I reached the spot, they had got the limber on to the track, and the waggon body within 7 feet of it, having lifted it up by inches. I got down underneath, and in half an hour we raised it up, and then scotching the wheels, placed it on to the limber. The hill was so steep that the men could not carry up the loads, so they formed line, and passed up the articles.

There were two sacks of "mealies" (Indian corn) which were too heavy for the men to carry, so I made Fox and Walkinshaw take either end of the sacks, while I lay with my face against the side of the hill lower down, and with chest and elbows forced up the centre of the sacks, rolling them upwards.

When we got the load (a very small one) up, I found that the driver and the mules were demoralised, and so decided to run the waggon down by hand. Two men went to the pole, but I said laughingly, "If anyone is to be killed over this job, it had better be an officer; you go behind," and as I tied the lantern, which belonged to my friend Woodgate, in front of the waggon, I added, "If the waggon fetches away, he will never see his lantern again." I took the pole, and at Maude's request let him help me. At the end of it there was a ring, through this we passed a reim, (rope made of ox hide), and knotted it, each taking an end round our wrists.

Although I did not anticipate the serious accident which ensued, I thought it would be safer if we "reimed" up the wheel, for which there was no drag chain, but our united strength failed to move the waggon, and so I was obliged to take off the reim, and with a strong pull we started it. For 30 or 40 yards we did well; then the waggon came faster, and presently, to my horror, I found we had lost control over it. It flashed across my mind that my jest might come true, as, though holding back all I could, I had to increase my pace. I realised in the darkness that Maude had stumbled by the increased weight on my arm. Running on my heels, I made a heavy tug at the pole, and hanging back drew the waggon so close to me that I felt the fore rack on my shoulder and feared I should soon be like a pancake! (I measured the track next morning and found I had taken the wheel to within 5 inches of the scarped outside of the hill.)

As the waggon pressed more heavily on me, putting my left hand on the ledge of the hill, which was about the height of my waist, I vaulted better than I had ever done before, or have done since, rolling over above the waggon. As I scrambled on to the track I saw to my horror what seemed in the darkness to be a bundle, while the waggon, released from the guidance of my hand on the pole, turned to the right, and careered down the slope out of sight. Hastening to the bundle, I found it was Maude on his face, doubled up, senseless. When after some minutes he said, "Oh! my chest is knocked in!" I was so miserable that I could not answer him. He murmured, "Lay me on my back."

I sent a man down the hill after the waggon, to fetch a table. He brought back a broken half of it, on to which we lifted my friend. As we carried him down the hill, the front men being so much lower than those behind, Maude's body began to slip off, so I had to walk backwards, holding his feet, until I noticed Private Stringer was much exhausted, when I changed places with him. Now Paliso was 2½ inches taller than I, so I got an undue weight, and before I reached the tent had no breath left in my body. We placed Maude on the bed in the tent, cutting off his clothes, he groaning all the time. I poured some brandy and water down his throat and put a hot-water bottle to his feet, which were icy.

I then wrote a hasty note to Major Clery at Luneberg and sent Private Stringer and Paliso off with it. It was 25 miles away, on a track neither of them had ever seen, and although the rain had ceased, the mist was so thick it was difficult to see 50 yards off. They had, however, the guiding line of a mountain range, and a river along which they rode. I said to Stringer as they started, "You must ride till you and your horse drop from fatigue to get a doctor, and his quiet "Yes, sir," assured me that if he failed it would only be from one of these causes. As they disappeared in the mist, I shouted, "Borrow some of the officers' horses, and come back at once." They reached Luneberg about 3 a.m., and Stringer announced that he was then ready to start back, while the Kafir lay down and could with difficulty be aroused. He was a Fingoe, and had, moreover, ridden 16 miles with me in the morning, while Stringer had been in camp.

When I got back to Maude, I found he was able to speak, and ask for tea or soup, which I gave him through the tube of my syphon eye-douche; and about one o'clock I lay down and tried to sleep, but every time Maude moved, or groaned, he awoke me. About five in the morning he asked for cocoa, and I wrote a note to Mr. Henderson, whose house was close to us, for some Kafirs to pull out the waggon. I collected some articles from the wreck—the men's tent, and horse food, and washed more dirt off my friend's face.

When the doctor arrived he declared that, as far as he could see, there was no serious damage; the wheels had passed over Maude's chest, and he was very sore all over. When the Kafirs were ready we lifted him on to the stretcher, but he groaned so much from his weight pressing against the sides, that I stopped at Mr. Henderson's and got the loan of a rough bedstead, placing that on the stretcher. We were very tired, and the Zulus occasionally kept step, which gave poor Maude the movement of being tossed in a blanket. As night fell, and with it, rain, I decided to make my way into an empty house we found on the way. We got into Utrecht—45 miles—on the following evening, and at the end of ten days my friend was at work again.

I was up early on the 21st November and arranged for my Cape cart to start with our baggage at 1.30; but about eleven o'clock Captain Woodgate came in, and said that both the drivers were drunk, and nobody else could catch the mules. I observed philosophically, "Perhaps one may be sober by 1.30, which will be plenty of time, and one driver can get the cart to Newcastle, so send the more sober of the two."

I was harried all the forenoon by pressing business, but, to my delight, Major Moysey, Royal Engineers, came to join, and thus I was relieved of one part of my manifold duties. A succession of people,— the principal medical officer, the *landdrost*, and various settlers, and Captain McLeod, my assistant, the agent, (I had been appointed Political Agent for North Zululand and Swaziland in October), accredited to the King of the Swazis,—occupied the time until 3 p.m., when, just as I was starting, Faku, Cetewayo's representative near Luneberg, and another Induna, arrived with an important message. The message was amusing: the Zulu monarch declared that, when he sent orders for the Germans to leave Luneberg, he did not know it was Transvaal territory; but that now he was aware of it, he would make Umbeline keep his people in order, and so perhaps I would be good enough to withdraw the soldiers. I declined this request but consoled the ambassador with a present of tobacco. At the close of the interview the post arrived with important letters from the general, one putting the 13th Light Infantry under my orders.

At 4.30 p.m. I started, with my orderly officer. Lieutenant Harry Lysons. (Son of my friend, General Sir Daniel Lysons.) The Cape cart had 27 miles to go, but Lysons knew a short cut, and a ford across the Buffalo River, just south of where it is joined by the Incandu and Ingagane Rivers. We cantered to the Buffalo, 12 miles, without drawing rein, well under two hours, including a stop at a Fingoe's *kraal*, from whom I hoped to buy mealies. He was a prosperous settler from the Cape Colony, speaking English well. The day was now closing in, and after we were across the river, Lysons hesitated. He had guided me as straight as a line drawn on the map hitherto, but the ground on the right bank of the Buffalo is difficult to understand, and there is no doubt that, having crossed the main stream once, we kept too far to our right, and came back to it.

We now realised we were wrong; but after turning northwards, darkness came over us, and "our rest" became, not "stones," but puddles. Vainly attempting to read my compass, for it was now quite dark, we plodded on at a walk. Light rain fell incessantly, and a black cloud, the precursor of heavy storms, blotted out every star, and compelled us to dismount and feel for footpaths, which crossed and recrossed each other in the most bewildering manner.

About eight o'clock we came to a river, the whirling waters of which we could just distinguish lying below us, with steep banks on either side. After wandering up and down for twenty minutes, our horses jumping round every few minutes, when the flashes of lightning were more than usually vivid, I found a place where oxen had descended, and holding the horses I sent Lysons down to explore, as on the far bank we thought we saw a light. He slipped twice going down, and when he reached the water, being nervous he might be drowned, I called to him to take off his waterproof coat, adding that, as I should probably not hear him, I would sing loudly until his return.

I waited an hour, the horses turning round and sliding about, endeavouring to get their faces away from the rain, and after the first quarter of an hour I sang "Far Away" till I was tired of the tone of my voice, but could not hear a sound. I began to calculate the chances of my ever getting "War-Game" and Lysons' pony down the bank, and came to the conclusion that I should either lose my orderly officer or my horse, who constantly rested his nose on my shoulder.

When the heavy rain came on about five o'clock, I had shifted my un-read English letters from my pocket to my wallets; but now, thinking I ought to try and find Lysons, even though I lost my horse, I put the letters back in my pockets, fearing, however, to find them in a shapeless pulp in the morning. Just then Lysons greeted me so cheerily from the opposite bank, I thought he must have a Kafir with him, but when, having again waded across the river, he rejoined me, he said he could not find the lights, and he believed he had wandered in a circle. As he reported very badly of the descent, we led the horses up stream for 300 yards, but the banks being more unfavourable we returned. So far as I could make out from my watch, it was about eleven p.m.

A heavy storm, obscuring everything, obliged us to stand still, and I sat down and slept for ten minutes, but a loud peal of thunder frightening "War-Game," made him jump so violently as to hurt my arm, which I had passed through the reins. I then decided to try and descend step by step, utilising the lightning for a light. I went down the bank, "War-Game" following me like a dog. It was nervous work walking exactly in front of him, but unless I did so he would not advance a foot! When he reached the water, I rewarded him with a piece of sugar, which I generally carried for my horses.

We got across the river about midnight, and after wandering for about an hour in and out of small ravines, another storm compelled us to halt. We lay down as close to each other as we could for warmth; but as "War-Game" jumped at every vivid flash of lightning, and pulled at my arms, I could not sleep. Lysons slept, not soundly, but still he did sleep. I stood up from about 12.30 a.m. till 4 a.m. wondering occasionally which of the two shivered most, master or horse. I felt nervously at my letters every five minutes to see whether they were still dry. About 4 a.m. the water was so deep under Lysons I made him get up, and he presently heard a cock crow, towards which we led our horses.

After walking for ten minutes I asked, "Do you hear him now?"

"No, not at all. Shall I challenge?" He then screamed such a cock-a-doodle-do that my horse jumped into the air, and nearly knocked Lysons over; but his challenge was immediately answered, and ten minutes' walk brought us to a *kraal*. After much shouting we got a Kafir out, and I let off my only Zulu sentence, asking the way to Newcastle. I could not say "Come and show us," but a half-crown in my left hand, and a grip of his neck with my right, indicated what I wanted, and the Kafir trotted off, bringing us to the bank of a river, through which we waded with some difficulty. The water came in over the top of my boots, Lysons on his pony going in up to his waist. When we got to the far side, being now sure of the track, I threw the half-crown to the astonished Kafir, who probably never earned one so easily before, and we cantered into Newcastle.

After an hour's sleep, and having had some breakfast, we drove northwards, but the jolting of the Cape cart was intolerable. Presently, looking back, I observed a farmer following us in a "Spider," (light four-wheeled American carriage.) I knew him as a man who had ox-waggons for sale and suggested he should take me into his carriage. This he did, and in a four hours' drive I learnt a good deal about Colonial life. While we sheltered in one of his farms, occupied by a Dutchman, who could not speak a word of English, but who made some tea for us, frying beef and eggs together in one pan, we escaped one of the heaviest storms I ever saw.

I have often read with incredulity travellers' stories of hailstones being as large as walnuts, and can scarcely, therefore, hope my readers will believe my statements when I say that I have seen many such under the Drakensberg range of mountains. I bought a span of oxen during the storm, and then started again at three o'clock. The farmer was to have taken us a short cut, but what was generally a little rivulet was now a whirling river, and we had to go round by the ordinary track.

We stopped that night at Meek's farm, 30 miles north of Newcastle, and next morning, rising at daybreak, got the loan of the Spider and two of Mr. Meek's ponies. The ground was heavy, and neither animal would pull, so we started in a somewhat undignified fashion, my orderly officer pushed the cart behind, while Paliso, the interpreter, and I hauled on the shafts until we got up the hill and could start with the advantage of the downward incline.

When we reached the farm of Andries Pretorius, there were twenty of his kindred awaiting my arrival. They were all surly, and although it is customary in that part of the country for the host and his family to come out and assist in unharnessing a guest's horse, nobody offered to help, except Pretorius. He apologised for his kindred, explaining they detested the sight of an Englishman. He was careful to impress on me, however, that were I not his guest he would be equally discourteous. He had a remarkable face, hard, resolute, and unyielding. When we went in—Mr. Meek interpreting—I explained the object of my visit.

"I know," I said, "there is a strong feeling against the Imperial Government, but you have many relatives on the border, and their farms, now valueless, will be very valuable when we settle the question."

Pretorius replied: "We have sworn an oath to be true to Messrs. Kruger and Joubert, who went to England to see your Government, and we will not move till we hear the answer to the deputation, and we will not help you till the Transvaal is given back to us."

"I shall not, then, have the pleasure of your assistance."

We talked for two hours as "friends." Pretorius argued on the Annexation question, and, as I thought, got the worst of it. He said, "You came into my house, saying 'How dirty it is; turn out.' And now you cannot clean one little room named Sekukuni! And what a small broom you have got, to try and sweep up Cetewayo! He will destroy that broom."

I observed, "Well, your house was very dirty, and tumbling down; moreover, it had just then taken fire. My house was next yours, and as you could not put out your fire, I was obliged to try to do it. It is true that the broom was not large enough to sweep up Sekukuni, and it may be destroyed in sweeping up Cetewayo, but my queen can send out 45 regiments instead of the 5 stationed here, and if the little broom is destroyed you will soon see more brooms."

"But why do you light a big fire before you put out a little one?"

"We hope when we put out the big fire, that the little one will go out of itself."

"Then," said he, tell me honestly—do you prefer to have with you your own soldiers, or Dutchmen, when fighting natives?"

"For shooting natives and taking cattle, I prefer Dutchmen. In the Perie Bush, in Kaffraria, I had 300 Dutchmen in my command, but when I had a position to carry, and the Kafirs were standing up to us, I took soldiers. In four months I never had a Dutchman killed in action."

Although this honest opinion was not appreciated by Pretorius or by his family, we had much conversation, and finally, when I left the farm, all the Dutchmen came out and expressed the hope that personally I might come safely out of the Zulu War.

I did not abandon the general's scheme, on account of this failure, and when at the end of November the staff at Maritzburg wrote that the Cabinet had finally decided not to accede to the general's request for reinforcements, expressing the hope that war would be avoided, I made an effort to win over the Dutchmen living in the Wakkerstroom and Utrecht districts. On the 4th December, after a conference which lasted from 9 a.m. to 5 p.m., I induced some of them to say that in the event of war they would accompany me. The man of most influence won over was Piet Uys, who, for himself and his sons and nephews, declined to receive pay.

★★★★★★

Extract from a letter from Lord Chelmsford to Colonel Evelyn Wood:—

Maritzburg, 10th December 1878.

You have done wonders with the Dutchmen, and I am quite sure the High Commissioner will be as much obliged to you from a Political point of view as I am from a Military one.— Chelmsford.

Sir B. Frere to the Secretary of State for the Colonies:—

Maritzburg, 23rd December 1878.

I have but little doubt but that the firm, conciliatory, and judicious treatment of these gentlemen by Colonel Evelyn Wood will have an excellent effect, not only locally, but generally throughout the South-eastern Transvaal districts.—B. Frere.

★★★★★★

I spent the next three weeks in purchasing transport, and having sketches made of all tracks leading over the Transvaal frontier towards Ulundi.

Chapter 7

Christmas 1878.—The Invasion of Zululand

Sir Theophilus Shepstone came to stay with me, Christmas Eve 1878, for three days, and gave me much valuable information about the Zulus. He was particularly kind, and I appreciated it the more because the high commissioner having made me a Political Agent for North Zululand and Swaziland, had virtually taken the control of our policy in those countries, as regards the natives, out of his hands. This, however, increased my work, and I had more than I could do. My diary shows that at 6.30 a.m. I was inspecting mounted infantry, and a more ragged crew perhaps was never got together, except the professional beggars on a stage. I was much dissatisfied, for the first horse I looked at was about to get a sore back, his saddle cloth being twisted up under the saddle. Many of the men had only 10 rounds of ammunition, instead of 75.

I got back to breakfast at 8 a.m., when Captain Barton rode in from Major Buller's camp, where he was doing good work, which justified my recommendation of him for Special service. (Captain

105

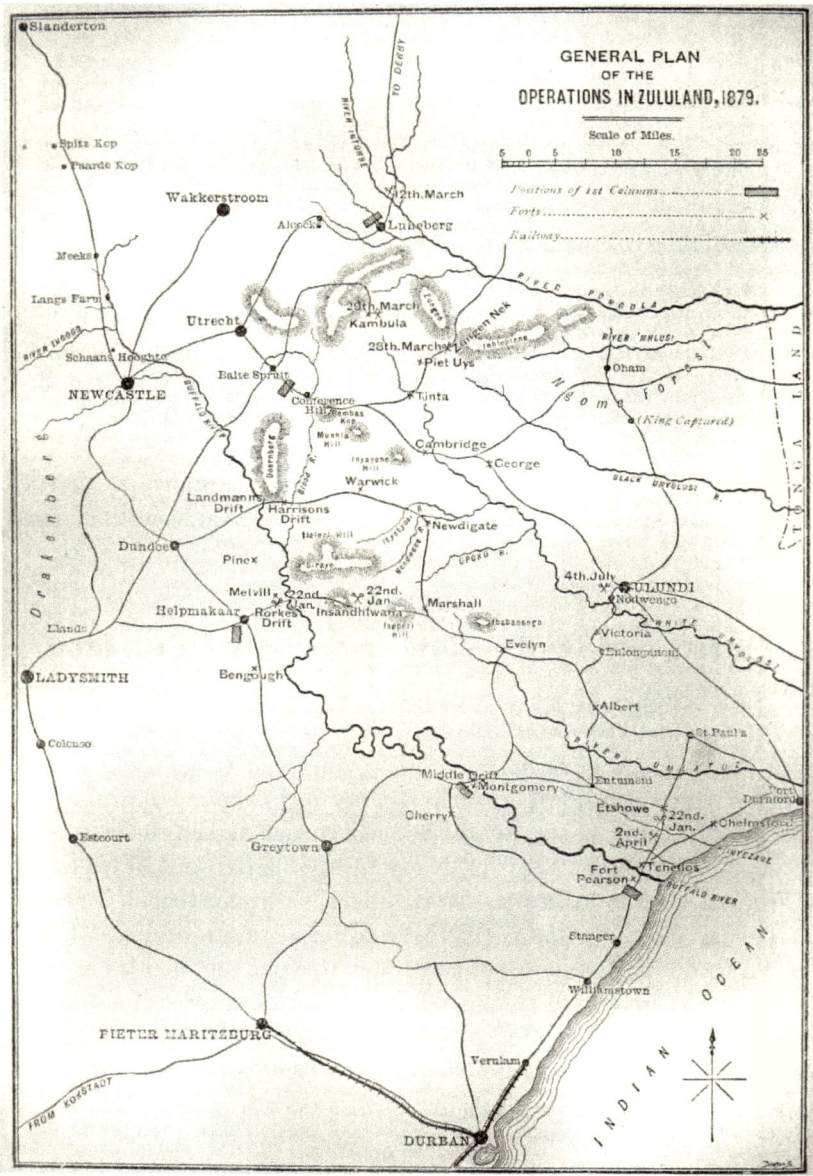

GENERAL PLAN
OF THE
OPERATIONS IN ZULULAND, 1879.

Barton, Coldstream Guards, serving in Frontier Light Horse; he was *aide-de-camp* to Sir Hope Grant at Aldershot in 1870-1871.) During breakfast time, a hurried meal, I gave him instructions, as he was going to Wesselstroom to buy horses, grain, and vegetables.

At nine o'clock I had a second inspection of the 90th Light Infantry, looking at every man's boots, which were unsatisfactory; this took till 11.30. My excellent major was much vexed by my telling him that the kits of no two companies were laid out in the same manner, for this, though perhaps not of great importance in itself, takes the inspecting officer more time. Nor were his men's "small books" signed for the previous month. Then I passed on, telling the Royal Engineer officer what was required in the *laager* to make it defensible.

The *landdrost* now appeared, with the townspeople, and asked how many soldiers were to be left to protect them.

"I am not going to leave any, except the halt and the maimed. The townspeople can defend the *laager*, and the halt and maimed my stores, and if I lose them it won't much matter to me."

One of the local leaders said, "If you lose your stores you will starve!"

I replied, "I shall have two months' supplies at Balte Spruit, 20 miles in advance; and all I promise the Utrecht Townspeople is a decent burial on my return."

Then the senior doctor came and asked me our plan of campaign. Surgeon-Major Cuffe, however, was a good organiser, and took all trouble in that respect off my hands. Then a captain came and told me he could not work with his senior officer and must leave him. I suspected that the complainant had a hot temper but sent him to work on transport duty. Next, Major Clery appeared, (now Major-General Sir C. Clery, K.C.B.), and said that Captain Barton had annexed a waggon. The dispute turned on a point of grammar.

Clery wrote, "Send them back." Barton read this to mean "oxen." Clery meant "waggon and oxen." They both quoted Lindley Murray at length. Captain Woodgate then wanted me to look at, and buy, two horses which were outside. I told him to ask Clery to buy, or reject, the horses. At this moment I was reminded that I was to give an address on the Zulu nation and its army on the following Friday night, to which I had not yet given a thought! When I could obtain ten minutes without interruption, I was considering how to equip 1000 natives without any means at hand. To this number I later added another 1000, and as officers speaking Zulu had to be found, as well as blankets, guns, and something to carry powder and bullets, or ammunition, it will be understood the work was of an engrossing nature.

I began work at daylight on Christmas Day 1878, and went to a Church parade at 7 a.m., and then did some odd jobs till 8.30, when we had a Sacrament service, for which Major Buller and Captain Barton rode in ten miles. It was pleasant to see our boldest polo players, who had hustled me the previous evening, Bright, Hotham, and Lysons, at the service. All three were fine bold boys; Bright had been the stroke oar of the Eton Eight. They came in to breakfast, which caused some little difficulty about knives and forks, as Sir Theophilus Shepstone was still with me. He worked with me for a couple of hours after breakfast, and then I did business with the doctors and commissariat.

I saw my guest off about midday, but when I returned from a ride to Major Buller's camp, I found that Sir Theophilus had come back, for his mule driver was drunk, and all the mules were lost. This was, however, my gain, as I could not see too much of my guest, and it cleared up our relations. He wrote to me later from Newcastle, he had previously imagined Sir Bartle Frere was under the impression that he was not supporting me; the idea was, however, erroneous. Sir Theophilus and I had disagreed as to putting in force the Transvaal Commando law.

He thought it would be better to make it applicable to whites and blacks, and I wanted it enforced only for natives, in order to obtain drivers and *foreloupers* for my waggons, and the black men who formed Wood's regiment, many of whom, however, came voluntarily, as indeed they well might, at 1*s.* a day. I always received the warmest support from Sir Theophilus, and the misunderstanding was caused, I think, by my diffidence in expressing, after so short a residence in the country, any opinion which did not coincide with that of one who had spent his life in South Africa.

On the 26th December I started a company, 13th, and one of the 90th Light Infantry with a convoy of waggons to fill up Balte Spruit, a position I had selected 20 miles to the southward of Utrecht. About midday I received a message from Captain Woodgate that all the waggons were stuck in a ravine, 10 miles distant, and later it became necessary to encamp a company at three different places to assist the oxen when they were unable to "pull out" by themselves.

At the end of the month I got a very kind letter from the general—now Lord Chelmsford—relative to the *Gazette* of Honours and

Rewards for the Operations in the Amatola Mountains, which had just been received.

★★★★★★

He wrote: "I was sorry not to see your name in Orders for some reward, for all your good service, and for the help you have given me, but it is only deferred. Your loyal and excellent work will not, and shall not, go unrewarded, if I have anything to say to it."

★★★★★★

The confidence which the general gave me enabled me to urge a more concentrated advance than he had at first intended, and this was eventually adopted, as was another suggestion I made, that we should purchase all the Transport we might require, as being not only a cheaper arrangement, but the only feasible plan to ensure success. Any disappointment I felt about the *Gazette* was mitigated by the fact that several officers whom I had recommended received promotion, including two in the 90th Light Infantry, Some other selections, although made, no doubt, on what appeared to those in Pall Mall adequate grounds, caused much amusement in the Colony, for of two of the seniors who became Companions of the Bath, one had been relegated to the command of 30 privates and the regimental band, 500 miles from the scene of action, and the other assumed charge of a few loyal natives in a peaceful district.

The military secretary treated me with great kindness, and allowed me to write to him freely, so I urged on his attention the omission of Brevet Major Hackett's name; and took the opportunity of telling Sir Alfred Horsford that the delay in gazetting me to the command of the regiment had caused me to serve ten months in South Africa at 2*s.* a day less pay than Captain Woodgate, or indeed any of the captains employed on special service, received.

When my last company joined at Utrecht, the officer in command informed me he had heard all his way up that Colonel Wood was a wonderful judge of oxen. This was an unfounded reputation, for I knew very little about cattle. I had no veterinary surgeon and was therefore obliged to look closely at every beast myself; but the average price and quality was undoubtedly satisfactory.

The incessant work, however, now began to tell on me, and my glands swelled as they had done when I was overworked in the Amatola Mountains, although for pleasure and on principle I played either lawn-tennis or polo for an hour or two every evening, the subalterns of the 90th being always available for a game.

On the 1st January one of my spies informed me that Cetewayo had assured Sirayo that he should not be given up to the British Government. Sirayo was not himself in fault, but the action of his sons, and especially of the elder, Melokazulu, (reported as killed in Bambaata's rebellion, June 1906), was the ultimate cause of Cetewayo's downfall.

Sirayo, whose district was on the borders of Zululand, adjoining the Buffalo River, had, like all important chiefs, many wives, and two of the younger ones absconded with young Zulus resident in Natal. Melokazulu followed with an armed party, and surrounding the *kraal*, took the women back into Zululand, where he shot them. In the following year I asked him in the course of conversation why he did not shoot the men, and he answered simply, "Oh, my father did not pay for them as he did for the women, for whom he gave cattle, and besides, the men were subjects of the British Government."

"Did your father know that you had gone after the wives?"

"No."

"Did he approve of your having shot them?"

"I don't know. I told him they were dead, and he made no remark."

I moved what was now called No. 4 column, consisting of the 13th and 90th Light Infantry, 4 guns, a varying number of horsemen, on the 3rd January to Balte Spruit, near the Blood River, which we crossed on the 6th, after hearing that Cetewayo had not accepted the terms offered by the high commissioner.

I received a letter on the 9th January from the general, requesting me to move down and demonstrate to the southward, to take pressure off him as he crossed the Buffalo, and also, if he was unopposed, to meet him personally about halfway from our respective positions.

I told the Zulus in our neighbourhood, and as far east as the White Umvolosi, that they must decide before daylight on the 11th January whether they intended to be friends, or foes. When, after the 11th, Colonel Buller seized a large number of cattle, I asked some of the Zulus why they had not driven them off, and they answered, "Oh, we never thought you would begin on the day you mentioned."

On the evening of the 10th, I moved with about two-thirds of the column, having *laagered* and entrenched one-third, towards Rorke's Drift. It rained incessantly, and the Blood River behind us, usually only 3 feet deep, became 11 feet in the course of a few hours, while it was impossible to move a waggon over slight watercourses, without putting on 50 men to help the oxen. I started at 2.30 a.m. for

CETEWAYO AFTER THE WAR

the Itilezi, and soon after nine o'clock met Lord Chelmsford on the Nkonjane Hill, 9 miles from Rorke's Drift. No. 3 column had started the previous day, but the difficulties of crossing the Buffalo were considerable.

I had an interesting talk with Lord Chelmsford for three hours, while Colonel Buller was sweeping up cattle to the south of the general's line of advance. After we had discussed the many affairs in which we had been interested since we met three months earlier, he pressed me, in the name of the high commissioner, to accept the office of Resident of Zululand. I urged that the Resident ought to speak the language, and that, moreover, I was too fond of soldiering to leave the 90th Light Infantry for political employment. He was greatly pleased to learn that I had got forty-two days' supplies for man and beast at Balte Spruit, besides a week's rations I had with me, as No. 3 column had only collected fifteen days'. Mr. Hughes, my commissariat officer, had been indefatigable in adding to my stores, for which purpose he had been sent three weeks earlier from the Transvaal.

Before I left Lord Chelmsford, I warned him that, according to the information given by my spies, the first serious Zulu attack would fall on the column which he was accompanying. Three days later, on the 14th, I informed His Lordship that no forward movement had been made from Ulundi, but on the 17th I wrote, "My spies say that the Zulu Army," or, as they expressed it, "Cetewayo, is moving westward."

On the 14th January I sent to tell Seketwayo, a chief of considerable importance, who had been negotiating with me since the 2nd, that I could no longer herd the 2000 head of cattle we held taken from his territory, but if he would come in, he should have them. The matter was complicated, as a considerable number of the cattle belonged to Cetewayo, or rather to the Royal House. The chief could not make up his mind and having waited five days I sent the cattle away to the Free State, where they were sold.

Being uneasy concerning Zulus to the north of our left flank, I directed Colonel Buller to send there the Frontier Light Horse under Captain Barton, who took between 500 and 600 head of cattle, clearing the Pemvane and lower Bevane Rivers, while the column was moving forward slowly, much impeded by heavy rain, to the Umvolosi.

I had obtained the general's approval to my going in a north-easterly direction to clear the Ityenteka Range, including the Inhlobane mountain, of Zulus under Umsebe and Umbeline, hoping to be back before the general was ready to advance with No. 3 column. Having reached the Umvolosi River on the 19th, we built a fort at Tinta's Kraal, which, humanly speaking, should have been impregnable if held by two companies, and off-loading seventy waggons I sent them in the afternoon back towards Balte Spruit, escorted by Captain Wilson's company of the 90th, with orders to fill up the waggons and return to Tinta's Kraal, where I intended to leave him, and a company of the 13th.

About 7 o'clock in the evening I got a note from Colonel Buller, saying that he had been engaged for some hours on the Zunguin mountain with several hundred of the Makulusi tribe, who were pressing him back, and, as he was writing at sunset, had crossed in small numbers to the right bank of the Umvolosi. This disturbed me considerably, for they were now within a few miles of our empty waggons, and it was not only the chance of the loss of the company and £21,000 worth of property, but it would have been difficult to replace the waggons. I knew that the convoy was not more than 3 or 4 miles off, for there was a muddy ravine which could only be passed with difficulty, and that Captain Wilson intended to begin to cross it at daylight.

Captain Woodgate, seeing I was perturbed, asked me the reason, and on reading to him Colonel Buller's note, at once went to the company, although we were just going to have something to eat. He had the oxen inspanned at once, the drivers and *foreloupers* on learning the news being anxious to get away to a place of safety. His unconsciousness of danger was shown by handing his horse to a Zulu when he dismounted to help the waggons across the ravine, with the result that he never saw it again for three days. Nothing of importance, however, occurred, for Colonel Buller, by showing a bold front to the Makulusi, held them on the river, and they retired after dark to their stronghold on the highest part of the mountain.

On the night of the 20-21st we made a long night march with the 90th Light Infantry, two guns and the mounted men starting at 11 p.m., and at daylight climbed the western end of the Zunguin mountain, along which we advanced during the day, taking some cattle and driving 1000 Zulus off it, they retiring to the *nek* connecting it with the Inhlobane. Looking down from the eastern extremity, we saw about 4000 Zulus drilling under the Ityenteka Nek; they formed in succession a circle, triangle, and square, with a partition about eight men thick in the centre.

We descended at night for water, and rejoined the 13th, the 90th Light Infantry having been nineteen hours out of the twenty-four

113

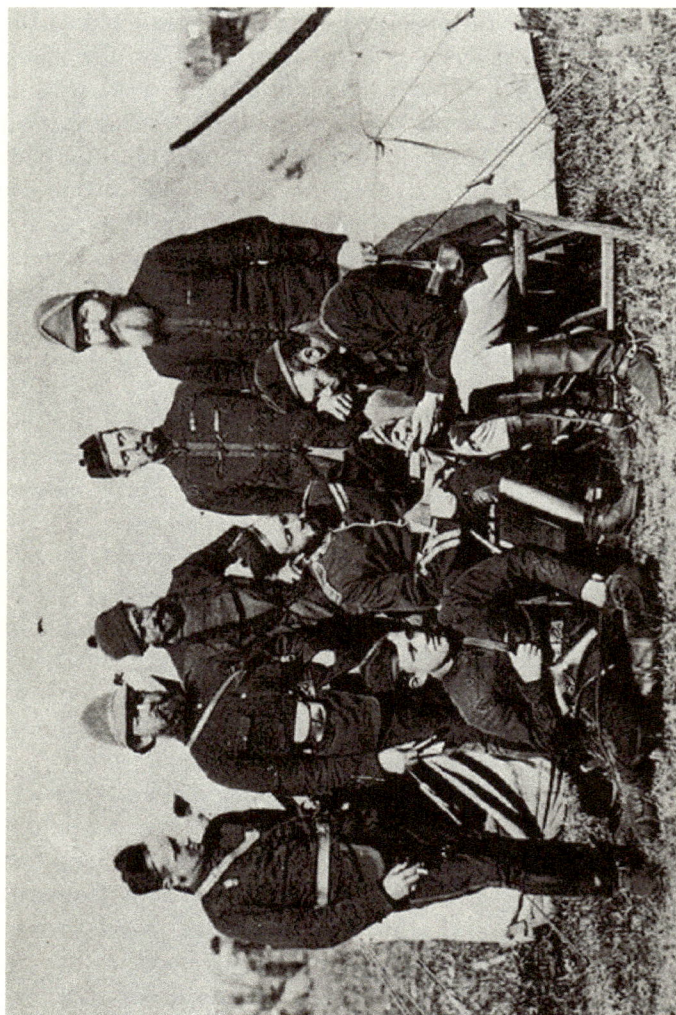

WOOD WITH HIS STAFF

under arms and having covered a considerable distance. In mileage, however, it was not so great as the distance covered by Wilson's company escorting the waggons, which filled up at once and returned to the Umvolosi, marching 34 miles in twenty-six hours.

We heard the guns fired at Isandwhlana, 50 miles off, that evening as we sat round a camp fire.

★★★★★★

These were fired by Lord Chelmsford's troops returning from Sirayo's district to the wrecked camp. Our Senior officers asked my opinion, what was the probable cause, and I said guns fired after dark indicated, I apprehended, an unfavourable situation.

★★★★★★

There was a thick mist on the morning of the 24th which delayed our advance, but when it cleared we moved forward and came under fire from Zulus hidden in the rocks under the south-western point of the Inhlobane. Leaving the 90th and two guns to follow the waggon track with the baggage, I went to the right with the 13th Light Infantry, Piet Uys and his troop of 40 *burghers*, with whom I was disappointed, as it was necessary for Piet and myself to ride in front to induce his men to go on to cover the advance of the guns. When we reached the rocks from whence the fire had come, it was clear we could not hope to get the guns down, so, after driving back a few Zulus who were in broken ground, I turned northwards, and went to a hill under which I had ordered the 90th to halt with the waggons and outspan.

When I got there the oxen had just been loosened from the Trektow, but to my great vexation they were without any guard, and the 90th, which ought to have been with them, was three-quarters of a mile in front, advancing rapidly in line, without any supports, against some 4000 Zulus.

★★★★★★

It appeared later I had greatly under-estimated the Zulu force, imagining it was the Makulusi regiment only, but the high commissioner learnt from his agent, and reported to the Secretary of State, not only was the Makulusi routed and dispersed, but that the Nodwengu and Udloko regiments shared in their fate. Later, Sir Bartle Frere wrote: "The Zulus are greatly impressed with the skill with which this force (Colonel Wood's) has been handled and are afraid it may push on to the Inhlazatze and threaten the Royal Kraal."

★★★★★★

I looked up the ravine, which farther to the southward had stopped my onward progress with the 13th Light Infantry and guns and was concerned to see about 200 Zulus coming down it towards the 90th's ammunition carts, which had been left with some bugler boys, who had no firearms.

I had just told an orderly to call Colonel Buller, when I was accosted by a Kafir who had ridden 48 miles from Utrecht bringing a note from Captain Gardner, recounting the disaster of Isandwhlana, of which he had been an eye-witness. Buller came to me at once and telling him in one sentence of the misfortune which had befallen No. 3 column, I sent him up the ravine to drive back the Zulus, while I galloped to the 90th and expressed a strong opinion to the senior officer—not belonging to the regiment—who had contravened my orders. The Zulus in front of them made no stand.

The young soldiers were very steady and expended less than two rounds of ammunition per man; but the Zulus filed from the sight of the advancing line and went ten paces to one covered by our men. The Frontier Light Horse and the Dutchmen pursued them until they climbed the Inhlobane mountain, and then after a halt of two hours I ordered the column to fall in, and, against the advice of some of the senior officers, read to the men the note I had received.

We moved back as far as our camp of the previous day, and next morning returned to our fort on the Umvolosi River. I was now in some difficulty. I did not want to abandon supplies, and I had 70 loads for which I had no waggons. The Dutchmen, who were well provided with waggons, and were themselves wonderful drivers of oxen, came to my aid. Piet Uys and his men, who had only about 1000 lbs. weight on each waggon, loaded up to 8000 lbs., and then we moved slowly westwards, halting on the 28th at Venter's Drift, where I was within reach of firewood, our greatest want in that part of the country. There were trees growing in the ravines south of the Ngaba Ka Hawane Mountain.

Here I received a considerate note from Lord Chelmsford, giving me a brief account of the disaster at Isandwhlana, and telling me I had a free hand to go anywhere or adopt any measures I might think best, ending:

> You must now be prepared to have the whole of the Zulu Army on your hands any day. . . . No. 3 Column, when re-equipped, is to subordinate its movements to your column. Let

A Zulu attack

me know how it can assist you.

I replied to Lord Chelmsford on the 31st January that I was in a position on Kambula Hill which I anticipated being able to hold even against the whole of the Zulu Army. I understood he did not wish me to incur risk by advancing, and I would not move unless it became necessary to do so in order to save Natal.

In spite of the carriage for stores lent to us by the Dutchmen, we had some trouble before we succeeded in finding a good military and sanitary position, and even to men who did not feel much compassion for oxen, to make them pull 8000 lbs. through swamps is trying to their feelings as well as to the oxen's hides. It has often been a wonder to soldiers in South Africa how the Dutch, under Pretorius and other leaders forty years earlier, took waggons up and down mountains which appear to us impracticable for wheel traffic, but the maximum weight in a waggon on commando was 1500 lbs., five adults being allowed a waggon between them, which of course made a great difference on a bad track. The difficulties of transport caused me to halt every second or third day, as I was obliged to make two journeys with my loads, and I soon had warning that I could not remain in the valley of the Umvolosi, by the loss of horses and oxen, followed by that of a man of the 90th, who died of very rapid enteric fever.

The military situation, although I tried to conceal the fact, affected my health. I never slept more than two or three hours at a time, going round the sentries for the next three months at least twice every night. We shifted camp five times before we finally took up the position in which the greater part of the Zulu Army attacked us on the 29th March, and as we constructed slight entrenchments in every camp, and improved the formation of the encampment so as to obtain the greatest amount of fire from all sides, the men were kept employed, and gained valuable experience.

We worked on Sundays, saying our prayers in a practical manner, for I had Divine Service parade on ground immediately adjoining the spot where two companies were at work throwing up redoubts, and let the men put down their picks and shovels and join in the service, which, during the sixteen months in which I either read it myself or caused one of the staff officers to do so, never kept the men standing more than ten minutes, and I have never seen soldiers so attentive.

From December 1878 I had native scouts 20 miles in front of our force, and patrols 6 miles out an hour before daylight, but in the afternoon we amused ourselves, although the early morning was a period of anxiety. My spies informed me of impending attacks, which were predicted for each new and full moon, which periods are held by the Zulus to be auspicious. Mounted men were stationed 6 miles in front by day, and two companies beyond our cattle at grass.

The arrangements for security during night were peculiar. It rained regularly when the sun went down, throughout the months of February and March, which added to our difficulty of ensuring security without impairing the health of the soldiers. To save them, the outlying pickets were allowed tents pitched in a circle, 200 yards outside the *laager*. Groups of 8 men were placed 100 yards farther out, 6 lying down under blanket shelters, while 2 watched and listened.

Beyond on the paths most convenient for the enemy's approach, under a British officer, were small parties of Zulus, whose marvellous hearing by night, and sight by day, enhanced the value of our precautions.

★★★★★★

They were drawn from the Border Zulus I enlisted at Luneberg in November, and attached to battalions, 6 to each company; their powers of hearing were extraordinary; they could see farther than we could with field glasses—their vision was surpassed only by the telescope. They lived near the battalion cooking fires and were the cause of considerable difficulty with respect to their clothing. I could not buy soldiers' greatcoats in Africa, but it was the dumping ground of cast-off full dress uniforms of the British Army, and I obtained from Maritzburg old cavalry tunics, those of the Heavy Dragoon Guards being the only ones into which the Zulus could squeeze their bodies, and in these it was only the top buttons that would meet.

★★★★★★

After the disaster on the Intombe these men asked to speak to me, and said: "We want to go home to our families, for you are going to be attacked by the whole of the Zulu Army."

"Well, that is just the reason why you should stop with me; I have been paying you all these months, and you have never yet been in danger."

"Oh, we are not nervous about ourselves, you are sure to repulse the attack, but some of the Cetewayo's men will sweep round in raiding parties on both flanks, and kill our women and children, who are near Luneberg."

119

"I promise you I will insure your wives and your cattle if any harm comes to them while you are with me," on which they saluted and went back to the kitchen fires quite content.

It is interesting that at some athletic sports on the 19th February, in the country pastime of throwing the *assegai*, the Zulus, who since Chaka's time had been taught not to throw long distances, but to rush on their foe and stab him with the short *assegai*, were easily beaten, the first prize being won by a Hottentot about 5 foot in height, who propelled an *assegai* 70 yards, the second man being a Colonial born Englishman, while no Zulu threw an *assegai* farther than 50 yards.

Our team in the tug-of-war, which had only been once defeated, was thoroughly beaten by Piet Uys and his Dutchmen. In 1872, when we were at Aldershot, I wished the battalion to enter a team for Divisional Athletic sports. I could get no volunteers, the battalion had never pulled in a tug-of-war, and showed no inclination to begin; eventually I had to appeal to the sergeant-major, who practically coerced the colour sergeants into producing one man a company. When I looked at them, selecting a man who seemed to be about my own size, I said: "I do not think you will be much good for this job—I doubt whether you can pull me over."

"I can do that, sir, and without much trouble."

Taking up a rope, I told him to try. He gave one look at me, and then pulled me off my feet; and although I sacrificed my spurs by digging them into the ground, he took me across the parade ground without any apparent effort. My judgment was decidedly faulty; although he was not more than a stone heavier than I was, his arms and back were abnormally powerful. I was much interested in training the team, which beat in succession every battalion at Aldershot, the Garrison Artillery at Portsmouth, every regiment of the Guards, a Brigade team of the Guards, a team from H.M.S. *Excellent* at Portsmouth, and a team of the Royal Marines. We sent it about to different garrisons, and it was never beaten until it met the 96th Regiment, which had an equally well-trained team, each man being about half a stone heavier in weight, the effect of which was decisive.

When we were marching up from King William's Town to Natal, our men vanquished the Frontier Light Horse, composed of fine men, as they did when at Utrecht, and again at Kambula Hill, but they could not make the Dutchmen take their pipes out of their mouths. I said to Piet Uys, "I do not think your pipe will be alight in a quarter of an hour." He laughed, and at the end of the quarter of an hour the

FORT ESHOWE

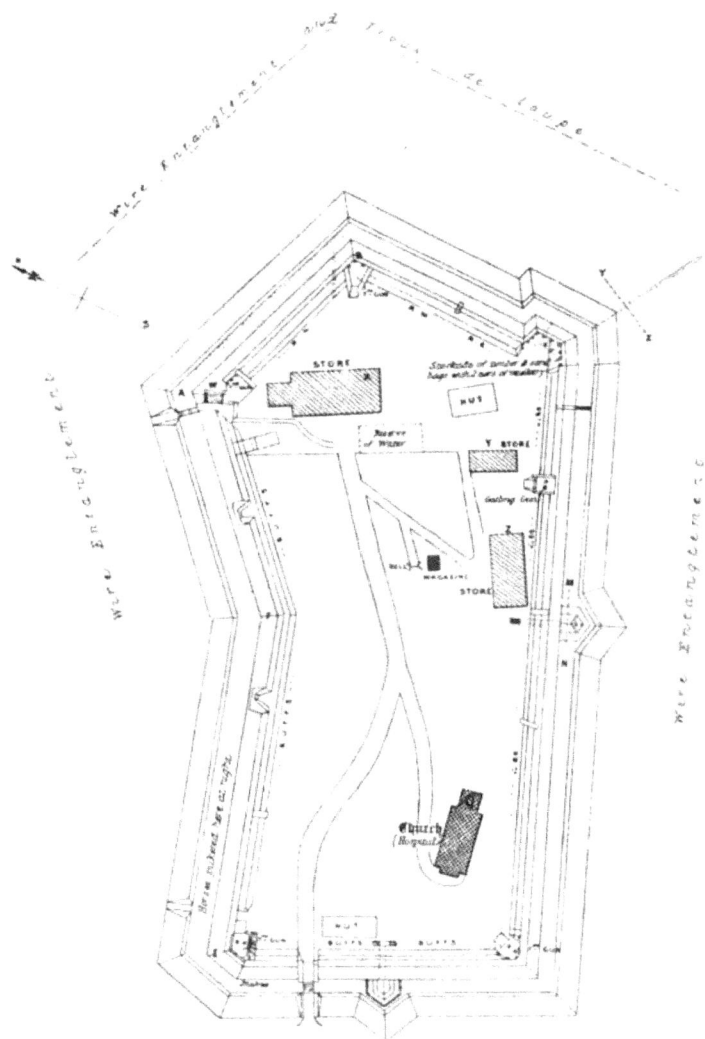

laugh was against me, for the Dutchmen, averaging 14 or 15 stone, with enormous knotted arms, and hands like iron, waited until the 90th were exhausted, and then without an effort pulled them over.

In each camp we occupied I made a lawn-tennis ground, playing it, and polo on alternate afternoons, when I was not out on reconnoitring expeditions.

CHAPTER 8

1879—In Zululand

At some athletic sports held in February, I was strolling amongst the competitors when I received a vigorous slap on the back, and, turning round, was greeted effusively by an officer with the exclamation: "How are you, old boy?" He was not able to stand steady, and I sent him away under arrest, in charge of Captain Ronald Campbell.

Next day, when he was brought before me, I asked: "What have you got to say?" Now, I have had to deal with many similar offenders, but never before had such an honest answer; most men attribute their inebriety to an incongruous mixture with salad, or to the effects of a very small amount of alcohol on an empty stomach under a hot sun, but my officer replied: "Drunk, sir, drunk; nothing but drunk."

"This is very serious, and I should like some hours to think over your case."

"Quite simple, sir; you must either let me off, or try me by court martial."

When I saw him again I said: "It is not the question of our safety only, but also of our honour as soldiers; if you are in charge of the piquets when this happens again, you might cause a great disaster."

"In the language of the soldiers, sir," he replied, "if you give me a chance I shall never be drunk again while under your command." He kept his promise, showed great courage in action some weeks later (for which, indeed, he had been noted when tiger shooting on foot in India), and his reformation was complete. A year later, when in Cape Town, I came across him one day when I had arranged a dinner to many of my former comrades, the club being placed at my disposal for the purpose. Although the dinner was convivial, and I invited my bibulous comrade, I should have been doubtful of his reformation if he had abstained altogether, but he took an ordinary amount of wine, and left about midnight perfectly sober.

Before he joined me in 1878 he was drinking heavily, while attached to another regiment at Maritzburg. One day the mess sergeant

122

ROUGH SKETCH

of

INTOMBE RIVER DRIFT

[Not drawn to scale]

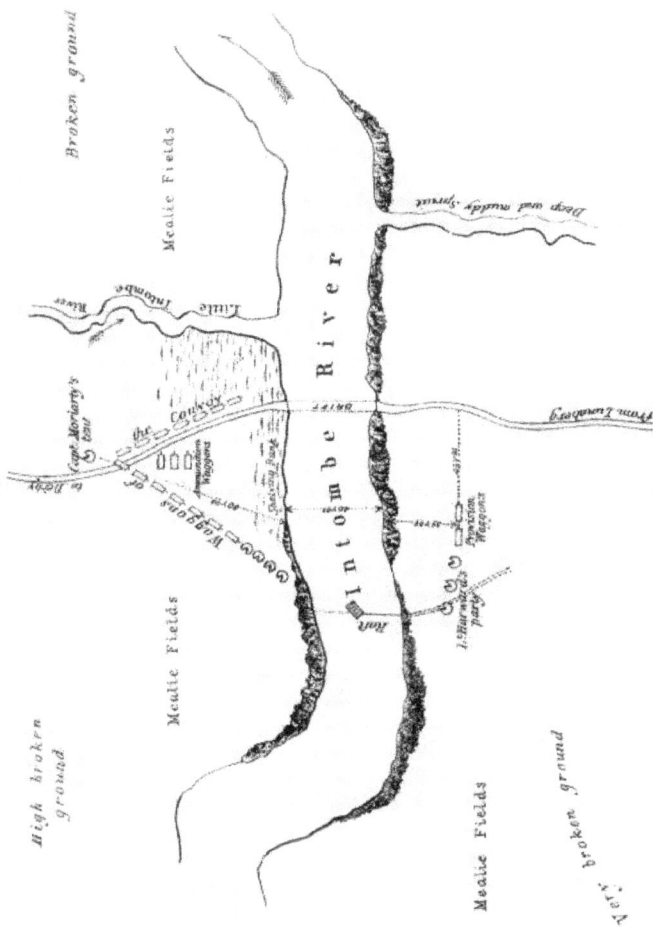

High broken ground

Broken ground

Mealie Fields

Little Intombe River

Intombe River

Mealie Fields

the Cattle

to Capt. Moriarty's tent

Wagons

Ammunition Waggon

Sinking Sand

104.50

104.50

104.50

81 yds

to Derby

Mealie Fields

Raft

Lieut. Harward's party

Provision Waggons

from Luneberg

Deep and muddy Spruit

Mealie Fields

Very broken ground

said to the officer managing the mess: "Unless I get some relief, sir, I must go back to duty."

"Why, what is wrong?"

"So-and-so goes to sleep every night on the sofa in the ante-room, and as he never wakes up till between one and two o'clock, I cannot close the mess."

"Sergeant, don't mind him—lock it up, and go to bed," the officer replied; and so, he did.

Next morning about 2 a.m. the honorary member awoke, and, rolling off the sofa, collided with the coal scuttle, and then fell over a high fender guard. This alarmed him considerably and crawling away he clutched the legs of a centre table, which he overturned. The crash aroused the sergeant, who hurried in undressed, grasping a lighted candle, when the officer exclaimed in a piteous tone: "Where am I—in Hell?"

"The sergeant, standing erect in his night-shirt, said: "No, sir, officers' mess."

The officer sat up, and at once asserted his authority, saying decidedly: "Then, bring me a brandy and soda."

During the night of the 12th-13th March I was awakened by a messenger with the news of the disaster to a company of the 80th Regiment, which was marching from Derby to Luneberg. Four companies crossing the Intombe River, 5 miles from Luneberg, had camped at the station when the water rose, and the 5th Company was unable to cross. A raft was employed, and one-third of the company had reached the west side of the stream of the river at nightfall. Half an hour before daylight next day an attack was made by Umbeline, assisted by Manyoba's tribe. (The nervous chief who feared I was going to arrest him in September).

Nearly everyone on the east bank of the river was *assegaied*, many in their tents, and the Zulus, taking to the water like otter hounds, crossed and endeavoured to overwhelm the 34 men on the western bank. Some 10 of these, however, were not only skilfully but courageously handled by Sergeant Booth, who successfully brought the party back. In all 40 of our men were killed.

I went over at daylight to the scene—40 miles distant—to inquire into the disaster, and to ensure our system for security being adopted for the future, returning in the afternoon to camp, as I had arranged a long ride for next day.

Uhamu, a brother of Cetewayo's, came into our camp in the Cape cart which I sent for him, he being so enormously bulky that it was difficult to find a horse to carry him.

★★★★★★

Sir Bartle Frere eulogised my agent, Captain Macleod, and me for our "temper, judgment, and patience" in getting Uhamu over from his brother; and a Zulu agent told Bishop Colenso, and Sir Bartle later, that Cetewayo's altered tone was due to the defection of Uhamu.

★★★★★★

He had made many appointments, but in the procrastinating Zulu fashion had failed for various reasons to keep them, until Colonel Buller had ceased to believe in his being willing to come over to us. Finally, he went to my assistant political agent, Norman Macleod, in Swaziland. He was no sooner in our camp than he asked me if I would be good enough to go after his wives.

"How many are there, Uhamu?"

"I don't know but about 300," he replied vaguely.

"But you have got two now with you," I urged.

"These are only slaves—I should like to have the others."

"I am not willing to take the responsibility of escorting all your wives unless you will come with me."

"Oh, in such a case, Great Commander, I would sooner do without them."

Uhamu's head place was in a rugged country, 45 miles from our camp, between the Black Umvolosi and Mkusi Rivers, and Ulundi being within 40 miles of the kraal, there was the possibility of our return being cut off if either of Uhamu's men let it be known, by Cetewayo's adherents, they were collecting the women in anticipation of our arrival.

Looking, however, to the political effect of getting out the tribe, I decided to go down, and on the 14th March started with 360 mounted men under Buller, and 200 of Uhamu's men, many of whom had fought against No. 3 Column at Isandwhlana. Some of my officers objected to my leaving Buller and the white men and accompanying Uhamu's people, by a short cut over the Zunguin Mountain, which would save three hours' travelling. I argued that there was absolutely no danger while their chief was located in my camp, especially as the men looked forward to bringing their wives and children back with them.

I took with me Captain Woodgate, (General Woodgate, mortally wounded at Spion Kop), Mr. Llewellyn Lloyd, (killed in action a fortnight later), my interpreter, Lieutenants Bigge, (now Colonel Sir

125

Arthur Bigge), Bright, (killed in action a fortnight later), and Lysons, (lately Colonel Commanding a battalion of the Bedfordshire Regiment; now on Staff in India.) We joined Colonel Buller under the Inhlobane, down the slopes of which some aggressive Zulus came, and fired at us at long ranges. I allowed two or three men to return the fire, and then had two shots myself, and the bullets falling amongst the Makulusi—for they occupied the mountain, silenced their fire.

About 2 p.m. we saw a few cattle to the south of us, and Piet Uys despatched his two boys, aged fifteen and thirteen, with half a dozen men to drive them to us. Master Dirks Uys shot a Zulu. When the father heard the firing, he tried to look unconcerned, and was too proud to ask me (for his eyes were not as good as mine) if I could see what the lad was doing, Lysons told me later that he kept on repeating, "Are they coming back yet?"

The men brought back about100 head of cattle, and I said to my friend Piet, "I am glad the lad has come back. I saw that you were nervous."

"Yes," he said, "I am always nervous if I am not there myself," a feeling which I understood. Nevertheless, he risked them in every skirmish, though the warmth of his affection for his youngest born— Piet was a widower—was evident.

In an argument he said something which I thought unworthy of the bigness of his character, and I remarked, "Why, you risk Dirks for us, you should not talk of farms and property"; and he replied, his eyes filling, "You are quite right, I would not give Dirks for all Zululand!"

An hour or two later Piet called out that he saw Zulus, and galloped off with his two boys, but on this occasion, nothing happened, for the Zulus he had sighted were some of Uhamu's men, who, taking advantage of our presence, were coming to join us.

We marched steadily till sunset, when we off-saddled for an hour, to let the horses graze, and, moving off again at dusk, at 9.30 p.m. reached the spot I had arranged with Uhamu, having taken three hours to pass over the last seven miles. We descended a mountain by a goat path, and all the Europeans dismounted; but I, being tired from having been touched by the sun in the forenoon, threw the reins on my pony's neck and let him choose, or rather feel, the path—it was too dark to see, and we got down without accident.

At sunset Uhamu's 200 men who accompanied me had asked me to stop, declaring they were tired. This I refused, and when we got down they had nearly cooked their food, having passed down by a

SKETCH MAP
of the
ISANDHLWANA
showing the positions
of the
Graves of those who fell & were buried

by Lieut. Mainwaring

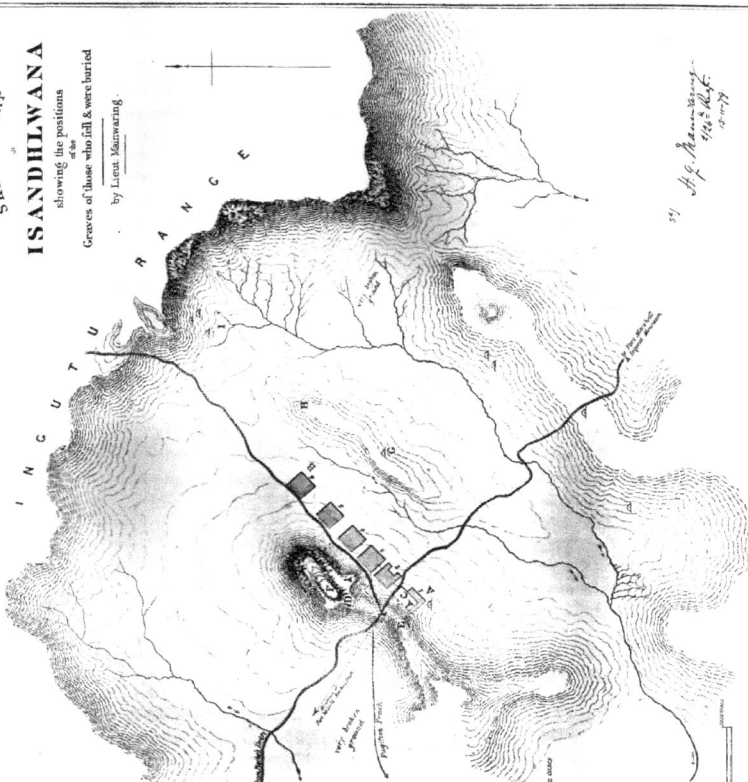

REFERENCE TABLE

A to B Site of Camp 22nd January, 1879.
1. 1. 24th Regiment. } Mounted Infantry, N.N.P.
2. Mounted Camp. } N. Carabiniers and N.M.B.
3. Col. Harness's Battery.
4. 2-24th Regiment.
5. N.N.C.
6. N.N.C.

C. Col. Durnford R.E. Capt. Wardell 7-24th Reg.t.
Lieut. Dyer 2-24th Reg.t. Lieut. Scott N.Car.[??]
Lieut. Bradstreet N.M.R. Quar.t.r. Hitchcock N.M.R.
1 Officer 24th Reg.t unrecognizable and about 150 men
(mostly 24th Reg.t) buried here.

D. Capt.A. Younghusband 1-24th Reg.t, 2 Officers 24th Reg.t
unrecognizable and about 60 men 24th Reg.t buried here.

E. Black's Kopje.
About 100 white bodies buried on each hollow, close to road,
also many single bodies along road which runs at head of camp
as far as B.

F. Isandhlwana Rock

G & H. Signs of heavy fighting and determined stand having been
made here.
K and. at G Full of dead Zulus.
Colar. Serj.t Wolf and 20 men (24th Reg.t) found amongst rocks
just above G.
The southern crest line from G all strewn with empty cartridge cases.
Camp of 2-24 were lying for some time from point H to kraals
at I which were afterwards found full of dead Zulus.

✝ Cairns
⌒ Kraals

(s.d.) H. G. Mainwaring
1/24th Reg.t
12 - 11 - 79

still steeper but shorter path. Before I went to sleep I had some of the women, for whom I came, brought out of a cave, three miles off, as I foresaw there would be delay next morning, and every hour added to the chance of our being caught by some of Cetewayo's regiments.

During the night I sent 6 miles away to some caves where I heard there were more women, being unable to sleep soundly, although greatly fatigued, for one troop of the Frontier Light Horse, linked in line, (horses are linked by a headrope being passed through the head collar, and then through that of the next horse), nearly walked over me, after they had eaten all the grass within reach. Buller came and pulled them away; indeed, every time I awoke in the night I saw him walking up and down, for he felt we were in a precarious position.

At daylight we shook ourselves and began to start—a long stream of humanity. The refugees numbered between 900 and 1000, men, women, and children. Many of the latter, although only five years old, walked from 6,30 a.m. till 9.30 p.m., when they had covered 30 miles. I sent Captain Barton on in front, while Colonel Buller and I remained behind. At 8.30 we were assured by Messrs. Calverley and Rorke—two traders who had often been in the district—that we had got the whole of the women and children. My engagement was that I would remain till daylight—that is, six o'clock.

At 8.30 Colonel Buller marched, a small rear guard, remaining with me till 10.30, as even then stragglers were coming in, the last few being shot at, and two *assegaied* in our sight but too far off for us to save them. My friend Buller had stoutly declared that he would have nothing to do with the verminous children, nevertheless during the march I more than once saw him with six little black bodies in front of and behind his saddle, children under five years of age.

As we passed under the Inhlobane, the Makulusi tribe, which had been reinforced by one of Cetewayo's regiments from Ulundi, fired a few shots at us without any effect, and we bivouacked at nightfall on a small effluent of the White Umvolosi, where Vryheid now stands.

Next morning, I started the procession at daylight, remaining myself on the top of the Zungu in range to see the rear guard into camp. I had sent in for all mule waggons available, to save the children a farther walk of 10 miles, and was waiting at the top of the pass, up which we had climbed on the 22nd January, for a dozen women who were loitering half up the mountain. It was past noon when I desired Piet Uys to descend and hurry them up, holding his horse for him, for it was too steep to ride down. When he returned he said, in his curious mixture of Dutch, German, and English, "*Kurnall, die vrow sie sagt* now too sick, presently have baby, then come quick."

"Piet," I exclaimed, "oughtn't we to send some of these women back to see after her?"

"Not necessary, *Kurnall*, she come."

Calling Mr. Llewellyn Lloyd, my interpreter, I apprised him of the situation, and said, "You are not to go into camp until that woman gets there." Finally, waiting for the waggons longer than I expected, I did not reach camp till 5 p.m., and, having had nothing to eat or drink since our morning cocoa at daylight, I was annoyed to see Lloyd sitting in his tent with a cup of tea, and observed in a somewhat irritable tone, "I thought I told you not to come into camp until the woman who was about to bring a baby into the world had arrived."

"Yes, quite so," he replied, "but she has been in camp a long time. Half an hour after you told me, she passed me like one of Waukenphast's pictures, doing five miles an hour easily, and I, suspecting that she had left her baby in the rocks, made her angry by insisting on seeing it, but she had it right enough under her arm."

Throughout the weeks of waiting for reinforcements I had frequent letters of encouragement from the high commissioner and Lord Chelmsford; the latter writing to me frankly, said I had caused irritation amongst the local Civil authorities by the insistent tone of my communications. I have no doubt that this was accurate, but on the other hand many were supine, some actually obstructive. I was unable to induce the Field Cornet of Wesselstroom to take any effectual steps to send back 400 men who had deserted, out of the 600 enlisted when we crossed the border.

The Transvaal Boers rejoiced in our misfortune, and openly stated that they intended to rise; some of the Natal authorities objected to my sending any refugees into the colony, advancing the most absurd reasons. The political agent, sent from Pretoria to Utrecht to assist me, instead of doing so wrote at length that he was advised that the action of the Administrator of the Transvaal, in putting the Commando law in force for the Kafirs, was illegal. The Civil authorities on the Natal and Transvaal border clamoured for protection, and urged me, but in vain, to fall back to ensure the protection of certain villages.

The Utrecht *landdrost* begged me to encamp close to that village, while the *landdrost* of Wesselstroom, the chief village of the Wakkerstroom district, spent much time in endeavouring to persuade me to encamp in front of his village. When I intimated that I was not inter-

YOUNG KAFFIR ARMED.

ested in Utrecht, as I had ample supplies at Balte Spruit, they expressed anxiety for the safety of that depot, and importuned Lord Chelmsford on the subject, who referred the correspondence to me, and to whom on the 3rd March I wrote in reply:

"I have often considered your proposition about the Zulus masking this position and going on to attack Balte Spruit and Utrecht. I do not believe they are equal to such a manoeuvre and are incapable of remaining in presence of a force without attacking it or running away. If all our mounted men were absent I should feel anxious, but so long as they are here I could always make the Zulus attack us by sending the mounted men to follow them if they marched to Balte Spruit. I doubt Cetewayo turning out more than 30,000 men; if he does, he would do better to send 20,000 here and 10,000 against you. Moreover, the moral effect of our being in Zululand is considerable, both on the Swazis and the Boers."

I discussed fully in this letter a scheme I had long considered about attacking the Inhlobane, but when Colonel Buller burnt the Makulusi Kraals, bringing away 500 of their cattle, the necessity was less apparent, and I did not recur to the plan until asked to take pressure off the force relieving Ekowe.

The Civil authorities were not, however, the only demoralised people. The general, in deference to the apprehensions of the inhabitants, sent a garrison to hold a village, 30 miles behind our camp, and the commanding officer marched round by Newcastle, adding 12 miles to his journey to avoid crossing a bit of Zululand 10 miles on the safe side of Kambula, and on arrival pitched his men's tents inside the cattle *laager*, which was several feet deep in manure; he became sick in a few days and went away.

The next senior officer, on hearing of the disaster to the company of the 80th, on the Intombe 45 miles distant, recalled a company which was 10 miles behind our camp, at Kambula, for fear of its being surprised, although there were still four companies 80th Regiment at Luneberg, and another company from our camp, coal digging, all between him and the enemy. Indeed, the overweening confidence felt by many before the war had now changed into unreasoning apprehension.

The one great heroic figure throughout the time when men's minds were depressed was undoubtedly the high commissioner, Sir Bartle Frere. He spent many days and nights in supporting all my demands, and in coercing unwilling and timorous Civil subordinates. With great address and moral courage, he prevented an outbreak of the Boers, projected after the destruction of No. 3 Column.

On the 12th March I took the opportunity, when acknowledging the thanks by the high commissioner and the general, to point out how much I owed to the staff officers, Mr. Llewellyn Lloyd, my interpreter and assistant political agent, Captain Ronald Campbell of the Coldstream Guards, Captain Vaughan, R.A., Director of Transport, and Mr. Hughes, assistant commissary-general, who worked literally day and night to carry out my wishes.

The difficulties of transport for the increased force, which was coming out to reinforce Lord Chelmsford's command, being always before me, I wrote urging that we should purchase sufficient at once, as hiring was not only extravagant but impracticable. The chief replied on the 14th March that he had handed my offer to provide waggons to the commissary-general, and was surprised that he did not jump at the offer, but added:

> I do not like to interfere with his arrangements; please do as you like best yourself. I congratulate you on the surrender of Uhamu, the entire credit of which belongs to you. You can do anything you like with your column; if you like to attack the Inhlobane, pray do so.

I had previously asked permission to send officers to the Free State to purchase mule transport, foreseeing that the final advance on Ulundi might be delayed until the grass on the veldt would no longer suffice for oxen, and thus render the movement impossible without mule transport. After writing in vain repeated reminders for five weeks, I decided to act on the qualified sanction of my chief in his letter of the 14th, "Please do as you like best yourself"; and on the 23rd sent two officers to the Free State, giving the senior. Captain Bradshaw, 13th Light Infantry, a cheque for £56,000, drawn on the Standard Bank of South Africa. They did very well indeed, enabling me to supply the 2nd Division, without which, as Lord Chelmsford wrote later, the advance would have been impossible.

The only comment made by the War Office on my action was to the effect that, as the money could not be all expended at once, I ought to have drawn two cheques, each for £28,000 at different dates, as I should thus have saved the amount of interest unnecessarily paid to the bank. In my reply, while admitting my mistake, I remarked I had already spent for the Government over £50,000 without the assistance of a paymaster, and it was therefore reasonable to debit the salary of such an officer against the amount of interest I had unnecessarily incurred.

The day Captain Bradshaw left was one of some anxiety. I had arranged a raid, by all the mounted men, in a north-easterly direction to the southward of Luneberg, to destroy the crops of one of our most troublesome foes. A convoy of 40 waggons was going in the opposite direction, south-south west to Balte Spruit, escorted by infantry, and there was a working party, with an infantry escort, employed in removing Potter's Store, which I had purchased and was moving from the Pemvane River to Balte Spruit. When we stood to our arms an hour before daylight the fog was so thick that we could not see 40 yards, and it did not clear off till the forenoon. I decided, however, to let the movement proceed as ordered, preferring the risk of surprise while I was present, to any which might occur in my absence.

Next morning, when I saw the convoys safe back in camp, I started and, overtaking Colonel Buller's 300 men, and 500 of Wood's Irregulars, reached Luneberg at sunset on the 24th. Next day we spread out over the basin of the Intombe River, cultivated by Umbiline's tribe, who were Zulus, although he was a renegade Swazi. We destroyed all the crops we could, and after two long days' work returned, on the evening of the 26th, to Kambula Hill.

In a letter dated the 19th, Lord Chelmsford called my attention to a paragraph in a Maritzburg newspaper, from a correspondent with No. 4 Column, alleging that I was fretting at the inaction imposed on me by the general, and wrote:

> You can undertake any operations you like, and I shall hear of it with pleasure. I hear all Cetewayo's army will be concentrated about Ekowe in a few days, so we shall have a hottish encounter.

I replied on the 27th:

> I do not often see the letters of the correspondent and hold no communication with him. If I did I should certainly tell him I am perfectly unfettered, your only action being to support me in every way. Buller has started, and at 3 p.m. I follow, to try to get up the Inhlobane at daylight tomorrow. I am not very sanguine of success. We do not know how steep the Eastern end may be, but I think we ought to make a stir here, to divert attention from you, although, as you see by our last reports, it is asserted that you have only Coast tribes against you, and that all Cetewayo's people are coming here.

In the forenoon of the 27th March, the two columns which were to attack the Inhlobane at daylight next morning marched; I followed in the evening, intending to lie down 5 miles under the Western edge of the Inhlobane. The more important part of the operation was intrusted to Colonel Buller, under whose orders I placed the two battalions of Wood's regiment. The 1st battalion, under Major Leet, bivouacking near the White Umvolosi, where Vryheid now stands, was intended to ascend the Western end of the mountain; both columns were to get as high up as they could before daylight on the 28th. In the orders I stated that, as Cetewayo was said to be advancing with his whole army, scouts were to be sent to the South and south-west, to watch the avenues of approach from Ulundi.

I took with me Mr. Lloyd, assistant political agent and interpreter, Captain the Honourable Ronald Campbell, Coldstream Guards, and Lieutenant Lysons, 90th Light Infantry, orderly officer, my personal escort, eight mounted men of the battalion, and seven mounted Zulus under Umtonga, a half-brother of Cetewayo's, whom the father, Umpande, had originally designated to succeed him. Before I went to sleep I had a long talk with Piet Uys, who was to accompany Colonel Buller, and had stayed behind to see me, while the colonel had bivouacked 5 miles farther to the east. Mr. Potter, a captain in the 1st Battalion, Wood's Irregulars, also came to me.

Both men knew the Inhlobane, and Potter had often been up on it. I asked whether, if we should have the bad luck after taking the mountain to see Cetewayo's army advancing, we could get down on the north side, and Mr. Potter assured me that we could—by leading our horses. Piet Uys was confident that Colonel Buller would get up, without serious loss, and we agreed that, except in the probable contingency of the Zulu main army coming in sight, our operation ought to be a success; then Piet turning to me, said, "Kurnall, if you are killed I will take care of your children, and if I am killed you do the same for mine."

We had heard, indeed, for several days that Kambula was to be attacked, but were informed that the Zulu Army could not leave till the 27th, as there had been a delay in "doctoring" one of the largest regiments. This was inaccurate. It had started on the 25th March.

CHAPTER 9

1879—The Inhlobane, 28th March

At 3 a.m. on the 28th I rode Eastward, with the staff officers and escort. Captain Campbell and I were silent, but the two younger men chattered till I wondered whether their voices could reach the Zulus on the Inhlobane. When Ronald Campbell spoke on Lloyd's challenge for his thoughts, he replied, "I am hoping my wife is well and happy."

Lloyd and Lysons, jubilant at the prospect of a fight, remarking on my silence, asked, "Are you doubtful, sir, of our getting up to the top of the mountain?"

"Oh no, we shall get up."

"Then, of what are you thinking?"

"Well, which of you will be writing to my wife tonight, or about which of you young men I shall be writing to parents or wife?"

Colonel Buller, to avoid risk of being surprised, had shifted bivouac twice during the night, but at daylight we struck his track and followed it. We met a squadron of his force coming westwards, the *commandant* having lost his way the previous night, and I directed him to move to the sound of the firing, which was now audible on the north east face of the mountain, where we could just discern the rear of Colonel Buller's column mounting the summit. I followed the squadron, but when it came under fire, as it did not advance rapidly, I passed to the front, the track at first being easy to follow, from worn grass and dead horses of Colonel Buller's command lying on it.

Hard rock now replaced the beaten down grass, and as we came under fire I unconsciously, by leading directly towards the rocks whence the bullets came, missed the easier gradient, up which Buller's men had ridden, losing only one officer. The ground was now steep and very rugged, so we dismounted and put the horses of my white and black escort in a cattle *kraal*, the walls of which were 21 feet high. Campbell invited me to leave my horse. I said, "No; I am a bad walker," and pulled it after me, Mr. Lloyd being close on my left hand. Half a dozen of the foremost of the irregulars had dismounted sooner and followed me until Lloyd and I were within 100 feet of the crest of the mountain, and we came under well-directed fire in our front, and from both flanks, the enemy being concealed behind huge boulders of rock.

The men of the squadron 200 yards behind us now opened fire, and Mr. Lloyd said, "I am glad of that, for it will make the Zulus shoot badly."

He had scarcely spoken these words when a Zulu rose up from behind a rock 50 yards above us, and, touching Lloyd with my elbow,

INHLOBANA MOUNTAIN.

Attacked March 28th, 1879.

by Lieut: Slade R. A.

Scale $\frac{1}{15840}$, or 15 inches to 1 mile.

2 miles

Col. Buller's Retreat

Col. Russell's

Col. Buller's track

Zulu army first seen from here by Col. Wood two miles distant.

Col. Wood

Copied from a Map done at the Intelligence Dep.t, War Off.

I observed, "He won't hit us in the face," for he laid his gun directly at my waist-belt.

He fired, and Lloyd fell back, exclaiming, "I am hit!"

"Badly?"

"Yes, very badly; my back's broken!"

I tried to lift him on my shoulders, but he was taller than I, and the ground being steep I stumbled, when Captain Campbell climbing up said, "Let me lift him," and carried him on his shoulder 50 yards down to where the horses were standing in the cattle *kraal*, under the walls of which the escort were sheltering.

I climbed a few yards higher, when a Zulu fired at me from underneath a rock, 20 yards distant. The charge struck my horse immediately in front of the girth, killing it instantaneously, and as it fell, striking my shoulder with its head, knocked me down. I heard an exclamation from my comrades, and scrambling up called, "No, I am not hit!" and as they began climbing the hill, added, "Please stop where you are. I am coming down, for it's too steep to get on any farther, in this place."

When I got down to the *kraal*, I saw Mr. Lloyd was dying. He could no longer speak; obtaining some brandy from Lysons, I tried to pour a little down his throat, but his teeth were already set.

I told Captain Campbell to order the irregular horsemen, who were taking cover under rocks below us, to clear the caves from whence the firing had come which killed my horse. He found much difficulty in inducing the men to advance, as they alleged the position was unassailable; and eventually, leading four of my personal escort, with Lieutenant Lysons, he climbed up, Bugler Walkinshaw going with him. I called Walkinshaw back before he was out of sight, for I wanted help for Mr. Lloyd; and thus he, one of the bravest men in the army, missed the chance of gaining the Victoria Cross.

In a few moments one of the men told me that the cave was cleared, but that Ronald Campbell was dead. He had led the small party of three or four men, passing up a narrow passage only 2 feet wide between rocks 12 feet high for several yards, and was looking down into the cave, when a Zulu fired, almost touching him, and he fell dead. Lieutenant Lysons and Private Fowler, (they both received the Victoria Cross), 90th Light Infantry, undauntedly passing over the body, fired into the cave, and the few Zulus in it disappeared through another opening.

By the time the men brought Ronald Campbell's body down, Mr. Lloyd was dead. Telling Walkinshaw to put his ear down to his heart,

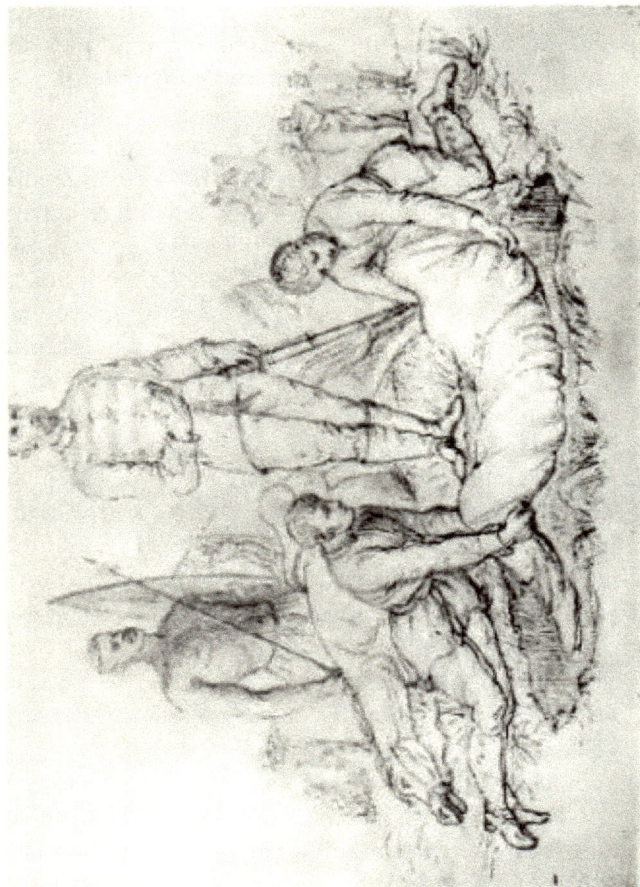

INHLOBANE, 28th MARCH, 1879

GENERAL BUFFALO HORN. To LORD CHELMSFORD. "Mr. ELIOT FELL MORTALLY WOUNDED AT MY SIDE. CAPTAIN CAMPBELL LEAPING IN THE MOST GALLANT AND DETERMINED MANNER WAS SHOT DEAD. WE BROUGHT THEM BODIES HALF-WAY DOWN THE HILL, WHERE WE BURIED THEM, BEING COMPELLED . . ."

he made sure, and then I tried to put the bodies up on my baggage animal. The fire from the rocks on all sides was fairly accurate, killing many out of the 21 ponies we had with us. As bullets were striking all round me on the stones, my pony moved every time I got Campbell's body on my shoulder. Walkinshaw, who was entirely unconcerned at the bullets, said, "If you will hold it, sir, I will put the bodies up"; and this he did.

It then occurred to me that in the wallets of the saddle under my horse, which was lying with all four feet in the air, was Campbell's wife's Prayer book, a small one I had borrowed before starting from Kambula, as my own was a large Church Service, and I said to Walkinshaw, "Climb up the hill, and get the prayer book in my wallets; while I do not want you to get shot for the saddle, you are to take all risks for the sake of the prayer book." He climbed up in a leisurely fashion, and, pulling the saddle from underneath the horse, brought it safely down on his head. We then moved down the mountain 300 yards, to find a spot on soil clear of rocks.

The operation of digging a grave was laborious, as our only implements were the *assegais* of the native escort, and when it had been completed to about 4 feet in depth, the men got flurried by the approach of some 300 Zulus from the Ityenteka Nek, and, lifting the bodies, placed them in the grave. It was not long enough, and although I realised the possibility of our having trouble with the approaching Zulus, yet as they were still 600 yards off and were most of them bad shots at that range, I had the bodies lifted out, and the grave made a proper length to receive them without the lower limbs being doubled up.

When I was satisfied, I read an abridged form of the Burial Service from Mrs. Campbell's prayer book. We were now assisted by the fire of some of Colonel Buller's men, who, seeing our difficulty, opened on the advancing Zulus, and, being above them, checked their approach. The officer commanding the Irregulars asked permission to move down the hill to regain Colonel Buller's track, and by it he finally reached the summit without further casualties. He had lost only 6 men dead, and 7 wounded, up to this hour.

As all firing on top of the mountain had now ceased, I decided to move back, and see how the other column had fared. Passing one of the Irregulars who had been shot in the thigh, I put him up on one of the dead men's horses, and as there was no apparent hurry, Umtonga's men drove with us a flock of sheep and goats. We stopped occasionally to give the wounded man stimulants, being unconscious that the main Zulu Army was moving on our left, across, and towards our path. When we were under the centre of the mountain, Umtonga, whom I had sent out to a ridge on our danger flank, gesticulated excitedly, explaining by signs that there was a large army near us. Cantering up, I had a good view of the force, which was marching in 5 columns, with the flanks advanced, and a dense centre—the normal Zulu attack formation.

I sent Lieutenant Lysons to the officer commanding the western party with the following order:—

> Below the Inhlobane, 10.30a.m. 28/3/79.
> There is a large army coming this way from the South. Get into position on the Zunguin Nek. E.W.

The plateau which Colonel Buller's force had cleared was 150 feet higher than the Lower Plateau on which the western column stood, but both parties saw the Zulu Army a considerable time before I did, as I was 1000 feet below them. Buller had seen it at 9 a.m., and the western force had seen it rather earlier, Buller being engaged in covering a party of 25 of the Frontier Light Horse under Captain Barton, Coldstream Guards, who were descending the eastern slope to bury one or two men killed in the assault. Sending word to Captain Barton to retire, Buller fell back to the western end of the mountain, and forming some selected men into a rear guard, he took them down the almost precipitous edge of the Upper Plateau. The path was down the apex of a salient angle, with long sides, and the head of the descent was well suited for defence. Buller's men had previously collected a great number of cattle, which had been driven down towards the Zunguin Nek at 7 a.m.

Colonel Buller and all his party would have got safely away had not the Makulusi, and the men of the regular regiment with it, taking courage at the advance of the Zulu Army, emerged from their caves and harassed the retreat, during which some valuable lives were lost. Colonel Buller came down, practically the last man, and was at the foot of the descent from the Upper Plateau, when, seeing men nearly surrounded by Zulus, he went back on two occasions, and brought out in succession two on his horse. Piet Uys came down with him, until he saw one of his sons having difficulty with his horse, and, going back, was *assegaied* by a Zulu crouching behind him.

★★★★★★

The death of Piet Uys was a great loss to us, and Lord Chelmsford supported the earnest representations I made in his favour, as did also Sir Bartle Frere, who knew a great deal about him. He was intensely patriotic and had done not only good service to No. 4 column, but to South Africa, for although he had opposed the Annexation, the justice of which he denied as regards his countrymen, he admitted its necessity in the interests of the country at large, and he lent all his great influence, in opposition to many of his oldest and dearest friends, in pressing on the attention of his countrymen their duty in combatting our savage foes. He had armed, equipped, mounted, and provisioned his numerous family at his own expense, bringing all his sons into the field. He had persistently refused to accept pay for himself, or for any of his relatives, who, after his death, declined to accept the arrears of pay which I offered.

He constantly acted as Arbitrator in compensation cases for damage done in the operations to the property of Dutchmen, and no decision was ever questioned by the sufferers, or by myself, who had to decide on the claim. When one of his own farms was accidentally damaged, he would not allow it to be reported. I asked for 36,000 acres of Government land to be set apart for his nine children, and was supported in my request by the high commissioner, whose last official letter before leaving Natal some months later was to urge on the Colonial Office the importance of giving effect to my recommendation; but I doubt if it would ever have been carried into effect had I not been afforded the opportunity of stating the case personally to Her Gracious Majesty the Queen, who ensured the provision being made.

★★★★★★

About 80 of the First Battalion of Wood's Irregulars were overtaken and killed, and with them, to my great regret, Captain Potter, and Lieutenant Williams of the 58th regiment.

★★★★★★

When the latter joined me, not very long before, I had a very favourable report of him from the Assistant Military Secretary, Colonel North Crealock, and my experience during the few days in which he worked under my command fully justified it.

★★★★★★

The main Zulu Army being exhausted by their march, halted near where Vryheid now stands, but some of their mounted men came on, and a few of the more active and younger footmen. Before leaving camp, I had given orders for a barricade of planks, 5 feet high, to be erected, and securely bolted into the ground with supporting struts, to run between the redoubt and the south end of the cattle laager, to stop a rush from the ravine on to the fort.

To those who objected that the Zulus would charge and knock it down by the weight of their bodies, I replied it would cause a delay of several minutes, during which 300 or 400 rifles, at 250 yards range, ought to make an additional barricade of human bodies, and I now sent an order to the senior officer in camp, to chain up the waggons, and to continue the strengthening of the barricade. I wrote I had seen between 20,000 and 25,000 Zulus, and remained on the Zunguin Mountain till 7 p.m., hoping to cover the retreat of any more of our men who might come up, being particularly anxious about Captain Barton, of whom we had had no news since he descended the eastern end of the mountain.

★★★★★★

I tell now the manner of Robert Barton's noble end, although it was fourteen months later that I obtained the details. He had shown not only distinguished courage, but in actions great humanity, and in the previous January nearly lost his life in trying to take a Zulu prisoner, the man firing his gun so close to Barton as to burn the skin off his face.

When, on receipt of Colonel Buller's warning, he descended the mountain, he trotted on westward, followed by the men of the Irregular Squadron who had been with me at the eastern end, and who, before I returned, had gained the summit without further loss. As they reached the western base of the mountain, some of the Ngobamakosi regiment headed them, and they tried to cut their way through, but, after losing some men, retraced their steps eastwards, and, though many fell, Barton got safely down over the Ityenteka Nek.

When I was with Her Imperial Majesty the Empress Eugénie, in May 1880, on the Ityatosi River, I asked Sirayo's son, Melo-kazulo, (reported as having been killed in Bambaata's rebellion, 1906), who was a mounted officer of the Ngobomakosi tribe, if he could tell me whether any of his men had killed my friend, whose body had never been found.

He said, "No; for I followed you, although you were not aware of it, and, when failing to overtake you, I turned back, I was too late to overtake those who were going eastward, and the pursuit was taken up by mounted men of the Umcityu regiment. I know a man named Chicheeli, who was a mounted officer of the Umcityu, and I believe saw what took place."

I said, "Send for him," to which he replied, "He won't come unless you send for him. He will believe Lakuni." (This was my name among the Zulus. The word describes the hard wood of which Zulus make their *knobkerries*, or bludgeons.)

Chicheeli came, and talked quite frankly, giving me a still higher opinion of the powers of observation of the savage than I already had. After describing the coat and other clothes that Barton wore, he said, "The white man was slightly pitted by smallpox."

Now I had lived at Aldershot for two years in daily intercourse with Robert Barton, and at once said, "Then it is not the man I mean." Chicheeli, however, declined to be shaken from his statement, and repeated that the marks on his face were slight, but that there was no doubt that he had had smallpox. Opening my portmanteau, I took out a cabinet-sized photograph and a magnifier, and, examining the face closely, I then perceived that what I had for two years taken to be roughness of skin was really the marks of smallpox, which Chicheeli had noticed as he stood over the dead body.

Chicheeli told me that on the Ityenteka Nek he followed several white men and killed them, one man, as he approached, turning his carbine and shooting himself. When he, with several others, got down on the plain, 7 miles from the mountain, he overtook Captain Barton, who had taken Lieutenant Poole up on his horse. He fired at them, and when the horse, being exhausted, could no longer struggle under the double weight, the riders dismounted and separated. Chicheeli first shot Lieutenant Poole, and was going up towards Barton, when the latter pulled the trigger of his revolver, which did not go off. Chicheeli then put down his gun and *assegai* and made signs to Barton to surrender.

I asked, "Did you really want to spare him?"

"Yes," he replied; "Cetewayo had ordered us to bring one or two *Indunas* down to Ulundi, and I had already killed seven men."

Barton lifted his hat, and the men were close together when a Zulu fired at him, and he fell mortally wounded; and then, said Chicheeli, "I could not let anyone else kill him, so I ran up and *assegaied* him."

I said, "Do you think you can find the body?"

"Yes, certainly," he said; "but you must lend me a horse, for it is a day and a half," (equal to 60 miles.) I sent Trooper Brown, V.C., with him next day, and, with the marvellous instinct of a savage, he rode to within 300 yards of the spot where fourteen months previously he had killed my friend, and then said, "Now we can off-saddle, for we are close to the spot," and, casting round like a harrier, came in less than five minutes upon Barton's body, which had apparently never been disturbed by any beast or bird of prey. The clothes and boots were rotten and ant-eaten and tumbled to pieces on being touched. Brown cut off some buttons from the breeches, and took a squadron pay book from the pocket filled with Barton's writing, and then buried the remains, placing over them a small wooden cross painted black, on which is cut "Robert Barton, killed in action, 28th March 1879," and then he and Chicheeli buried the body of Lieutenant Poole.

★★★★★★

I never knew until that day the depth of regard which Buller felt for me. I was sitting on the summit of the Zunguin range when he climbed up it, and, seeing me suddenly, uttered so fervent a "Thank God!" that I asked for what he was thankful, and he explained that he thought I had been cut off at the eastern end of the mountain. It rained heavily on the evening of the 28th. All the mounted men had been on the move day and night since the 23rd, when we went to Luneberg; but at 9 p.m., when a straggler came in to say that there were some Europeans coming back by Potter's Store, Redvers Buller immediately saddled up, and, taking out led horses, brought in 7 men, who were, as we believed, the sole survivors of the parties at the east end of the mountain.

So far as I know, the only officer who got down the western end of the Inhlobane on horseback was Major Leet, who commanded the 1st battalion Wood's Irregulars. Six weeks earlier, at the Athletic Sports, we had a tug-of-war between the officers of the 13th and 90th Light Infantry, captained by Leet and myself, and as the 90th pulled over the 13th Leet wrenched his knee out of joint, and I had told him to remain in camp on the 27th. This, however, he did not do, and as he could only hobble, he tried, and successfully, to ride down the mountain. I believe he got down before the counter attack; but while on the Lower Plateau, and being followed up closely by the enemy, he showed distinguished courage in going back to help a dismounted officer, for which he received the Victoria Cross.

On the night of the 28th March, as I sat at dinner, I could not keep my mind off Ronald Campbell, who had sat opposite me for three months, and had anticipated every want with the utmost devotion, and I cannot write now, even after the lapse of a quarter of a century, without pain of the loss the army sustained when my friend fell. As I visited the outposts at least twice every night from the date of Isand-whana till after Ulandi, 4th July, my clothes were nearly always damp from walking through the long grass, which, when not wet from the heavy rain which fell constantly through the months of February and March, was soaked with dew, and I had forbidden either of the staff accompanying me, because, as we slept in our boots and clothes, any-one who walked round the sentries got saturated up to the waist-belt.

I had, however, once or twice suspected that I was being followed, and one night, turning suddenly in the darkness, I knocked against a man, and then recognised Campbell's voice, as he answered my challenge. I said sharply, "Why are you disobeying orders? What are you doing here?"

"I have always the fear, sir," he replied, "that one night you won't hear the challenge of one of the sentries, and you will be shot."

On two occasions on which I was in bed with fever for three days, he nursed me as tenderly as could a woman, and I never saw anyone play a more heroic part than he did on the morning of the 28th March 1879.

CHAPTER 10

1879—Kambula, 29th March

I went round the sentries twice during the night, although I did not anticipate an attack until daylight, feeling sure the large masses of Zulus I had seen could not make a combined movement in the dark. When the night was past, the mist was so thick that we could not see more than a hundred yards. Captain Maude, who had temporarily re-placed Ronald Campbell, asked me if the wood-cutting party of two companies was to go out as usual. Our practice was that they should

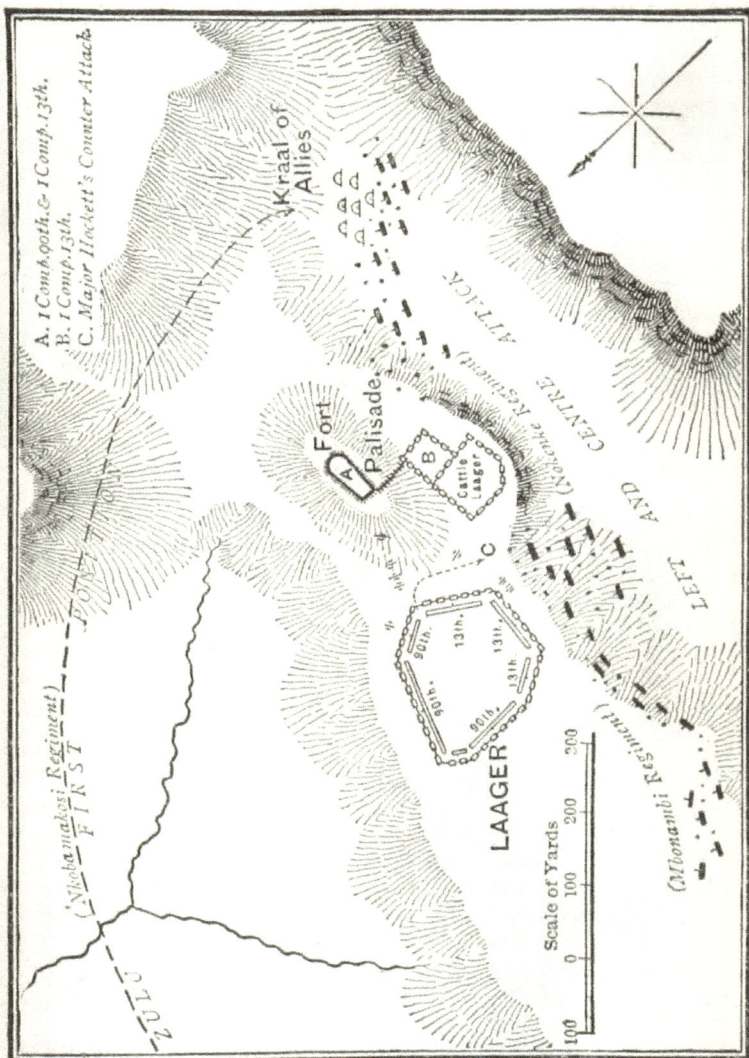

A. 1 Comp. 90th. & 1 Comp. 13th.
B. 1 Comp. 13th.
C. Major Hackett's Counter Attack.

Kraal of Allies

(Nokeuke Regiment) CENTRE ATTACK

LEFT AND

Fort
Palisade

A

B
Cattle
Laager

C

90th
13th
90th
13th
13th
LAAGER

(Nkobamakosi Regiment)
FIRST ATTACK

ZULU

(Mbonambi Regiment)

Scale of Yards
100   0   100   200   300

PLAN OF THE BATTLE OF KAMBULA.

not start till the front was reported clear for 10 miles, but until the sun came out there was no chance of the mist clearing off, and after thinking over the matter I decided the party should go, because we had never been able to get up reserve of fuel, and it was possible the Zulus might not attack that day. Our men would certainly fight better in two or three days' time if they had cooked food, and so I accepted the risk, but ordered two subalterns to keep ponies saddled to recall the companies in good time. Fortunately, though 5 miles away, the place was behind the camp.

All the mounted men had been continuously in the saddle since daylight on the 23rd, and it was difficult to get a trot out of the horses, (one of my ponies had carried me 94 miles in fifty-four hours, without corn, getting only the grass he could find when knee-haltered); but Commandant Raaf went out with 20 men to the edge of the Zunguin plateau, and when the mist lifted, about 10 a.m., reported the Zulu Army was cooking on the Umvolosi and a tributary stream. (Where Vryheid now stands.) He remained out himself to warn me when they advanced.

All our arrangements in camp were perfected, with the exception of the barricade, to which we had added some strengthening pieces.

The Dutchmen came to see me early in the day, to say that, as Piet Uys was dead they wished to go home, and, except half a dozen who had hired waggons to us, they departed. Great pressure had been brought on my gallant friend Piet to induce him to withdraw from the column. His friends told him he was a traitor to their cause, but Uys always replied that although he disliked our policy, he thought it was the duty of a white man to stand up with those who were fighting the Zulus.

★★★★★★

When in December 1878 I was endeavouring to get Dutchmen to join, some queried my impartiality as arbitrator in deciding claims for captured cattle—the South African form of prize money—and I rejoined, "I'll not take any for my personal use." I gave my share towards erecting a memorial to Piet Uys in Utrecht, and all the soldiers of the column contributed.

★★★★★★

Between 80 and 100 of Uhamu's men, who held on to the cattle they had driven from the Inhlobane, were overtaken and killed near the Zunguin Mountain on the 28th, but in the battalion which had gone out with Colonel Buller there were very few casualties. Nevertheless, Zulu-like after a reverse, the two battalions of Wood's Irregulars, about 2000 strong, dispersed,

I spent the forenoon, after saying goodbye to the Uys detachment, in writing a report on the previous day's reconnaissance, and letters to the bereaved relatives of those who had fallen.

At 11 o'clock Raaf reported that the Zulu Army was advancing, and I sent the officers to recall the wood-cutting parties, and had all the Trek oxen driven in, except about 200 which had strayed away from the drivers, whose duty it was to herd them. We got the two companies back in time for the men to have a hasty dinner before the attack actually began. The commanding officers asked if the battalions might not be told to hurry their dinners, but I said, "No; there is plenty of time," for by the system enforced in the column during daylight, as Lord Chelmsford saw five weeks later, our tents could be struck, and the men be in position in the *laager*, within seventy seconds from the last sound of the "Alert."

At 1.30 p.m. Colonel Buller suggested he should go out and harry the Zulus into a premature attack, and this he did admirably.

We had shifted camp several times for sanitary reasons. My friends the Dutchmen could never be persuaded to use the latrines, although I had one dug specially for them; moreover, Wood's Irregulars and the oxen had so fouled the ground as to induce fever, unless the camp was often shifted. The position in which we received the attack was on a ridge running in a south-westerly direction, an under feature of the Ngaba-ka-Hwane Mountain.

The waggons of the 13th Light Infantry formed the right front and flank, 4 guns were in front of the centre, and the 90th Light Infantry on the left. The horse lines were in the middle, and the rear face of the *laager* was held by the Irregular Horse; 280 yards in front, on ground 20 feet higher than the *laager*, was a redoubt, its main lines of fire being in a northerly and southerly direction, while 150 yards to the right front of the main *laager* was a cattle *laager*, into which we crammed upwards of 2000 oxen. The outer side of it stood on the edge of a deep ravine, into which the *laager* drained. The wheels of the waggons were securely chained together, and the space between the forepart of one and the rear of the other was rendered difficult of ingress by the poles (or *dyssel*-booms), being lashed across the intervals.

Two guns under Lieutenant Nicholson were placed *en barbette*, (placed on raised ground, thus firing over the parapet), at the front end of the redoubt. The other four guns came into action under Lieuten-

148

ant A. Bigge, (now Colonel Sir Arthur Bigge, K.C.B.), and Lieutenant Slade, (General F. Slade, C.B., lately Inspector-General, Royal Artillery), by sections on the ridge, connecting the redoubt with the main *laager*. The men belonged to garrison companies, but I have never known a battery so exceptionally fortunate in its subalterns. Lieutenant Nicholson, standing on the gun platform, fought his guns with the unmoved stoical courage habitual to his nature.

Major Tremlett was renowned as a fearless sportsman, and both Bigge and Slade were unsurpassable; they with their gunners stood up in the open from 1.30 p.m. till the Zulus retreated at 5.30 p.m., and by utilising the ridge were enabled to find excellent targets with cover during the first attack on the southern slope, and later on the northern slope, and suffered but little loss.

The direction of the Zulu advance was, speaking generally, from south-east, but when they came in sight they stretched over the horizon from north-east to south-west, covering all approaches from the Inhlobane to Bemba's Kop. When still 3 miles distant, 5000 men moved round to our left and attacked the side held by the 90th Light Infantry, prior to the remainder of the Zulu Army coming into action. This fortunate circumstance was due to Colonel Buller's skilful tactical handling of the mounted men, whom he took out and dismounted half a mile from the Zulus.

The Umbonambi regiment suffered a galling fire for some time, and then, losing patience, rushed forward to attack, when the horsemen, remounting, retired 400 yards, and, repeating their tactics, eventually brought on a determined attack from the Zulu right flank. The Umbonambi followed up the horsemen until they were within 300 yards of the *laager*, when their further advance was checked by the accurate firing of the 90th Light Infantry, greatly assisted by the enfilading fire poured in from the northern face of the redoubt. I saw a fine tall chief running on well in front of his men, until, hit in the leg, he fell to the ground. Two men endeavoured to help him back as he limped on one foot. One was immediately shot, but was replaced by another, and eventually all three were killed.

We now sent the artillery horses back into the *laager*, keeping the guns in the open, on the ridge between the redoubt and the main *laager*. I had instructed the officer commanding to serve his guns till the last moment, and then, if necessary, leaving them in the open, take his men back to the *laager*, which was within 188 yards.

The attack on our left had so slackened as to give me no further

ZULU WARRIORS

anxiety, when at 2.15 p.m. heavy masses attacked our right front and right rear, having passed under cover up the deep ravine, on the edge of which the cattle *laager* stood.

Some 40 Zulus, using Martini-Henry rifles which they had taken at Isandwhlana, occupied ground between the edge of the ravine and the rear of the *laager*, from the fire of which they were partly covered by the refuse from the horse lines which had been there deposited, for, with the extraordinary fertility of South Africa, induced by copious rains and burning midday sun, a patch of mealies 4 feet high afforded cover to men lying down, and it was from thence that our serious losses occurred somewhat later. The Zulu fire induced me to withdraw a company of the 13th, posted at the right rear of the cattle *laager*, although the front was held by another half company for some time longer.

I could see from where I stood on the ridge of land just outside the fort, leaning against the barricade, which reached down to the cattle *laager*, that there were large bodies in the ravine, the Ngobamakosi in front, and 30 men (leaders) showed over the edge, endeavouring to encourage the regiment to leave the shelter, and charge. I, in consequence, sent Captain Maude to order out two companies of the 90th, under Major Hackett, with instructions to double over the slope down to the ravine with fixed bayonets, and to fall back at once when they had driven the Zulus below the crest.

A 13th man coming away late from the cattle *laager*, not having heard the order to retire, was shot by the Zulus lying in the refuse heap and followed by four from the cattle *laager*. I was running out to pick him up, when Captain Maude exclaimed, "Really it isn't your place to pick up single men," and went out himself, followed by Lieutenants Lysons and Smith, 90th Light Infantry; they were bringing the man in, who was shot in the leg, when, as they were raising the stretcher. Smith was shot through the arm. I was firing at the time at a leader of the Ngobamakosi, who, with a red flag, was urging his comrades to come up out of the ravine and assault the *laager*.

Private Fowler, one of my personal escort, who was lying in the ditch of the fort, had asked me, "Would you kindly take a shot at that chief, sir? it's a quarter of an hour I am shooting him, and cannot hit him at all." He handed me his Swinburne-Henry carbine, and looking at the sight, which was at 250 yards, I threw the rifle into my shoulder, and as I pressed it into the hollow, the barrel being very hot, I pulled the trigger before I was ready—indeed, as I was bringing up

THE ATTEMPT TO SAVE THE COLOURS

the muzzle from the Zulu's feet. Hit in the pit of the stomach, he fell over backwards: another leader at once took his place, cheering his comrades on.

At him I was obliged to fire, unpleasantly close to the line of our officers leading the counter attack. I saw the bullet strike some few yards over the man's shoulder, and, laying the carbine next time at the Zulu's feet, the bullet struck him on the breastbone. As he reeled lifeless backward, another leader seized and waved the flag, but he knelt only, though he continued to cheer. The fourth shot struck the ground just over his shoulder, and then, thinking the carbine was over-sighted, (we paced it afterwards—195 yards), I aimed on the ground 2 yards short, and the fifth bullet struck him on the chest in the same place as his predecessor had been hit. This and the counter attack so damped the ardour of the leaders that no further attempt was made in that direction, although several brave charges were made to the south of the cattle *laager*, against the right flank of the Redoubt.

While I was firing at the leaders of the Ngobamakosi Regiment, who, from the ground falling away towards the ravine, were out of sight of the main *laager*, the two companies 90th Light Infantry came out at a steady "Double," Major Hackett leading, guided by Captain Woodgate, who knew exactly where I wished the companies to go, and how far the offensive movement was to be carried out. Lieutenant Strong, who had recently joined us, ran well in front of his company, sword in hand, and the Zulus retired into the ravine. The companies, however, were fired on heavily from the refuse heaps, at 350 yards range, and Major Hackett was shot through the head; Arthur Bright fell mortally wounded, and the colour-sergeant of Bright's company, Allen, a clever young man, not twenty-three years of age, who had been wounded in the first attack, and, having had his arm dressed, rejoined his company as it charged, was killed.

The Umcityu and Unkandampenvu had charged so determinedly over the open on our left front, as had part of the Ngobamakosi up the slope to the redoubt, from the south side of the cattle Laager, that I did not at first realise the full effect of Hackett's counter attack, and apprehended the mass still crouching below the crest would rush the right face of the *laager*. They would have had some 200 yards to pass over from the edge of the ravine to the waggons, but, owing to the ground falling rapidly, would have been under fire from the *laager* for 100 yards only. I therefore went into the main *laager*, being met by Colonel Buller, who asked me cheerily for what I had come, and I

153

replied, "Because I think you are just going to have a rough and tumble"; but Hackett's charge had done even more than I had hoped and having looked round I went back to my position just outside the fort.

At 5.30 p.m., when the vigour of the attack was lessening, I sent Captain Thurlow and Waddy's companies of the 13th Light Infantry to the right rear of the cattle *laager*, to turn out some Zulus who were amongst the oxen, which they had, however, been unable to remove; and I took Captain Laye's (now General Laye, C.B.), company to the edge of the *krantz* on the right front of the Laager, where they did great execution with the bayonet amongst the Undi Regiment, who were now falling back. I then sent a note to Buller, asking him to take out the mounted men, which he did, pursuing from 5.30 p.m. till dark, and killing, as it happened, chiefly the Makulusi tribe, who had been his foes on the previous day.

When the enemy fell back in the direction in which they had come, they were so thick as to blot out all signs of grass on the hillside, which was covered by their black bodies, and for perhaps the only time in anyone's experience it was sound to say, "Don't wait to aim, fire into the black of them."

At 3 a.m. on the 30th, one or two shots from the outpost line roused the camp, and the Colonial corps opened a rapid fire to the Front, immediately over the heads of the two line battalions and artillery, who stood perfectly steady. Rain was falling, so, while Maude was ascertaining the cause of the firing, which was a Zulu who, having concealed himself till then, jumped up close to one of our sentries, I sat in an ambulance near the battery until the Colonials having put three bullets into the top of it, I thought it would be better to get wet than be shot by our own men. After five minutes the firing was stopped. The scare was excusable, for the nerves of the mounted men had been highly strung for some hours, a fourth of those who had ridden up the Inhlobane having been killed.

In the next few days we buried 785 men within 300 yards of our *laager*, which we were afterwards obliged to shift on account of the number of bodies which lay unseen in the hollows. We learnt after the battle that when the Zulus saw our tents go down they thought it was in preparation for flight, and that unsteadied their right wing. (Zulu chiefs told me in 1880, when they saw our tents struck at 1.15 p.m., they made certain of victory, believing we were about to retreat, and they were greatly depressed by our stubborn resistance.) They never fought again with the same vigour and determination.

The line battalions were very steady, expending in four hours on an average 33 rounds a man; though that evening I heard that some of them had thought the possibility of resisting such overwhelming numbers of brave savages, 13 or 14 to one man, was more than doubtful. I had no doubt, and lost all sense of personal danger, except momentarily, when, as on five occasions, a plank of the hoarding on which I leant was struck. This jarred my head and reminded me that the Zulus firing from the refuse heap in the right rear of the *laager* were fair shots. A few had been employed as hunters and understood the use of the Martini rifles taken at Isandwhana.

Besides the men killed, we had 70 wounded, and amongst them my friend Robert Hackett. Born in King's County, Ireland, he was one of several soldier brothers. He was decidedly old-fashioned, and I have now before me an indignant letter, written four years before his terrible wound, urging me to use my influence to stop what he regarded as the craze for examining officers like himself, nearly forty years of age. He pointed out the injustice of expecting old dogs to learn these new tricks and argued that as he had bought his commission without any liability to be examined for promotion, it was unjust to exact any such test from him now; and added that, as no staff appointment would tempt him to leave the battalion, and it was generally admitted that he was efficient in all regimental duties, all he wanted was to be left alone, and not troubled with books.

He was, indeed, a good regimental officer; he managed the mess, the canteen, and the sports club, and, indeed, was a pillar of the regiment. He kept a horse, but seldom, or never, rode, putting it generally at the disposal of the subaltern of his company. He played no games and lived for nothing but the welfare of the men of his company, and the reputation of the regiment.

At Aldershot, in 1873, he gave me a lesson which I have never forgotten. I was senior major, being in temporary command of the regiment, and spoke to him about three young officers who did not pay their mess bills when due, and when the delay recurred the third time, I said, "Unless these bills are paid tomorrow morning, you will put the three officers under arrest."

The commanding officer being away, I was in the orderly-room when he reported, "The bills you spoke of have been paid, sir."

"You see," I remarked, "it only required a little firmness on our part to get the Queen's Regulations obeyed."

He saluted, but said nothing, and when I saw him in the afternoon

I said, "Hackett, I do not quite understand your reticence. Why don't you help me in making these young officers pay their bills by the proper time? Why do they delay?"

"Oh, it's not wilful, sir," he replied—"only impecuniosity."

"Oh, that can't be the case," I argued, "because when they had to pay, they paid."

He only answered "Yes"; but something in his tone made me say, "If you are right, can you explain how they got the money at such short notice?"

"That's quite simple, sir," he answered; "I paid the bills myself."

After this I thought less of the effect of my firmness!

When I visited him in the hospital the morning after the action, he was a piteous sight, for a bullet had passed from one temple to another, and, without actually hitting the eyes, had protruded the eyeballs, injuring the brain. He was unconscious of the terrible nature of his wounds, possibly from pressure on the brain, and observed to me, "Your Commissariat officers are very stingy in not lighting up this hospital tent; the place is in absolute darkness." We were all so fond of him that nobody ventured to tell him the truth, and it was not until he was in Maritzburg that the doctors begged a lady, who was a constant visitor at the hospital, to break the news to him.

When we received, on the 4th January 1879, the *Gazette* of the Promotions and Honours for the suppression of the Gaika outbreak, I addressed the military secretary as follows:

> Lord Chelmsford writes to me a kind letter about the omission of my name when honours were being served out, but I am not likely to trouble you on my own account, especially as one commanding officer rewarded has never been within 500 miles of bloodshed, but I confess Brevet Major Hackett might have attracted your, or His Royal Highness', favourable eye. A man of long service, old enough to be father of the junior captains, he has, I believe, been for many years the bed-rock of the 90th Light Infantry. An excellent regimental officer, ever ready to counsel or aid those of his brothers whose follies, or scanty purses, brought them into trouble. He has successfully neutralised the bad points of two commanding officers.

When in the hospital at the close of the action, I did not speak to Arthur Bright, who was dozing, but after we had had something to eat I sent Maude over to see how he was going on. Maude came back saying that he was sensible, but very depressed, although the doctors said a bullet which had passed through his thigh had not touched any artery or bone. The two doctors had more than they could do and may therefore be readily excused for not having noticed that the other thigh bone had been shattered; and Bright died, happily without pain, before morning. Over six feet in height, and very handsome, he exercised, through his high moral tone, great influence amongst the subalterns. He had been captain of a boat at Eton, was our boldest and best Polo player, and was a gifted draughtsman, possessing also a beautiful tenor voice. He had only fifteen months' service when he took command of the company of which Maude was the captain. This company had been unfortunate, for Stevens, its captain, was dangerously wounded on the 30th April 1878, when Saltmarshe was killed; and now, in one day it had lost its only duty officer, Bright, and the gallant Colour-Sergeant Allen.

For two or three days after our victory I had some anxiety on account of our convoy of wounded men, which Buller escorted to the Blood River. My battalion was unfortunate, for, in addition to the two officers of the 90th whom we buried, we sent away three wounded in the convoy. I was obliged to keep Maude to help me, in spite of his company being without an officer.

Lieutenant Smith, whose arm was badly hit, was invalided to England. After seeing his family, he went to stay with Lady Wood, and, while he was giving his account of the fight in the drawing-room, his soldier servant was telling my wife's servants about it in the kitchen; and, alluding to the time when I walked across the open to the *laager*, he said, "We saw three Zulus following him, and we knew he couldn't hear 'em, so we turned our faces away that we might not see him *assegaied!*"

"Ah," the cook said, with deep emotion, "that would have been a sad day for his wife and children!" when the soldier observed cheerfully, "Oh, we weren't thinking of them, or of him either, for the matter of that, but what would have become of *us* if 'e'd been killed?"

I heard from Lord Chelmsford, who said he observed in my official report of my attack on the Inhlobane that I had made no reference to his having induced it; and, while thanking him for his generosity, I replied that I considered I was bound to help him, and that the operation I undertook was, moreover, feasible, and would have been carried out without any serious loss except for the coincidence of the approach of the Zulu main army.

30th March.—Although nearly all of Wood's Irregulars had deserted the previous evening, we still had the Zulus attached to the companies, as well as the drivers and *foreloupers* of the waggons, and, knowing
it was hopeless to expect them to bring in, without reward, any Zulus
as prisoners, I made it known I would give a "stick" of tobacco for
any wounded or unwounded Zulu who was brought into camp. During the fight it was difficult to spare wounded Zulus who could sit
up, for, when I took out a company from the redoubt for a counter
attack at 5.30, an officer shouted, "Look out for that wounded Zulu
behind you." He fired immediately, killing a soldier who followed me.
When all resistance was over, I was anxious, not only for the sake of
humanity, but in order to make an accurate report, to ascertain what
regiments had attacked us. So, I instructed our men to bring me, if
possible, a representative of every Zulu regiment engaged.

Next morning, 15 or 20 grand specimens of savage humanity
stood in front of me, while the interpreter took down their names
and the names of the officers commanding the regiment to which
they belonged, and we learnt that the Zulu Army had numbered over
23,000 men. When I had obtained all the information I required, I
said, "Before Isandwhlana, we treated all your wounded men in our
hospital, but when you attacked our camp, your brethren, our black
patients, rose and helped to kill those who had been attending on
them. Can any of you advance any reason why I should not kill you?"

One of the younger men, with an intelligent face, asked, "May I
speak?"

"Yes."

"There is a very good reason why you should not kill us. We kill
you because it is the custom of the black men, but it isn't the white
men's custom!"

So, putting them in charge of an officer and a couple of Colonel
Buller's men, I had them sent safely past our outposts, as far as the
Zunguin mountain.

We got in a considerable number of wounded Zulus, and as our
hospital establishment was not capable of dealing with our own cases,
I was obliged to hand them over to their countrymen attached to the
companies of infantry; and to ensure the wounded men being well
treated, I promised our Zulus an ox to eat at the end of the week.
There was, however, but little animosity when once the fight was over,
because all the border Zulus were so intermarried that we had cases
of men fighting in Cetewayo's regiments against brothers in Wood's

158

Irregulars.

It is not often that the narratives of victors and vanquished agree, so it is interesting to note that the Governor of Natal, in reporting to the high commissioner on the 21st April, wrote:

> The whole of the Zulu border population have returned to their homes. In conversation with our natives, they give accounts of the two days' fighting with Colonel Wood, which agree with the published accounts in every respect. The Zulu losses on the first day are stated to have been severe. The Europeans who fell selling their lives dearly.

I had heard many stories of the gallantry shown by Colonel Buller in the retreat from the western end of the Inhlobane, but I had some difficulty in arriving at anything definite, because he guarded closely all the mounted men from receiving orders except through him, and I knew from his character that he would repudiate the notion of having done anything more than his duty.

A few days after the fight he went out with a troop of the Frontier Light Horse to endeavour to find Captain Barton's body, but could not reach the spot, as he was opposed by Zulus in force, making a raid in the direction of Luneberg, carrying off cattle, and killing men, women, and children. While he was out I received written statements from Lieutenants D'Arcy and Everitt and trooper Rundall, whom he had rescued at the risk of his life, and their reports were verified by those of other officers who were present. This enabled me to put forward a strong recommendation that his name should be considered for the Victoria Cross. A day or two later, on his return from another raid, in which he had been unsuccessful, I said, as he was leaving the tent after making his report, "I think you may be interested in something I have written," and I handed him the letter-book.

He was very tired, and observed somewhat ungraciously, "Some nonsense, I suppose!" to which I replied, "Yes, I think I have been rather eulogistic."

When he handed me back the book his face was a study.

CHAPTER 11

1879—The Prince Imperial

Five companies of the 80th Regiment now joined my column from Luneberg; and, the evening before they marched in, Buller came to me and asked if a protecting certificate might be given to his regi-

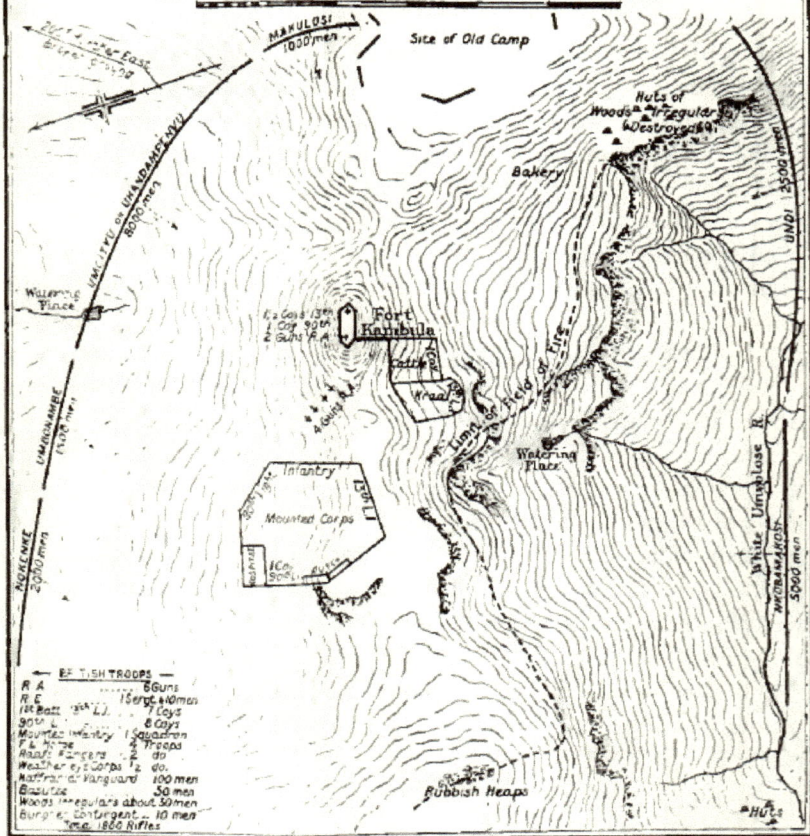

Sketch of the Camp of Nº 4 Column

KAMBULA HILL
ZULULAND

ATTACKED BY ZULU ARMY 29ᵗʰ MARCH 1879

NMYAMANE
Prime Minister

HᵈGᴿˢ
TYINGWAYO
General in Command

Scale of Yards
Yards 100   50   0   100   200   300   400   500 Yards

Port-La-Tête-East
Bridge Crossing

MAKULOSI
1000 men

Site of Old Camp

Huts of
Woods Irregular
Destroyed 691

UMITHI OR UMANDAHLOVU 8000 men

Bakery

UNDI 2500 men

Watering Place

Ea Coys 13ᵗʰ
1 Coy 90ᵗʰ
2 Guns R.A
Fort
Kambula

Cattle

Kraal

4 Guns R.A

Limit or Field of Fire

Watering Place

Infantry

White Umgiose R.

NOKENKE 2000 men

UMGINSANDE Exist Path

13ᵗʰ L.I

Mounted Corps

IMBAUDGOTI 5000 men

1 Coy
90ᵗʰ L.I

Rubbish Heaps

Huts

— BRITISH TROOPS —
R.A   .... 6 Guns
R.E   1 Sergt. & 10 men
1ˢᵗ Batt 13ᵗʰ L.I.   .... 7 Coys
90ᵗʰ L.I   8 Coys
Mounted Infantry 1 Squadron
F.L. Horse   4 Troops
Raaf's Rangers   1 ½ do.
Wetherleys Corps 1 ½ do.
Kaffrarian Vanguard 100 men
Basutos   50 men
Woods Irregulars about 50 men
Burgher Contingent .. 10 men
Total 1800 Rifles

mental sergeant-major.

"What do you mean?" I asked.

"Well, he is about the best man in the Frontier Light Horse," he replied, "but he has just been to me to say that he is a deserter from the 80th, and as he is sure to be recognised tomorrow, he intends to be off tonight, unless you will condone his offence, and give him a protecting certificate."

This I did, and the man served with credit until the end of the war.

I spent the next two months in collecting provisions, not only for my own column, now numbering 2500 Europeans, but in anticipation of the wants of others, as I knew insufficient steps were being taken at Helpmakaar; and by the 15th May I had succeeded in collecting at Balte Spruit 100 days' food for 4000 Europeans, and a fortnight's food for the horses and animals of No. 4 Column.

In February, when the column was encamped at Kambula, a trader, who had a brother-in-law in the Volksraad at Pretoria, came into camp with waggons, asking to be allowed to sell groceries to the troops. I saw the man, and he assured me that he had no alcohol of any description; but I would not allow him to unpack his waggons until he had given me a certificate in writing that his verbal statement was accurate.

In the evening I received a report that a small raiding party of Zulus was murdering natives to the north of Rorke's Drift, and I ordered Captain Maude to go with a few mounted men and two companies of Wood's Irregulars to the spot. At nine o'clock the party was still in camp, waiting for some of the natives who had not finished cooking, and I sent Ronald Campbell down to try and start them. He came on the trader, who was selling trade gin at 1s. a glass to the soldiers, some of whom were already drunk. Campbell had the man seized and sent for me. There was a full moon, and I executed summary justice by its light: ordering the man to be tied up to the wheel of his own waggon, I sent for two buglers, and gave him two dozen lashes on the spot, upset the whole of his liquor (which must have been a considerable loss, for he had a large quantity under the groceries), and informed him that unless he trekked at daylight, I would impound his waggons and oxen for the rest of the campaign.

I received, a few weeks later, various legal letters concerning an action with damages laid at £5000, to which I paid no attention, as I was in an enemy's country. The administrator and I had interfered with the sale of liquor at Utrecht, and the trader, who got summary justice, also wished to "take the law of me."

In the month of May I was riding one morning into Utrecht, attended by bugler Walkinshaw, when, a few miles to the north of Balte Spruit, we met a horseman, who, stopping me, asked if he "was on the right track to Colonel Wood's Camp, and also whether the road was safe?" I told him he was quite safe until he got to Balte Spruit, as there was a company there, but that after he turned out of the valley to the eastward, there was a certain amount of risk, unarmed people travelling only with an escort.

"What sort of a man is this Colonel Wood?" he asked.

"Well," I replied, "some people like him, and some dislike him."

"I have been told that he is very rough."

"Yes, that is so, when he is vexed."

"I am an officer of the High Court of the Transvaal, and I am going to him with a writ. Do you think he will be violent with me?"

"Oh no, I'm certain he won't."

"Then you think there is no risk as far as he is concerned?"

"None whatever; but you had better not mention your business in the camp, as his own battalion is at Kambula Hill, and it might be bad for you if the men got to know your errand."

"Why? What do you think they would do to me—kill me?"

"Oh no; the worst that would happen to you would be to be tarred and feathered."

"I don't like this job that I am on. I think, if you'll allow me, I'd like to turn back and ride with you into Utrecht and send the document by post."

Accordingly, we rode along together, and I showed him the post office in the little town before I went about my business.

Lord Chelmsford came to visit me early in May, and stopped for several days, bringing with him the prince imperial, who returned to me as a guest a fortnight later. The young prince impressed me much by his soldier-like ideas and habits and was unwearied in endeavouring to acquire knowledge and military experience. The prince accompanied Colonel Redvers Buller on some patrols, and on his return from one on the 21st May I observed at dinner, "Well, you have not been *assegaied*, as yet?"

"No; but while I have no wish to be killed, if it were to be I would rather fall by *assegai* than bullets, as that would show we were at close quarters."

I went out to the north side of the Inhlobane and buried Charles Potter and Mr. Williams. Uhamus' men had stood bravely by the white men. Many dead Makulusi lay around, and Captain Potter's body was alongside that of a chief of Uhamus' tribe. I was obliged to postpone till later the burial of Piet Uys, whose body lay on the lower plateau of the mountain, 1000 feet above us, as Makulusi held the ground.

Though my relations with the Commissariat Departments were friendly, it was, I thought, essential to write forcibly, and on the 25th April Lord Chelmsford supported my views in a letter.

"It is of no use, however, thinking of Ulundi, until Commissariat and Transport are in better order."

I irritated the heads of departments—for there were "heads" although there were no bodies—by my plain speaking. I represented frequently that an Ordnance Department scarcely existed, and that the hospital arrangements were totally inadequate. I pointed out that No. 4 Column had been for a fortnight without castor-oil, in spite of the fact that there was a daily post from Newcastle to the column, and that from Maritzburg up to Newcastle there were two mail carts weekly. I was taken to task for having used the word "disgraceful," but maintained it, asserting that there was no other word which adequately expressed the want of system.

Eventually, after much expenditure of time occupied in angry correspondence with Civil authorities, showing that the natives sent to me from the Wakkerstroom district who had deserted, carrying away government horses, guns, and blankets, had never been sent back, my friend Mr. Rudolph, the *landdrost*, was placed over the two districts of Utrecht and Wakkerstroom, and then attention was paid to my requisitions.

Lord Chelmsford consulted me at this time with reference to an expedition proposed against Sekukuni, although we were less prepared to undertake such than we were when the previous attack was abandoned in September. I wrote to his Lordship:

In my opinion we are not strong enough, either in generals, troops, or departmental officers, to attempt more than we have on hand.

And he decided that the matter must stand over until we had settled with Cetewayo.

No. 4 was now renamed "The Flying Column," and I was told during the month that I was to help General Newdigate by offering him the results of my experiences, and also by supplying him with waggons. This I did to the extent of 37, about the number I had then bought in the Free State, Lord Chelmsford writing to me that the 2nd Division would be unable to advance until I provided the waggons.

I had been cutting firewood and digging coal for General New-digate, and from the 19th of the month sent to the Second Division 40,000 lbs. daily. By Rudolph's exertions I got Zulus to act as drivers and was enabled to use the waggons which had been lying idle and had already cost us in a short time £4000. As the nominal strength of the 2nd Division was only about 2500, we soon handed over as much coal as they could carry; its great economy consisted in that 1 lb. was of better value for cooking purposes than 3 lbs. of wood. I should have been ready to advance by the middle of May had not I been obliged to lend waggons, for I had collected sufficient to carry twenty-five days' food for men and ten days' mealies for horses.

A draft of 80 men for the 13th Light Infantry landed early in May, but only 45 came into the field, the others being invalided between Durban and Utrecht, a march of about 250 miles.

On the 1st of June we encamped on the Umvunyana River within a short distance of the 2nd Division, and I describe here the system by which I kept the Flying Column supplied with fresh bread through-out our advance, which was necessarily slow, to enable the cattle to graze.

I generally accompanied the Advance guard, and when satisfied there were no considerable force of the enemy within striking dis-tance, the bakers with the ovens followed me in mule waggons. Hav-ing chosen the site for the camp, I personally selected the site for the bakery, which was at once dug out, and fires lighted. Although the weather was no longer as wet as it had been, yet we seldom got the first batch of bread out under eight hours, for if the "sponge" was put in before the ground was thoroughly dry, the bread was not fit for consumption. The bakers worked all night and stopping behind the next day until the rear guard moved off, baked up to the last moment; sleeping that day and the following night, they started again on the third day with the advance guard, and thus worked throughout alter-nate nights. The boon to the column was great. I sent a daily present to the headquarters staff, and to General Newdigate, under whom I had served at Aldershot.

I attribute the health of the Flying Column to some extent to the fresh bread, but also to the fact that the men invariably had a meat breakfast. Early in June the commissariat wrote to me complaining that I had overdrawn thousands of rations. This did not perturb me.

Sending for Colonel Buller, I told him my difficulty; and, going out himself with a squadron, he returned in a few hours with enough cattle to repay our overdraw, and to leave a handsome surplus in the hands of the commissariat.

Our difficulties may to some extent be realised by the statement that on the 1st June it took us two hours and a half to start our ox waggons, owing to the inexperience of the drivers; but in the evening we encamped near the 2nd Division, from which the prince imperial, with an escort of six colonials, had gone out that morning on duty.

At sunset the British officer and four survivors of the party rode into the 2nd Division camp, reporting that the prince, who had been sketching sites for camps, had been killed. Next morning, we sent forward a party of Basutos, who picked up the prince's body, shortly before a squadron of the 17th Lancers, sent out from the 2nd Division, arrived. I defer the story of his death, as I learned it from the mouths of the attacking party, 17 of whom told me the facts on the spot in the following year; but I may here state the body was unmutilated except for wounds, for he had fought until the end, and was pierced by eighteen *assegais*. Two white men were lying 50 yards from him.

The officer, arraigned before a court-martial for misbehaviour, alleged the prince was in command of the party, but I have had a strange and convincing piece of evidence before me for many years, in the prince's own hand-writing, that he was serving under the British officer, and was therefore in no sense responsible for the disaster. Light rain was falling early on the 1st June, and when the party started the prince was wearing a Pocket Siphonia. (A very light waterproof of the day, advertised: "To be carried in the pocket.") He had been unusually well taught; his plans submitted for redoubts to defend depots showing not only great natural talent, but that he had thoroughly assimilated the sound instruction imparted at the Royal Military Academy at Woolwich. On previous patrols he had taken full notes, and on the 1st June had filled the sheet of a writing pad thus:

1st June.—Started from Itilezi to find camping-ground for 2nd Division; party under Captain ——

And then follows an itinerary with a panoramic sketch, the last entry being dated 1.30 p.m. The prince, tearing these notes off the pad, had put the paper into the ticket pocket of the waterproof; and when, after the war, various articles belonging to His Imperial Highness were recovered, the coat, having been sent to Chislehurst, was

165

being sponged and straightened out, for the waterproofing had caused it to stick together, a lump in the ticket pocket was noticed, which was found to be the sheet of the writing pad. I was kept up very late that night, many correspondents coming to me to furnish natives to ride to the nearest telegraph office with an account of the misfortune.

A young transport officer appeared from the base and reported he had lost three of his waggons; disregarding the remonstrances of his superior officers, who wished me to send a conductor, I insisted on the young man going back himself. Although he did not find the waggons, which arrived safely next morning, yet the Transport officers realised that it was useless to come into the Flying Column camp until they had brought in all their party.

On the 5th June, when the two columns were encamped 20 miles from Ibabanango, the headquarters staff were having tea with me when my orderly officer Lysons arrived with a message from Redvers Buller. He was skirmishing with a large Zulu force, which was following him up. As the staff departed, they shook me warmly by the hand, wishing me good luck. Taking out my watch, I laughed, saying "I am obliged to you, but you are much mistaken if you think we are going to have a fight It is half-past three, and there are less than two hours of daylight; and, with the Zulus 5 miles off us, there is no chance of our being engaged tonight." My forecast was correct.

On the 7th of June the Flying Column was sent back to Natal to bring up more provisions, off-loading our food, and taking back the empty waggons of both forces. Oxen make no difficulty in crossing any place with an empty waggon, but as the rivers can only be entered and traversed at certain places, especially the Nondweni, (locally called the Upoko), the crossing of such was a question of many hours and gave rise to some anxiety. Although we now knew that Umbiline was dead, and that renegade Swazi had been our most active foe on the sources of the White Umvolosi, I nevertheless kept two squadrons out 10 miles on the north, or danger flank; and to ensure them being on the alert, always visited them before daylight, which gave me little opportunity for sleep; but we arrived without incident at Landtman's Drift on the 9th of June.

We started back again on the 13th, and as I had just received a report that our scouts covering the coal-cutting parties had been driven in, considering that I had 660 vehicles to convoy, my position was one of considerable anxiety. On the *veldt* they were able to travel fifteen abreast; but when we crossed the Nondweni on the 16th there were only three practical places, and each required repairing parties of a hundred men with pick and shovel. The drivers all knew which was the danger flank, and I foresaw that they would try to cut in as the front of the column became reduced from fifteen to three waggons, and therefore placed officers on the top of the steep bank of the river to ensure that the waggons had halted, and descended in regular rotation; for once a collision occurred on a slope, the oxen telescoped, and it took us a quarter of an hour to disentangle them.

I was in the river superintending a party digging out the egress on the south side, when, looking round, I saw five waggon drivers racing for the descent on the north side, while the officer on duty was sitting with his back to them smoking, apparently quite unconcerned. The water being up to the horse girths, and the bottom strewn with rocks, rendered rapid movement impossible, which added to the irritation I felt. I was overworked, had had no sleep while on the line of march, and, forgetting manners and propriety, I lifted up my voice and cursed him, saying, "You d——d infernal idiot of an officer."

The words were no sooner out of my mouth than I regretted the vulgarity and want of dignity shown in losing my temper. It flashed across my mind that the lazy officer belonged to another corps. Regimental feeling would allow me (a 90th man) great latitude in addressing one of my comrades, but the fact of my nominally commanding the 90th would add to the vexation of an officer of another regiment on hearing such language applied to him.

My contrition was increased by the echo: in the deep valley, seven times those vulgar swear words were repeated, gradually becoming fainter in the distance. Suddenly I heard the cheery voice of the lazy one's (lately commanding a district in the United Kingdom), commanding officer, "Ay, ay, sir, I'll talk to him;" and then followed a string of expletives in comparison to which my language might be considered fit for a drawing-room.

My want of self-control was excusable, since I had come to the end of my physical strength. From the 2nd of January, except to wash, I had never undressed nor had my boots off, and had been sleeping like a watch-dog! and, besides my military duties, I was still acting as political agent, which took up a certain amount of time. When I rejoined Lord Chelmsford on the Nondweni River, I was obliged to have my face tied up for a week, suffering from continuous neuralgic pains in the eyes, coupled with gastric neuralgia.

CHAPTER 12

1879—Ulundi

General Newdigate played a joke on me as we passed his camp. When leaving for the frontier with the empty waggons, I sent him a very old woman, virtually nothing but skin and bone. She was bright and intelligent, but so emaciated that we lifted her about in a basket no larger than a fish basket given in a London shop. I had personally carried her out of a burning *kraal* to save her life, and, not wanting to take her farther from her own people, I sent her over to General Newdigate on the day I marched back to Landtman's Drift, with my compliments, and expression of a hope that he would feed her.

This he did; but when I returned to my camp on the evening of the 16th, for I had ridden nearly to the spot where we intended to encamp next day, I found the old woman waiting for me, the general having sent her back by an orderly, who carried her as if she were a parcel of fish, saying, "General Newdigate's compliments, and he thinks you would like to have the old woman back again."

I was ahead with the advanced guard, when the bands of the 13th and 90th Light Infantry, as they passed the 2nd Division camp, played with fine sarcasm, "Wait for the Waggon," there having been considerable emulation in the two columns, the 2nd Division wanting to lead, and the Flying Column wanting to keep its place. It did so, led into Ulundi, and followed in the rear of the 2nd Division when Lord Chelmsford came back to the high ground.

On the 1st of July we descended the Entonjaneni to the White Umvolosi, 5 miles south of Ulundi. Moving off before 7 a.m., it was nearly two o'clock before the last of the 100 waggons of the Flying Column were *laagered*, and had the Zulus shown the initiative and audacity which characterised them early in the war, they might have inflicted severe loss upon us, if they had not indeed destroyed a portion of the force. They were, however, then discussing the terms of peace to be offered to Lord Chelmsford, and on the 2nd of July, at a meeting attended by the Prime Minister, Mnyamane, who was present at the attack at Kambula, and Sirayo, and four other chiefs, it was resolved to send to the British general "the Royal Coronation white cattle." These had indeed started and were within 5 miles of our camp when the Umcityu (sharp pointed) Regiment drove them back and insisted on the chiefs giving battle.

On the 3rd of July I sent Colonel Redvers Buller across the Um-

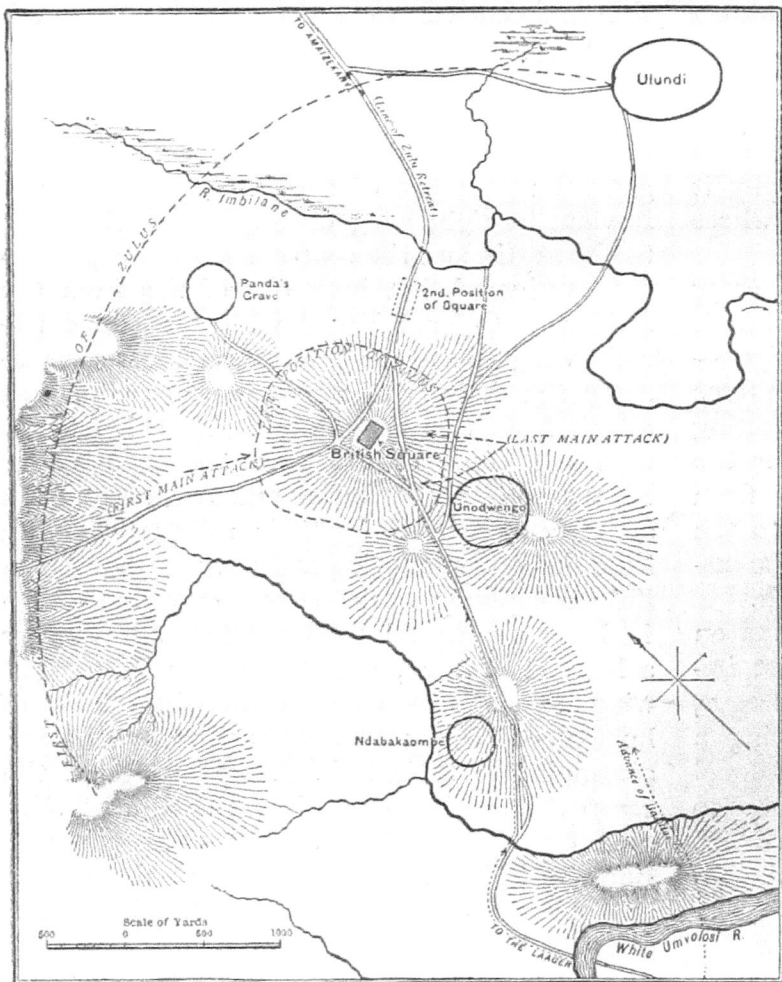

PLAN OF THE BATTLE OF ULUNDI: JULY 4, 1879.

volosi to reconnoitre the ground on which Lord Chelmsford fought on the following day, and although he lost three men killed and the same number wounded, the information obtained was worth more than the lives of a larger number of soldiers. That day at twelve o'clock I had 120 of our trek oxen, which, taken at Isandwhlana, had been sent by Cetewayo to us, driven back across the Umvolosi. These cattle had been accepted only on the condition that Cetewayo complied with the demands which the High Commissioner had made on him.

That afternoon Lord Chelmsford told me he wished the Flying Column to lead the attack. Parading the column, I said:

> Now, my men, we have done with *laagering*, and we are going to meet the Zulus in the open; you will remember how on the 24th of January I read out to you the news of the disaster at Isandwhlana, so I expect that you will today believe that anything I tell you is, to the best of my judgment, correct. I cannot promise that you will all be alive tomorrow evening, but if you remain steady, and wait for the word of the officers before delivering your fire, I promise you that at sundown there will be no Zulu within reach of our mounted men, and that you will not see any from an early hour in the day.

At 6.30 next morning we moved over the river, marching in hollow square; we stood on some rising ground selected by Colonel Buller the previous day, and on which for five-and twenty minutes we were attacked by 12,000 or 15,000 Zulus. The regiments came on in a hurried, disorderly manner, which contrasted strangely with the methodical, steady order in which they had advanced at Kambula on the 29th of March, for now not only battalions, but regiments, became mixed up before they came under fire. There were most regiments represented on our left; the actual front of the square was attacked by the Udloko and Amahwenkwee, about 3000 men. Usibebu was the only chief who came within 600 yards of us, and when he was wounded, his regiment, the Udloko, generally lost heart, although, the moment the firing ceased and I rode out to the front of the square to where Lieutenant H. M. L. Rundle, Royal Artillery, had been working two machine guns, I counted sixty dead bodies in the long grass within seventy paces of the front of the Gatlings.

When the attack slackened and our men began to cheer, led by men who had not been at Kambula, I angrily ordered them to be silent, saying, "The fun has scarcely begun;" but their instinct was more accurate than mine, who, having seen the Zulus come on grandly for over four hours in March, could not believe they would make so half-hearted an attack.

As we marched back to our camp the men remarked that their general's forecast of the previous day was accurate.

Although I was satisfied that the war was now over, inasmuch as single men of Wood's Irregulars, of which there were about 500, were willing to go anywhere in Zululand with a message, we did not omit any precautions. Scouting parties preceded the column, and flankers were pushed out, as we moved towards the coast to meet Sir Garnet Wolseley, and not until the 20th of July did I take my clothes off at night. The day after the action, I wrote to Lord Chelmsford's staff officer:

> His Excellency has frequently been good enough to speak with approbation of the order, regularity, and celerity of this column. I feel that eighteen months of incessant work in the field, which has not been without anxiety, more or less constant, makes it advisable, both in the interest of the service, and for the sake of my own health and efficiency, that I should have a relaxation of work if only for a short time. I desire, therefore, to place on record that the good service done by this column is due to the cheerful, untiring obedience of soldiers of all ranks, which has rendered my executive duties a source of continued pleasure, and to the efforts of the undermentioned staff, regimental, and departmental officers, many of whom have worked day and night to carry out my wishes. . . .

Lord Chelmsford that evening published a congratulatory order to the troops, ending thus:—

> The two columns being about to separate, the lieutenant-general begs to tender his best thanks to Brigadier-General E. Wood, V.C., C.B., for the assistance rendered him during the recent operations.

★★★★★★

Lord Chelmsford to the Secretary of State for War:—

Entonjaneni, 7th July 1879.

I cannot refrain from bringing again to your special notice the names of Brigadier-General Evelyn Wood, V.C, C.B., . . . whose service during the advance towards Ulundi from the advanced Base, and during the recent successful operations near Ulundi,

DEATH OF ZULU WARRIOR AT ULUNDI

have been invaluable.

Brigadier-General Wood, although suffering at times severely in bodily health, has never spared himself, but has laboured incessantly night and day to overcome the innumerable difficulties which have had to be encountered during the advance through a country possessing no roads.

★★★★★★

I received a letter dated the 9th July, Port Durnford, from Sir Garnet Wolseley:

Just a line to congratulate you on all you have done for the State. You and Buller have been the bright spots in this miserable war, and all through I have felt proud that I numbered you among my friends, and companions-in-arms.

On the 15th of July, Sir Garnet Wolseley and his staff arrived at sunset, and intimated his intention of seeing the column next morning. In order to mark the difference between war and peace service, I had caused a supply of pipeclay to be brought from Natal, and throughout the night of the 14th our men were employed in washing out the coffee colour with which we had stained our white belts in January, and pipeclaying them, so that next day when we marched past, although the clothing was ragged, the men's belts and rifles were as clean as if they had been parading in Hyde Park.

I entertained the general and his staff, and at dinner Sir Garnet Wolseley asked me: "Who were the natives I saw going westwards over the hill at the rear of the camp?"

I replied: "Wood's Irregulars, who were engaged to serve only with me personally; I paid them up and sent them home."

He said, "You were in a great hurry."

I reminded him that in December 1873, when one of my Sierra Leone men had lost his eye in action, he disapproved of the Regimental Board which I had convened, and which had awarded him £5. I did not mention I had personally paid the £5 but added: "I was so afraid of your economical spirit that I have compensated Wood's Irregulars and let them go."

Next morning Sir Garnet Wolseley spoke to me on his proposed arrangements for attacking Sekukuni. I knew what was coming, as I had seen a letter he had written to Lord Chelmsford, saying:

I mean to send Wood up, as we can trust him, to settle Sekukuni.

Sir Garnet said: "Now, I know that you have had hard work, but I want you to do some more, and propose to give you an adequate Force to bring Sekukuni to terms."

I replied: "I haven't had an unbroken night's rest for eight months and am not of the same value as I was last January, and therefore do not feel justified in accepting any command for the present. If you will not let me go to England, I must go to sea for a fortnight or so, for without a rest it is impossible for me to do for you, or the country, good service."

"Well, then, how about Buller, is he fit?"

"No, he has said nothing about it; but he is even more 'run down' than I am, his legs being covered with suppurating Natal sores;"—and so the chief acquiesced in our departure, and issued the following order:—

In notifying the army in South Africa that Brigadier-General Wood, V.C., C.B., and Lieutenant-Colonel Buller, C.B., are about to leave Zululand for England, Sir Garnet Wolseley desires to place on record his high appreciation of the services they have rendered during the war, which their military ability and untiring energy have so largely contributed in bringing to an end. The success which has attended the operations of the Flying Column is largely due to General Wood's genius for war, to the admirable system he has established in his command, and to the zeal and energy with which his ably conceived plans have been carried out by Colonel Buller.

Sir Garnet Wolseley informed me he would urge the commander-in-chief to promote me to the rank of major-general, and did so, but the application was refused. Later he wrote from Pretoria:

I am sore at heart in not being able to address you as 'Major-General.' When will our Military Authorities learn wisdom?

On the 18th of July I left the Flying Column, and their shout, "God speed you," made my eyes moisten. We had served together, one battalion eight months, and the other for eighteen months. Much of the time had been fraught with anxiety; the good-bye of these men, of whom it was commonly said in South Africa, "I worked their souls out," and whom I had necessarily treated with the sternest discipline, was such that I have never forgotten.

As I was leaving camp the natives attached to the companies of the

90th Light Infantry asked to speak to me, and their leader said: "Are you not going for a long journey?"

"Yes."

"How far?—For a moon?"

"Oh, longer than a moon."

"Well, you promised you would compensate us for the women killed by Umbiline after the Battle of Kambula."

"Yes, that is true; but, as I said at the time, I should not pay until I was convinced that you actually possessed the number of wives for which you have claimed, and the *landrost* has not yet certified to the numbers, although I have written to him many times."

Their spokesman said: "May we understand that it is you, Lakuni, (my Zulu name), who will decide the point, or shall you have to refer it to Government?"

"I can and will decide the point myself, for I have a large balance of cattle money forfeited by the men of Wood's Irregulars who left the column on the night of the 28th March, after their return from the Inhlobane, and when I am satisfied of your loss I will make it good."

They threw their sticks in the air, and shouted "Goodbye, we are content."

I no longer required an escort but told the ten men who had been with me for fifteen months, had incurred more danger than any other soldiers in the Column, and had worked longer hours, that if they liked to follow me to Maritzburg they could have a week's holiday, and I would give them as good a dinner as the city could produce; and they came with me.

Colonel Buller and I rode down together through Ekowe, where we learned that we had received a step in the Order of the Bath, Buller having been made a Companion of the Bath after the operations in the Amatola Mountains, My reward was induced by a letter written by Sir Bartle Frere on the 27th of March, two days before the battle of Kambula, in which he urged on the Secretary of State for the Colonies the great value of the service performed by Colonel Pearson and myself, dilating on the political effect of our maintaining positions so far advanced in Zululand as to render invasion of Natal by the Zulu Army in force an operation of extreme peril. My friend Pearson received the Companionship of the Bath. Lord Chelmsford, who had preceded me to Maritzburg, wrote me the following letter:—

My hearty congratulations on your promotion to K.C.B.; it

ought to have been given to you months ago. The authorities have apparently woke up and realised the fact that you had not in any way been rewarded for your good work in the old colony, and at the beginning of this war I hope they will also understand that a good deal is still due to you for Ulundi.

This kind wish was not, however, fulfilled.

The inhabitants of Maritzburg entertained Lord Chelmsford at dinner, and in speaking after it he took the opportunity of again thanking me in the following words:

> I never would have believed it possible for any general to receive such assistance and devotion as I have experienced from my men. . . . It would be invidious to particularise individuals and services, but when I look back eighteen months two names stand out in broad relief, the names of Wood and Buller. I can say that these two have been my right and left supporters during the whole of my time in the country.

I took some interest in the dinner I gave to my escort at the principal hotel. It was costly, and the variety of the liquids which my guests ordered was astonishing, for they drank beer and every sort of wine to be found in a hotel cellar. Sir Redvers Buller and I were occupying the same bedroom, the city being crowded, and when Walkinshaw, my orderly bugler, brought us our baths at 4 a.m. next day.

Sir Redvers asked Walkinshaw, "How is your head?"

"Not very well, sir."

I, being interested in discipline, asked as he left the room, "I hope they all got home?"

"Yes, sir."

He is an accurate and truthful man, for he put in his head and added,—"they had carts and wheelbarrows."

The Cape Town people also entertained us, and the ladies of the colony gave me in 1880 a very handsome embossed silver shield for my services in the suppression of the Gaika outbreak, and later I received an address with a beautiful service of plate from the inhabitants of Natal.

Steaming by St. Helena and Ascension, we reached Plymouth on the 26th August, where my wife, brother, and sisters met me, and I went as soon as possible on a visit to my brother-in-law at Belhus, where my mother was staying, Sir Thomas Lennard's tenantry giving me a great reception. The village of Aveley was decorated, and the inhabitants taking out the horses pulled the carriage up to the house.

The Fishmongers' Company, of which I had become a liveryman in 1874, entertained me at dinner on the 30th September. I took the opportunity, on being asked to speak on South Africa, to try to do justice to Sir Bartle Frere, whom I termed, and after twenty-five years' experience still regard, as the greatest High Commissioner South Africa has seen; the greatest not only in his treatment of barbaric peoples, but in unflinching courage and rectitude of purpose. The trust he placed in me was the means not only of winning over some valuable allies, but of neutralising the position of many colonists of Dutch extraction, who otherwise would have swelled the number of discontented Boers who assembled at Pretoria to protest against our Government.

I spoke also of my comrades, mostly deceased, who had done so much for England, purposely making no difference between officers, non-commissioned officers, and privates who had distinguished themselves. While some newspapers unduly praised me, I was taken to task for naming anyone by a few anonymous correspondents of the daily Press.

After paying this tribute of respect to the memory of those who had given up their lives while under my command in defending the interests of the country, I spoke of the prince imperial as follows:

In remembering those brave spirits and that gallant youth—the son of England's Ally—whose mother is our honoured guest, I am reminded of the question and answer in Shakespeare, for humanity is the same in all ages. When Rosse said to Siward—

'*Your son, My Lord, has paid a soldier's debt:*
He only lived but till he was a man,
The which, no sooner had his prowess confirm'd
In the unshrinking station where he fought,
But like a man he died,'

the bereaved parent asked, 'Had he his hurts before?' and on being told, 'Ay, on the front,' replied—

'*Why then, God's soldier be he,*
Had I as many sons as I have hairs,
I would not wish them to a fairer death.'

Of the gallant prince imperial we may say, 'Ay, all eighteen wounds on the front.'

CHAPTER 13

1879—Complimentary Honours

I attended on the 20th of September the sale of Sir Thomas Lennard's hunters at Belhus, then an annual event of much interest in the County, and it having been stated in the papers I should be there, many of the labouring classes came to see me. An elderly woman, who had walked many miles, pushing her way through the crowd round the show-ring, asked a policeman eagerly, "Which is 'im? "She had pictured in her mind an imposing heroic figure in a splendid uniform, and on my being pointed out, a middle-sized man in plain clothes, observed in a disappointed tone as she wiped her perspiring brow: "What, 'im kill all them Zulus! Why, my old man would clout un."

On the 14th of October the County of Essex entertained me at Chelmsford, presenting me with a handsome Sword of Honour and a service of plate, and in a speech at dinner, while thanking the inhabitants of Essex, I replied to the adverse anonymous critics who had objected to my naming my comrades in previous speeches by explaining the necessity of bringing the Nation into closer touch with its private soldiers. I had long thought that with a Voluntary Army it was useless to expect the best results, unless where bravery and devotion to the interests of the country is concerned, all ranks receive consideration, and I deliberately acted upon the conviction, in spite of adverse criticism. (Much has since been done in this direction. The parents of soldiers wounded on service are now relieved from painful anxiety by weekly telegraphic reports.)

A friend, the able editor of a newspaper, while remarking on my speeches in terms personally complimentary to me, observed:

"Sir Evelyn Wood does not appear capable of perceiving the seamy side of his profession."

I was too fond of my friend to answer him in print, for I feel sure that if I had written to his paper he would have put in my letter, but, as I told him privately, the occasion was not one for bringing to notice the seamy side, of which there is, doubtless, in military life more than anyone could desire, but there are also many noble aspects in such a career; for, as I remarked in speaking of the death of Ronald Campbell, Coldstream Guards:

When the noise and excitement of a war is over, the soldier who has seen men die for each other, or for duty's sake, can never again be altogether unheroic in his life.

I received in September a command to stay at Balmoral, and left town on the evening of the 8th. I was most graciously received by Her Majesty, who honoured me with her conversation throughout dinner, and again the next night, in addition to an hour's interview each forenoon and afternoon, and then on until the 11th. My original invitation was for one night only, and when I was told on Thursday that I was expected to stop till Saturday I was much concerned, as I had promised to visit Lord Cawdor, who was naturally anxious to hear about his son, Ronald Campbell; and moreover, Sunday travelling is practically impossible in Scotland.

The equerry-in-waiting informed me that it would not be etiquette for me to express any wish in the matter, so I approached Lady Ely, who was equally determined that she would not speak to the queen, and explain my position, I then said, "Well, Lady Ely, then I shall," believing that the queen, who had been so gracious, would not wish to put me to inconvenience, or disappoint Lord Cawdor.

This had the desired effect, and when Her Majesty sent for me in the afternoon she opened the conversation by saying, "I believe it will not be convenient to you to remain till Saturday?" and I replied, "Most inconvenient. Your Majesty."

I was greatly impressed, not only by the queen's accurate judgment, but by her profound knowledge of details of the recent operations.

I went by Elgin to Nairn and spent an interesting twenty-four hours with the family of my late friend. On my return south, I received the following courteous letter from Lord Beaconsfield, and I went to Hughenden on the 23rd.

Hughenden Manor, Sept. 15th, 1878,
Dear Sir Evelyn,—The queen wishes that I should see you, but it is not only in obedience to Her Majesty's commands, but for mine own honour and gratification, that I express a hope that your engagements may permit you to visit Hughenden on the 23rd inst., and remain there until the following Friday.—Your faithful servant,

Beaconsfield.

There was a house party, those interesting me most after my host being Mr. Edward Stanhope, then known as "Young Stanhope," afterwards Secretary of State for War, and Sir Drummond Wolff. Lord Beaconsfield asked me to come and stroll with him on the terrace the morning after my arrival—a walk which we shared with his peacocks—and he asked me many questions about soldiers and South Africa, I endeavouring to parry his queries respecting Sir Bartle Frere. In the course of his conversation he expressed unbounded admiration for Sir Garnet Wolseley, telling me that when he embarked for South Africa he had said to him: "Now, I trust you—you trust me." Then passing on to other soldiers, he asked if I had known Colonel Home.

I explained that I had lived for many weeks in a hut of leaves on the West Coast of Africa with him, and, moreover, had been associated with him at Aldershot. His Lordship said: "That man had the biggest brain of any soldier I have met." I agreed heartily, but then Lord Beaconsfield rather spoilt the value of his judgment by observing, "Why, it was Home who made me acquire Cyprus" Home foresaw clearly that England must, for the sake of India, acquire a predominant interest in Egypt, and at one time had made a plan for building a gigantic fort in the bed of the sea, three miles outside Port Said.

The second night, after the ladies had left the dining-room, somebody remarked on the news in the evening papers that Mr. Waddington had been appointed French Ambassador at the Court of St. James and went on to say how extraordinary it was that the French found it necessary to nominate an Englishman to that position, appealing to Lord Beaconsfield for his opinion. His Lordship replied: "The fact is, the French have never had a native Frenchman worthy of the name of statesman."

I observed gently: "My Lord, have you forgotten Colbert?"

He turned to me, saying somewhat sharply: "You don't seem to be aware that Colbert was a Swiss!"

I did not think it necessary to contradict my host, and a much older man, by stating the fact that, although educated in Switzerland, Colbert was born at Rheims, and submitted to the suppressing looks of my fellow guests, who chorused: "Yes, Colbert was a Swiss!"

I was sitting next but one to His Lordship, and then in a low tone observed: "My Lord, how about Sully?"

Sir Drummond Wolff from the end of the table called out: "What is that you are saying?"

"Oh, nothing, I only made another suggestion;" but our host, drawing himself up, said in his slow, measured voice:

"I now feel I made a rash and inaccurate statement. Sir Evelyn Wood challenged it, and I could not agree with him when he instanced Colbert, but he has now reminded me of Sully, who was not only a Frenchman, but a very great minister. I admit my mistake."

In the drawing-room, later in the evening, Drummond Wolff came up to me and said: "I say, how on earth did you manage to remember Sully?"

"When I was small," I replied, "my parents were poor, and we had few toys, but in our nursery, there was a French history book, *The Kings and Queens of France*, and I often looked at a picture of Sully standing at the door with a portfolio of papers, having surprised Henri IV., who was on his hands and knees carrying two of Gabrielle D'Estrées' children on his back."

I saw by Lord Beaconsfield's manner that if I stayed till the end of the week, as I had been invited, I should never escape a searching inquisition respecting Sir Bartle Frere's action in declaring war, so on Wednesday night I asked my host's permission to take my leave next morning. As we were going to bed, I said: "You will allow me to thank you, and say goodbye, as I am going by the earliest train."

He replied: "There is no earlier train than 8.23, and as I am always up at 7 I shall have the pleasure of seeing you."

As this was just what I wanted to avoid, I told the butler I would have my breakfast at 7.30 in my bedroom, and at that hour rang, and asked why it had not been brought. He answered that it was in an ante-room, close at hand, where a fire had been lighted. I had scarcely sat down before I heard the measured step of his Lordship on the stairs, and as he came in, after greeting him, I asked him whether he had read an article in a magazine which I had open on the table.

He replied somewhat shortly, "No," but he had come to talk to me about other matters, and he proceeded to put many searching questions as to Sir Bartle Frere's procedure with the Zulu Nation.

We all knew in December that the Government had refused General Thesiger the reinforcements he had asked, as the Cabinet wished to avoid war, but the high commissioner and the general were of opinion that matters had then gone too far to avoid it. Lord Beaconsfield asked me: "Will you please tell me whether, in your opinion, the war could have been postponed for six months?"

"No, sir."

"For three months?"

"I think possibly."

"For one month?"

"Certainly."

"Well, even a fortnight would have made all the difference to me, for at that time we were negotiating with Russia at San Stefano, and the fact of our having to send out more troops stiffened the Russian terms."

"But, sir," I said, "you surely do not mean to say the sending out of four or five battalions and two cavalry regiments altered our military position in Europe?"

He said: "Perhaps not—but it did in the opinion of the Russians, who imagined we were sending an army corps."

He then went on to say: "You are young; some day you may be abroad, and let me urge you to carry out, not only the letter of the Cabinet's orders, but also the spirit of its instructions."

Two years later, after Majuba, I had to ponder often on this admonition.

On the 16th October the military secretary informed me that the Colonial Office had brought to the notice of the commander-in-chief "the very valuable political services" I had rendered when in command of a column in Zululand. Sir Bartle Frere had brought the services of my friend Colonel Pearson also to notice, and the fact that the only result in my case was an expression of His Royal Highness's gratification, which caused him to make a note in the records of the War Office, did not detract from the pleasure I had on reading of Pearson's being made a Knight Commander of the Order of Saint Michael and St. George.

There were many discussions amongst the heads of the army on the question of my promotion. His Royal Highness the Commander-in-Chief was conscientiously opposed to it, and indeed to all promotion by selection, having been a consistent advocate of advancement by seniority. He held an officer should command a battalion when he was forty, but on the other hand maintained that a colonel should become a major-general only by seniority. He said more than once, "Men are much of a muchness; I find officers very much on a par." (Lord Penzance's Royal Commission on Army Promotion. August 1876.) Lord Penzance's committee pointed out, however, that if the system advocated by the commander-in-chief was maintained the average of majors-general would be sixty-four. The senior staff officers appointed by him naturally reflected his views. There was, however, a colonel of very decided opinions then in the office, for whom the adjutant-general sent, and asked: "Would you object to Evelyn Wood being put over your head?"

He replied: "Do you consider he would make a good general?"

"Yes, his reports are good."

"Then, sir, I think you should promote him; and having said that, may I further add I do not think you have any right to ask my opinion."

Sir Garnet Wolseley did his utmost to get me promoted on public grounds. In addressing the commander-in-chief from South Africa, on the 18th July, he wrote:

"I earnestly hope that Your Royal Highness will be enabled to recommend Colonel Wood to Her Majesty for the permanent rank of major-general, not as a reward for what he has done, but in the interests of the Queen's Army, and of the State." (*Military Life of H.R.H. Duke of Cambridge*, by Colonel Willoughby Verner: "I intend to send Brigadier Wood, he being the best Commander of those in South Africa. His name is in everyone's mouth, from bugler up through all ranks, as the man of the war . . .")

The chief, ignoring the public grounds question, replied:

Evelyn Wood I know as an excellent man. . . . . I have my doubts, however, whether Wood has not received his full reward with a K.C.B. and a Good Service Pension.

The commander-in-chief was misinformed as to the rewards he mentioned. He had given me the Good Service Pension in March 1879, on General Thesiger's strong remonstrance that I was the only officer unrewarded for the Gaika War, and the K.C.B. was given for my services in Northern Zululand, before the Battle of Kambula.

★★★★★★

Despatch from Lieutenant-General Thesiger to the Secretary of State for War:—

King William's Town, June 26th, 1878.
I am of opinion that his (Colonel Evelyn Wood) indefatigable exertions and personal influence have been mainly instrumental in bringing the war to a speedy close.

★★★★★★

On the 1st November the Bar of England gave me a dinner in the Middle Temple Hall, the first, I believe, to a soldier, unless we consider Drake belonged to both services, at which the Lord Chancellor paid me a gracious compliment:

The law is silent in the midst of arms, yet, as we see tonight, the lawyer and soldier combined can, after arms have been laid

183

aside, speak with the eloquence which befits the one and the vigour which characterises the other.

Early in December 1879 my mother's health gave us cause for anxiety, and on the 13th of that month my sister, Lady Leonard, in whose house she was staying, said: "I am afraid that you are feeling very ill."

"Yes, very ill!"

"Would you like us to telegraph for Evelyn to come and see you?"

"Yes, please do so."

As my sister was leaving the room, mother called her back, and asked: "What time is it?"

"About six."

"Then please write on the telegram, 'Not to be delivered till 11.15 p.m.'"

"Why?" my sister asked. "Because he is giving an important dinner party at his club, and if the telegram goes now he will leave the table, and it will spoil the party."

I was, in fact, entertaining the Attorney-General Sir John Holker, and some friends who had thrown themselves warmly into the dinner given to me by the bar. At 11.15 the telegram was placed in my hands as I was saying goodnight to my guests. My brother was with me, and we left by a luggage train at 2 a.m., reaching Belhus early on Sunday. My mother spoke to me about ten o'clock that night quite rationally, asking about the dinner party, and died at five o'clock next morning, so painlessly that I was unable to credit the fact that she had passed away.

Her last act of unselfishness was only similar to her conduct throughout her life. There are few men, I suppose, who remain in quite as close touch with mother and sisters when they marry as they were while bachelors; but in my case, with the mother, as with two sisters, my marriage only brought one more into the circle of devoted relations.

I assumed command of the Belfast District on the 22nd of December, and to this day am ignorant why I was sent there, as the commander-in-chief had given me on the 29th of October the command of the Chatham District, which I took over on the 12th of January 1880, from General (now Sir) Edward Bulwer, brother of Sir Henry Bulwer, who was Governor of Natal in 1879. My only difference of opinion with the general was as to the terms on which I purchased horses, furniture, *et cetera*, concerning which he showed much more consideration for me than for his own pecuniary interests.

When Her Imperial Majesty the Empress Eugénie read in the newspapers the account of the Fishmongers' banquet on the 30th of September, and the allusion to her noble son beautifully expressed in Shakespeare's language, she sent for me, and, after several prolonged interviews, I was commanded to Windsor, where Her Majesty was graciously pleased to honour me with the charge of the empress on a journey she was undertaking to the spot where her gallant son perished. The queen enjoined on me the greatest care for the safety of her sister, and I replied I could only accept full responsibility if H.I.M. the empress would follow my instructions as if she were a soldier in my command. This was arranged, and on the 25th of March the empress sailed from Southampton for Cape Town and Durban.

Her Imperial Majesty had sent me a cheque for £5000, desiring me to purchase everything required, and to defray all charges. I handed back on our return to the empress' secretary £3600. I was allowed to take my *aide-de-camp*, Captain Arthur Bigge, (now Colonel Sir Arthur Bigge, K.C.B., K. C.S.I.) and Lieutenant Slade (now General Slade, C.B., Royal Artillery), as an extra *aide-de-camp*. Both these officers had distinguished themselves by the courage with which they fought their guns in the open at Kambula twelve months earlier. The Marquis de Bassano, Lady Wood, and the Honourable Mrs. Ronald Campbell, the widow of my staff officer and friend who fell leading so determinedly at the Inhlobane, Dr. Scott of the Army Medical Department, two maids in the service of the Empress, Walkinshaw, my bugler, who had served with me in 1878 and 1879, and a complete establishment of servants, made up the party.

When we reached Cape Town, I had communications from well educated acquaintances in the old Colony and Natal, loyal to our Government from conviction and personal interest. I wrote to my uncle on the 20th April, after an interview with a Dutch gentleman:

> From what this gentleman told me, and from what I learn from other sources, it is clear to me that affairs in South Africa are in a very unsatisfactory state. Joubert and Kruger are now in this colony agitating amongst the Colony Boers for the restoration of the Transvaal. There are many members of the Cape House whose seats depend on the vote, and thus pressure is brought on the ministry here. I do not suppose we shall restore the Transvaal: if we do, we shall be obliged to re-annex it in ten years,

for the sake of both whites and blacks. If it is not to be restored, the cause of order and progress will be greatly strengthened by the Imperial Ministers saying, 'We cannot restore the Transvaal.

I suggested he should tell some of his friends in the Cabinet what I had learnt. He had long before resigned his seat on the Woolsack, owing to failing vision, but was on intimate terms with his former colleagues.

CHAPTER 14

1880—H.I.M. The Empress Eugénie

While we were at Cape Town I paid Cetewayo two visits and sat with him for some time. He expressed great pleasure, and, unless he was a good actor, felt such at seeing me. He was a man of considerable tact, for he had taken the trouble to procure a photograph of myself. He discussed the merits of his chiefs in the course of conversation, and said it was quite correct that he had ordered Faku to drive the settlers away from Luneberg. As he put it humorously, "I said they were to go away lest they should be hurt." He told me many interesting stories of my proceedings in Zululand and mentioned that he was always nervous lest I should make a raid with the mounted men and carry him off to Ulundi, thus confirming the information obtained by Sir Bartle Frere.

The ex-monarch asked me for a rug; and so, appropriating a thick handsome one belonging to my wife, I sent it when we got back to Government House, where the empress was staying. But Cetewayo returned it with a message that it was not nearly big enough to cover his body, and with some difficulty I found one which gave him satisfaction.

We left Maritzburg on Thursday the 29th of April, with waggons, cooks, servants, waggon drivers, and mules. The party consisting of eighty persons.

H.I.M. the Empress had proposed, in the first instance, to ride throughout her journey, but foreseeing that this might be inconvenient I had purchased a "Spider," and after our first day's journey, finding it too heavy for a pair, in spite of the predictions of the oldest inhabitants, that it was impossible to drive four horses from such a low seat, I drove the empress or one of the other ladies 800 miles before we re-embarked.

They greatly enjoyed the scenery in the Tugela Valley. The camp was pitched one day on a slope overlooking a ravine, 150 feet below the tents. Up to Helpmakaar, the track is carried through a beautiful though rugged country, and on the 5th May we mounted 650 feet in 5 miles, and descended 1800 feet in the next 5, travelling on an unfenced road, scarped out of the mountain-side.

When we reached Utrecht the whole of the population turned out to see me, and from the moment we crossed the Blood River I had a succession of black visitors, including 10 men enlisted in October 1878, who had been attached to companies of my battalion, and who had lost wives killed in the raid made by Umbilini after the Battle of Kambula. They were the men who had thrown their *knobkerries* in the air when they learned I was to decide and pay the amount they claimed for their wives. In every case the claim was certified by Mr. Rudolph, the *landdrost*, as correct, and I handed over cheques amounting to between eight and nine hundred pounds, which I told them would be honoured at Newcastle. They saluted according to their fashion and walked off without the slightest doubt of their getting gold for the pieces of paper tied up in the corner of their blankets.

When the last of them had departed, one man came forward and said, "Will you do something for me?"

"Oh! but you are not one of the men whose wives I insured?"

"No; but I was in Wood's Regiment, and my wife was killed."

"When was that?"

"In August."

"But then you could not have gone straight home when I dismissed you in the middle of July near Kwamagasa?"

"No; it is true I stayed for some little time with relatives in Sirayo's country, and the raid took place while I was there."

"That is, you contributed to your own loss?"

"Yes; I have no claim, but perhaps, as my wife was killed, you will do something for me?"

"How long had you had her?"

"Five years."

"What did you give for her?"

"Ten cows." (A cow is equal to £3, and a calf 30s.)

"That is a good deal."

"Well, it was the current price when I married her."

"Wives will be cheaper now, for we have killed a good many men, and no women. Had you any children?"

"Two."

"Boys or girls?"

"Girls."

"Were they killed?"

"No."

"Then they are worth a calf a piece?"

"That is so."

"What sort of value was your wife?"

"Excellent; she could hoe well."

"Well, for the sake of calculation, if you have had her five years she could not be as good as she was when you got her, and eight cows was the outside value when you married her, according to the current rate at this time; so, if we take off one cow for the two girls you have still got, and two cows for wear and tear, if you get the price of five cows you will be fully compensated?"

"Yes; I shall be perfectly content."

I satisfied myself that his loss was correctly stated, and then having prize money which was somewhat of a white elephant to me, I eventually gave him £24 with which he departed expressing deep gratitude.

While we were encamped on the Blood River the whole of the Uys family came to see me, as did also Sirayo and his two sons. They accompanied us to Kambula, and on the 16th the empress, standing in a little redoubt on the hill, was able to see not only where Lieutenants Bigge and Slade had fought their guns in the open for four hours, but also where the Ngobamakosi Regiment, of which Melokazulu was a mounted officer, attempted to come out of the ravine, to storm the *laager*. We had taken up a tombstone for the graves near the camp, and on the 21st, in Mrs. Campbell's presence, I had the tombstone to Ronald Campbell carried up the Inhlobane by men who were fighting against him when he lost his life on the 28th of March.

The empress rode and walked up the eastern end of the mountain where Colonel Buller ascended and descended by the Devil's Pass, at the foot of which he gained his Victoria Cross. The ruggedness and steepness of the descent may be gathered by the fact that I had all 14 ponies belonging to the party driven slowly, and allowed to pick their path down, and the only one which accomplished the descent without a heavy, fall was my own pony, which I led, and indicated to him where he should put his feet.

While we were near the Inhlobane I rode many miles to the eastward and to the north of the mountain searching for the body of my friend Robert Barton but was no more successful than were the 25 natives whom I employed for three weeks for the same purpose. Uhamu came to visit me at Tinta's Kraal. He naturally did not tell me, but I learned from others, that both he and Mnyamane, who were the most powerful chiefs, were oppressing their lesser brethren. Mnyamane had then taken 400 cattle from Sirayo, and 600 from his people, on the ground that it was his fault the Zulu dynasty had been destroyed.

We had arranged that the empress should reach the Ityatosi some days before the sad anniversary, the death of her only son, June the 1st. When we arrived there, we were troubled by the intrusive action of a lady correspondent of an American newspaper, who endeavoured with much persistence to obtain "copy" for her paper. I sent for the headman of the *kraal,*—and it is remarkable how the natives trust any Englishman whom they know,—and after an explanation of the case, he signed a witnessed deed of a lease of all his land on a radius of 2 miles from the spot where the prince fell. We explained the law of trespass, and after giving the Zulus some blankets they formed a long line, and clasping hands danced away, showing how they would resist passively the approach of any one who endeavoured to go on the property.

I have already described, by Chicheeli's help, how he killed Robert Barton. We were able to give the remains a Christian burial. When we arrived at the Ityatosi I sent out for all the men who had been engaged in the attack on the reconnoitring party when the prince lost his life, and while waiting for them to assemble. Lieutenant Bigge and I rode to the Inhlazatze Mountain, with the double purpose of returning Mr. Osborne's call, who had waited on the empress when she entered Zululand by crossing the Blood River, and also because I wanted to confer with him about the lease I had taken of the land around Scobuza's *kraal*, the spot where the prince was killed. Leaving at 1 a.m. we were able to spend several hours with Mr. Osborne, and got back in time for dinner, the ponies doing the 74 miles without any sign of distress.

I had long wanted to know the truth of the story of the death of Masipula. When we were marching on Ulundi the previous year I was out in advance of the column reconnoitring, and when sitting under a tree the interpreter said, "The last time I was under this tree I said goodbye to Masipula, Umpande's Prime Minister;" and he told me this story. During the later years of Umpande's long reign the position in Zululand was somewhat analogous to that in the days of our Regency, when George the Third was no longer capable of managing the affairs of the nation. Masipula felt it his duty to check Cetewayo continually in his desire of raising more regiments, and when the king died, Cetewayo delayed until he was crowned by Shepstone, and then sent a message to Masipula, "The King is dead."

The meaning of this intelligence thus formally delivered was, "As you were his minister so many years, you ought to die." Masipula not accepting the hint, sent back a message that he greatly regretted Umpande's death; and Cetewayo waited patiently for another three months, and finding that Masipula would not take the hint, sent for him. He told my informant he knew that Cetewayo would kill him, and the Englishman asked, "Then why go? Ride over the border into Natal and live there." The old chief drawing himself up proudly, observed, "And do you think that, after being his father's minister so long, I would refuse to obey the son's orders?"

I asked Mr. Osborne, "Can you tell me whether Cetewayo poisoned or strangled Masipula? for I have heard that he had his beer poisoned, and another story that, after receiving him, in the evening he sent men into the *kraal* assigned to him, and that when the executioners entered, Masipula placed his head in the noose which was already in the rope. Tell me if you can, was he poisoned, or strangled?"

Mr. Osborne was a cautious man, and his solitary life among the Zulus perhaps increased this habit, although within 40 miles of us not anyone except Captain Bigge and our orderlies could speak English, he dropped his voice, and in a low tone answered me in a monosyllable, "Both"; and added, the poison not having taken effect as quickly as was expected, the ex-prime minister was strangled.

While we were encamped on the Ityatosi, near Scobuza's *kraal*, I had prolonged interviews with 18 Zulus, whom I examined separately, and from them obtained a detailed account of the surprise of the reconnoitring party of the 1st June in the previous year, in which the prince imperial fell, the natives later putting themselves in the exact positions they held that afternoon. There were between 30 and 36 Zulus who took part in the attack.

The patrol having rested on a hill to the north of the river, descended at three o'clock to Scobuza's *kraal*, and the Zulu scouts who were watching it hastily assembled all the men within reach. These crept up the bed of the river and were close at hand concealed in a mealie field, when a friendly Zulu, who was acting as guide, and was killed a few minutes later, informed the British officer in command that he had seen Zulus near, and then it was that the party was ordered to mount. The Zulus purposely waited until this moment, realising that it would be the most favourable moment to attack, and fired a volley. The horse of one of the white escort was shot, and he was immediately *assegaied*. That of another soldier fell in an ant-bear hole, and the rider was stabbed before he could rise.

The rest of the party, except the prince, galloped hard to the ridge, not drawing rein until they reached some rocks 820 yards from the *kraal*, when one of them looked round, and they then rode away, still fast, but not at the headlong speed at which they had started. The Zulus in pursuit ran first after the two white soldiers who were on the flanks, three or four men, headed by Zabanga, following the prince. His horse had jumped just as he was mounting, and his sword fell out of the scabbard.

He was very active, and was vaulting on his horse in motion, when the wallet on the front of the saddle broke away, and he fell to the ground, being at this time only 60 yards behind the fugitives. There were seven men who actually fought the prince. When Langalabalele, pursuing the fugitives, first saw Zabanga (killed at Ulundi, 4th July 1879) he was running away from the prince, who was rushing at him. Zabanga, crouching in the grass, threw an *assegai* at him. The first *assegai* stuck in the prince's thigh, and withdrawing it from the wound, he kept his foes at bay for some minutes. In the native's words:

> He fought like a lion; he fired two shots, but without effect, and I threw an *assegai* at him, which struck him, as I said at the time, but I always allowed Zabanga's claim to have killed him, for his *assegai* hit the prince in the left shoulder, a mortal wound. He fought with my *assegai*, and we did not dare to close with him until he sank down facing us, when we rushed on him.

On the 1st of July I drove the empress and Lady Wood from Maritzburg to the foot of the Inchanga Mountain, where at the terminus of the railway a train was waiting. The road was engineered down the side of the mountain, and the empress liking to travel fast, I let the horses canter most of the way down. I was always nervous when driving Her Majesty, and when I handed my wife into the train, I said, "Now my personal responsibility is over I shall not mind if the train goes off the line."

We had indeed a narrow escape; when I had assisted the ladies out of the carriage I handed the reins to a sergeant of the Army Service Corps, who was waiting to take the team back. He had gone only half a mile at a steady trot when the connecting rod which fastens the fore-carriage to the after part of the "Spider "snapped in two. If this had happened half an hour earlier, when we were cantering down the mountain road, the empress and Lady Wood would have had a severe accident.

After giving a personal report of the journey to Her Majesty, for which purpose Lady Wood and I received a command to Osborne, I resumed my work at Chatham. (The War Minister, apprehensive of criticism in the House of Commons, declined to allow me to draw any, even half-pay as a colonel, for the six months I was absent from the command.)

This gave much interesting occupation, and an opportunity I had long desired of reducing the number of useless sentries who wasted their time in many places in the garrison.

The commissary-general at the War Office corresponded with me at this period, and later, on the question of my succeeding him, which he desired. I had been successful in providing food and transport in 1878-79, and now, being anxious for the efficiency of his department, in the absence of any specially qualified officer in it, he wished that I should succeed him. He proposed this to me on several occasions, once when writing with reference to the confidential reports I had furnished on officers who had served under me during the Zulu War, concerning which he wrote:

I take this opportunity of stating, with reference to the reports you have sent me, that no more faithful or honest descriptions of officers' characters have ever reached me.

South Africa, sometimes named "The land of Misfortune," may be more aptly termed "The land of Misunderstandings." The problem of ensuring good government in a vast country inhabited by a few dominant white men, in the midst of warlike native races, has always been difficult.

Many governors and generals have been recalled by a dissatisfied Home Government, mainly because it did not understand the local conditions of the country, and twenty-five years ago, (as at 1906), the solution of the Zulu question, instead of solving the Boer-British difficulties, brought their opposing interests into sharper antagonism.

Ashanti to the Zulu War

An extract from "The Life of Sir Henry Evelyn Wood"
By Charles Williams

CHAPTER 1: ASHANTI AND HOME AGAIN

Few of our little wars have excited more interest among the people than the expedition which Sir Garnet Wolseley commanded for the punishment of the aggression of King Coffee Calcalli upon our Gold Coast possessions. It was not, perhaps, the value of our territory there which contributed in any degree to the feeling among the great bulk of newspaper readers. For, indeed, the Gold Coast has a very bad name among folks at home. And the climate is as bad as ever fancy painted it. There is only one European in the colony to every ten thousand natives. In fact, the Coast is unworthy the name of colony, but it is an important trading territory, and it supplies us with a very large quantity of raw material for our manufactures. Although we had a station there from the year 1618 and were fully represented by an incorporated company as early as the year 1662, yet we and the Dutch had never precisely defined the limits of our land until 1868, when a separation of interests was effected.

Of this England took little or no notice. It was an affair of administration and went down pretty much as a matter of course. But this transfer led to very serious results. The Dutch had got on well with the Ashantis, in spite of the horrors of the local "customs," and the frequent massacres of human beings, for reasons half of superstition, wholly of savagery. In matters of commerce the fault of the Dutch has seldom been squeamishness. But every Sunday school child in England had been taught to look to Ashanti and Dahomey as contemporary illustrations of the "dark places of the earth, full of the habitations of cruelty," as King David put it. When the Ashantis, in what would nowadays be called the Hinterland, came to realise that they had lost their conveniently blind friends from the Netherlands, they did not like it. And they came to the conclusion that they could drive the few British into the sea.

So, they invaded the coast, and occupied a protectorate of ours owned by a tribe called Fantis. They also blockaded our forts, or stations. This sort of thing not even a government rapidly falling into decrepitude could well stand, and when news came that Colonel Festing, of the Royal Marine Artillery, had not without difficulty beaten back King Coffee's legions it was time to act. And the Government acted with characteristic vigour! It appointed Sir Garnet Wolseley to the command of the troops (half a battalion of marines) and it made him Administrator of the Gold Coast. It was not an appointment or a duty which most people would covet, and there did not seem to be any credit likely to be got out of it. But it was a mission of danger, and the post of danger is the post of honour. The general (local only at that time) would have had no difficulty in filling up a staff to ten times the dimensions he had fixed upon in his own mind. And among those officers on whom he most depended was Lieutenant-Colonel Evelyn Wood, V.C., who left Liverpool on September 12th, and reached the Gold Coast on October 2nd, when he received the following order from Sir John McNeill, Chief of the Staff:

I am desired by Major-General Sir Garnet Wolseley, C.B., K.C.M.G., to direct you to proceed to Elmina, accompanied by the officers specified in General Orders, for the purpose of raising a body of loyal natives for service against the Ashantees, at present invading the Protectorate of the Gold Coast.

Colonel Wood landed at Elmina the same day to take up his duties. He raised first of all a corps of coolies for transport and organised an Intelligence Department. And before the 14th October he had got together a small native force which, if it did not cover itself with glory in the whole of the campaign, was, nevertheless, good enough to march into the bush, in which the Ashantis trusted as much as to their own undoubted bravery, and inflict a defeat on the enemy at Essaman. The next morning, he received from the general a letter containing the following passages:

Cape Coast Castle, 5.30 a.m.
October 15th.

My Dear Wood,
What hour did you get back last night? I watched you through

a glass until you got close to the marines we left on the beach, and your movements looked so pretty that one might have thought them a strategic movement across the 'Long Valley'. . . . . . I have to congratulate you upon the very able manner in which you did everything yesterday. I am very much obliged to you. The operations were well carried out, and all your previous arrangements were admirable.

Without entering into the history of this brief and brilliant campaign, it may be said that the original idea of Mr. Gladstone's first government was that, save a few marines and West India troops, the bulk of the force was to consist of native allies. These allies, mostly Fantis, were already known to be among the most cowardly of mankind, and it could have been with no great confidence that Lieutenant-Colonel Evelyn Wood and Major Baker Russell began to raise and drill two native regiments.

Thanks to the co-operation of Captain, now Sir, Redvers Buller, Captain Fremantle, R.N., Colonel McNeill (who was badly wounded in the arm), Captain Brackenbury, R.A., and Captain Crease, R.M., the attack on Essaman was a success, and in the opinion of Sir Garnet Wolseley was the turning-point of the war, as it broke the spell regarding the invincibility of the Ashantis in the bush. The Ashanti commander-in-chief decided to retreat. But in spite of the success at Essaman, it became clear that nothing could be done in an effective way without European troops. Wood's troops consisted of Cape Coast volunteers, and of men from Elmina, Kossu, and Bonny, very unpromising raw material. When the news of the Essaman success got home it was acknowledged by Mr. Cardwell, who wrote:

> I have had the honour of laying this despatch and the enclosure before the queen and have received Her Majesty's commands to convey to you, and to Lieutenant-Colonel Wood, who, under your general direction, was in immediate command. Her Majesty's approbation of the able and gallant conduct of the officers, non-commissioned officers, and men on that occasion. I observe with great satisfaction the terms in which you speak of the services rendered by Lieutenant-Colonel Wood, V. C.

For ten days Colonel Wood was engaged in reconnoitring through the bush, and then he proceeded to the head of the road, but not before the Fantis had exhibited every variety of cowardice that might be expected from previous experience. Meanwhile Sir Garnet was down with Coast fever, dangerously; and when he recovered he ordered an advance by Mansu. On the 27th November, Colonel Wood, who had been directed to harass the enemy, "to hang on his rear and attack him without ceasing," was pushing the enemy's rear-guard near Faisowah when his troops became unsteady, and his column of less than 300 natives was nearly surrounded. He retired and was followed five miles by the Ashantis. But then it was the turn of the latter to become panic-stricken, and they "broke up their camp and retired precipitately through the night with torches, scarcely stopping till they reached the Prah." The king wrote to Sir Garnet complaining of this attack on his retreating force, and adding that his troops "lost all their sick men and all their property," and the General replied:

> As regards the attack upon your retreating army at Faisoo, it was made only by a small party of my undrilled black troops, who were ordered to fall back as soon as they found where your army was; yet it caused the whole of the Ashantee army to retreat in the utmost haste and confusion, leaving their dead and dying everywhere along the path.

This picture was certainly not overdrawn, for the main Prahsu road was found strewed with the corpses of Ashantis, disease and starvation having decimated their ranks more than the sword. The last verb in this sentence is decidedly inadequate to express the fact, if it be true that "of the 40,000 warriors who originally invaded the protectorate at least one half perished." In spite of the cowardice of the native levies, and with the assistance of but a few marines and blue-jackets, the first phase of the war was brought to a satisfactory ending, and the general was not wrong in attributing the result to "the untiring exertions of the few carefully selected Staff and Special Service officers who had accompanied him, and whose hard work, exposure, and privations had been so cheerfully endured for two and a half months before" he wrote. In the same sense he further said to the Secretary for War, under date of December 5th:—

> ....Of the special service officers, where all have worked so hard and so earnestly, it is no easy matter to particularise individuals. The two seniors, Lieutenant-Colonel Wood, V. C, and Major Russell, have each raised a regiment. . . . Lieutenant-Colonel Wood commanded at the engagement of Essaman, as mentioned in my despatch of the 15th October, in which I stated my appreciation of the manner in which he carried out the

orders he had received. He is now commanding the advanced posts from Mansu to the River Prah, and displays both zeal and ability in the discharge of his duties. . . . . I have great pleasure in bringing the names both of Lieutenant-Colonel Wood, V. C, and Major Russell to your special notice."

And the general was not alone in his views, for the Commanding Royal Engineer spoke to the same effect:

"I have to request you will bring to the notice of his Excellency the Major-General, the great assistance I have received from Lieutenant-Colonel Wood, V. C, who has aided me in every way. Indeed, I cannot express too strongly how much I am indebted to Colonel Wood for this assistance."

The help was very substantial which was thus handsomely acknowledged. Major Home has recorded one phase of it:

The great difficulty at Prahsu was the want of hutting materials. On the south bank the palm-leaves were almost entirely deficient, and they had to be procured from the north bank of the river . . . . 200 to 300 men of Colonel Wood's regiment-, with two or three European officers, were ferried across daily, to cut palm-leaves and stakes for hutting.

But this extract only tells a small part of the story how, on the arrival of the European troops, under Sir Archibald Alison as Brigadier, with Colonel Greaves as Chief of the Staff—"all that there was of a Chief of the Staff," as a great friend of his subsequently described him, with reference to a humorous affair in Cyprus—they found all the way from the coast to the Prah carefully constructed huts built by the native troops and labourers under Colonel Wood.

The general arrived at Prahsu in advance of the European troops on January 2nd, 1874, and by the 15th all was ready for the column, for which there were lying prepared a month's provisions for 3,520 fighting men and 3,000 carriers, in spite of continual desertions of Native allies. Negotiations which the general knew to be futile were carried on for some time with the Ashanti king, both before and after the crossing of the Prah by the force, between the 15th and the end of January, on the last day of which the savage "threw off the mask." The general advanced in four columns forming a sort of square, designed to meet the enveloping or outflanking tactics of the enemy.

Colonel Wood commanded on the right, where he "encountered so heavy a fire that he directed his men to lie down." Of the fire the general himself confessed he had not known one heavier, so it is no wonder that before the action was won, which it was at a quarter to two in the afternoon, having lasted for some six hours. Colonel Wood was badly hit in the chest by a slug and had to be carried several miles to the hospital. In a hurried despatch addressed to the Secretary of War the next day Sir Garnet Wolseley said:

...... My whole force divided into four columns ... Right column, Lieutenant-Colonel E. Wood, V.C.; Naval Brigade left wing. Wood's Regiment, Rait's artillery, two rocket detachments. Royal Engineers' detachment ... Up to 1.30 p.m. the enemy kept up a very heavy fire on Lieutenant-Colonel Wood's column, whose right was extended into the bush, east of Egginassie ... The officers commanding the columns performed their difficult task most excellently and were efficiently aided by their staff. Lieutenant-Colonel Evelyn Wood, V.C. was wounded while at the head of the troops.

But though the slug wound was so severe. Colonel Wood managed to get out of hospital on February 3rd, and, though weak, he marched throughout the night, and overtook the General at 4 a.m. the next day, in spite of a "pitiless storm," a "deluge of rain which never ceased throughout the night." He was thus in time for the final action at Ordahsu, which threw open the path to Coomassie, and in this he took his place at the head of his Native regiment and led the advance.

In the following months, like his general, Colonel Wood returned to England, to find that his services had been fully recognised in the despatch sent by Sir Garnet from Coomassie on the day after the occupation of that bloodstained capital, in the following passage:

.... The two native regiments raised on the coast were commanded throughout the war by Brevet-Lieutenant-Colonel E. Wood, V.C., 90th Light Infantry, and by Brevet-Major B.C. Russell, 13th Hussars. Both these officers have upon many occasions been placed in very difficult positions, requiring the exercise of high military qualities, and have invariably carried out their very arduous and trying duties most efficiently. I take the liberty of bringing to your especial notice, as those upon whom the brunt of this war has fallen, these and the other combatant officers named below, who originally came out with me or followed me by the first mail steamer.

In June, 1874, Colonel Wood delivered before the United Service Institution a lecture on the Ashanti Expedition, Mr. Gathorne Hardy, now Lord Cranbrook, in the chair. This lecture gives a capital word picture of the campaign; but, as the chairman said, the lecturer had spoken of everybody's services rather than his own. Nevertheless, there is one passage from which a fair idea may be gathered of the difficulties that were overcome in the native material on which ministers had originally intended to all but exclusively depend:

On the 7th November, 1000 Cape Coast men, who had been directed by Colonel Wood to join him at Essecroom, arrived at Abrakampa, in order, as they said, to fight under the general's eye. At 2 p.m. they were paraded, facing the bush, and a more extraordinary battle array was never seen. In the British Army, corps quarrel for the position on the right of the line; here each company struggled for and edged away to the left, I imagine because it was the point further removed from the Ashantis. In front was a line of stalwart men, bigger than the Ashantis, all well-armed with Enfield rifles. Behind them were their chiefs with whips.

Behind the Fantis chiefs, were Kossoos with drawn swords. When ordered to advance, the Fantis moved forward a dozen paces and then stopped. The chiefs belaboured, all within reach, and the Kossoos menaced the most backward, including many of the chiefs. In time all but the kings were out of sight, and they showed no intention of venturing into the bush, till some officers who were looking on, having been forbidden to go forward, used more than 'verbal persuasion,' to quote the words of a despatch; and, indeed, one gifted officer used so much persuasion towards a chief as to spoil a strong umbrella.

Yelling and firing, the Cape Coast men advanced as the ever-menacing Kossoos closed on them. Once in the bush, however, they were more at liberty, and, squatting down, they let the Abras pass to their right. These, on reaching Anismadi, the Ashanti camp, observed the last of Amanquatsia's army moving off. Not anticipating an attack, they had left much spoil and many slaves in camp, and several fell into our hands, though some were slaughtered in sight of the Abras, one Ashanti being shot while actually cutting a young mother's throat, a baby being on her back.

It is worth noting that, at this time, Sir Garnet Wolseley's substantive rank in the army, though he had acted as Major-General in Ashanti, was "Major, half-pay, late 90th Regiment," and that Colonel Wood's similar rank was "Major, 90th Foot." On the last day of March he was gazetted Brevet-Colonel, and had a Commandership of the Most Honourable Order of the Bath conferred on him. Within a month he was called to the Bar by the Honourable Society of the Middle Temple.

In the beginning of July, he rejoined the depot of his regiment at Hamilton, and little over two months later he was appointed Superintending Officer of Garrison Instruction for the United Kingdom, including Ireland. In the following August he served as A.Q.M.G. of General Herbert's Division in the Autumn Manoeuvres, and on St. George's Day, 1876, he was appointed to the like post in the Aldershot Division. After more than a year of sound and useful work, he arranged the concentration of a so-called Army Corps in Windsor Park on July 9th, what time it appeared more than likely the said Corps would soon have to see foreign service in the neighbourhood of the Black Sea. General Sir Thomas Steele thanked him before Head-Quarter Staff for "the perfect arrangements of the day."

In August, 1877, General Napier, Governor of the Royal Military College at Sandhurst, offered him the place of Commandant of that Institution, but the prospect of war prevented the acceptance of the post. A little later, the similar post at the Staff College was declined for a like reason. But Turkey was to be left to fight her foe unaided, and all hope of taking part in an Eastern Campaign was for the time being shattered, when the 90th Regiment was ordered to South Africa, and Colonel Wood, as its senior major, resigned his staff appointment to follow it, being employed on "Special Service "until the time came when he was ordered to take over the command. On the day after the Treaty of San Stefano was signed, he landed at East London, and nine days later was sent to command the troops near Keiskama Hoek, which was threatened by an attack from insurgent Kaffirs. Thus, began a service in South Africa which was to prove alike interesting and important.

CHAPTER 2: IN KAFFIRLAND AND ZULULAND

It would be foreign to the nature of this volume to enter into any question of colonial policy in which its subject had not an initiative or controlling hand. But it is necessary, for the sake of clearness, to trace the position of affairs from the time Colonel Wood landed at East London, which was the same day that the command of the troops in South Africa was handed over by General Sir A. T. Cunynghame to (local) Lieutenant-General the Hon. F. A. Thesiger, now Lord Chelmsford. For some time before this one of the periodical fits of restlessness had taken possession of the Kaffir and other tribes, and it had broken out into hostilities in or before February, 1878.

The Transvaal had been annexed in 1877, and with it the country of Sekukuni, a chief of Basuto descent, but the most powerful feudatory of King Ketchwayo of Zululand. The Transvaal Boers had no real right to the country, and previous to the annexation Sekukuni had beaten the Boers badly. But even before any Zulu troubles arose there had been a brisk little war with the Kaffirs, ending with the death of the chief Sandilli. This man had given a great deal of trouble; and Colonel Wood was destined to take a prominent part in breaking his power. Five days after taking command at Keiskama Hoek he led a column of regulars and volunteers up the Quilli mountain, and for the next ten days was employed in clearing the Kaffirs out of the Peri bush. On the 28th March, in the words of General Thesiger:

> The enemy showed themselves in considerable numbers on the open ground between the Goza heights and the precipice west of Haynes Mill; and I ordered an attack for the following morning. The combined movements of Colonel Wood and Commandant Frost were well carried out.

And this day there was a smart skirmish between Wood's mixed column and the enemy. The attack on the 29th did not lead to much more than another skirmish, so far as Colonel Wood was concerned, but what there was of it the general thus describes:

> The Kaffirs made an obstinate stand, and drove them (Fingoes), killing Captain Webster of this division while gallantly leading on his men. At this moment Colonel Wood's force . . . opportunely appeared on the high ground above the bush and effectually carried out its instructions.

The Kaffirs being driven off, Colonel Wood was employed until April 5th in the necessary but tiresome work of cutting tracks through dense bush. On that day the friendly natives searched the bush and reported it clear of foes. The next day he descended the mountain and had a skirmish at Burn's Hill, west of the Intaba Dodo River, and soon after he had the satisfaction of being joined by the headquarters and five companies of the 90th Regt., to the command of which he had succeeded at the beginning of the month. On the last day of the month he had a serious fight. He commanded three columns, in all about 1,500 men, which attacked and defeated the Kaffirs in the Intaba Dodo bush, himself accompanying the right column, which had the most of the fighting. The general reported that:

> About 6. 45 a.m., heavy firing was heard from Colonel Wood's direction. . . . . The path by which this column had to advance was surrounded by dense bush, which completely screened the Kaffirs . . . . By sunset the day's work had been satisfactorily concluded. . . . . Our loss, except Colonel Wood's right column, was slight.

On the 8th, Wood's column once more ascended the Goza heights, and had a skirmish at McNaughten's Kranz, Buffalo Range; while on the 12th, the Fingoes under his command had yet another skirmish, in accordance with the orders of the general "not to cease harassing the Kaffirs day or night." The general added "the officers in command are not likely to lose sight of these orders." Colonel Evelyn Wood was not likely to do so at any rate. From the 12th to the end of the month he was engaged in clearing the bush of the Buffalo River, and in searching for fugitives, the war being virtually at an end, as the general informed the Home Government on Waterloo Day, and even a week before. No hostile Kaffirs had been found in the Buffalo Bush; but there was always a chance of further fighting so long as Sandilli, the head and front of the rising, was at large. He was slain in a skirmish on the 30th, and the rising immediately collapsed. The general reported of Wood as follows:

> From the 9th to the 29th May, the troops under Colonel Sir Evelyn Wood gave the rebels no rest. . . . Colonel Evelyn Wood, V. C, C. B., 90th Light Infantry, on special service in South Africa, has had command of a separate column of Imperial and Colonial troops, from the time that I assumed the direction of military operations in the field. I cannot speak too highly of the good service rendered by this officer. He has exercised his command with marked ability and great tact. I am of opinion that his indefatigable exertions and personal influence have been mainly instrumental in bringing the war to a speedy close. I would beg to draw attention to the names of those officers who

are especially brought to notice by Colonel E. Wood.

On Midsummer day. Colonel Wood took command of a column which was ordered on a march of 510 miles from King William's Town to Natal by way of Pondo Land. He reached Maritsburg with the column on September 1st, having meanwhile paid a visit, on a political mission, to the town of Umfundisweni, in Pondo Land. Six days later he was appointed to the command of the troops in the Utrecht district, just over the border from Natal in the Transvaal, and his five companies of the 90th regiment were to follow him, as the other companies were already there. It was on the 17th that he took up the command, and in view of troubles coming fast and thick, he proceeded two days later to Luneburg, where he was engaged for some time in the purchase of transport.

Meanwhile Ketchwayo's men had destroyed all the Dutch home-steads from the River Pungolo to the River Pivan, the Zulu king hav-ing, as long before as February, instigated Sekukuni to make an attack on a chief named Pokwana, who was friendly to the English, and who was able, with a little help, to beat off the assailants. Captain Clarke, commissioner for the district, having remonstrated with Sekukuni, that chief replied that the English were afraid to fight, that the country was his, that the white people must leave, and that he was quite ready for war. (See *Official Narrative of the Field Operations* connected with the Zulu War of 1879.) The Boers also began to be restless, and to openly express discontent.

The local forces being slightly strengthened, one of Sekukuni's chiefs was terrified into submission, but the great man himself was very active in opposition. And before he could be suppressed, Ketchwayo was ready to take the field in person, nominally on account of some disputed ter-ritory near the Blood River, but really because he had transferred to the British the detestation which he had nourished against the Boers, so that the Zulu war which followed was in fact a heritage which we took over in connection with the annexation of Zululand. On October 1st the general wrote as follows to Colonel Wood:

Sir Bartle Frere is very anxious to give some encouragement to the German settlers at Luneberg, who have sent him a petition pointing out the precarious position in which they are placed. I have told him that at present it will be quite out of the question to send them any troops; and I doubt much when the whole of the 90th are concentrated at Utrecht it will be prudent to weaken that garrison.

Yet two companies of the 90th were taken to Luneberg, Colonel Wood reporting his action and stating that unless the settlers were protected they would leave their station. To this despatch he received the following reply:

> You have taken a serious responsibility upon yourself, and I doubt very much whether you have acted wisely. However, you may depend upon my backing you up, as of course in your position you were bound to act in whatever way you considered necessary, under what I presume were very pressing circumstances.

The high commissioner had no doubts on the matter, and Sir Bartle wrote:

> As regards Colonel Wood's advancement of a detachment to Luneberg, it is to my mind clear it was the right thing to do. . . . They appealed to Colonel Evelyn Wood for that protection which he was, as I conceive, as much bound to afford them as if they had been living in Pretoria. . . . . I think he deserves our gratitude and acknowledgments for taking the responsibility of saving us from such a disgrace.

And later on, he wrote to the Colonial Secretary as regards another raid:

> It will be in the recollection of Her Majesty's Government that this is by no means the first raid made by Umbelini, with the connivance if not under the orders of Cetewayo, in whose country he lives. It is simply a specimen of the horrors from which Colonel Wood saved the German settlers in the little town of Luneberg by sending a company of troops to their protection when threatened by Umbelini two or three months ago.

On the same subject Sir H. Bulwer, Governor of Natal, wrote of Umbelini's raid:

> About the same time, or a few days later, another *kraal* across the Pongolo, this time close to the Luneberg settlement, was attacked by his people, who killed men, women, and children. This act, following upon the notice given by the Zulu headman, Faku, caused a great deal of excitement among the Ger-

man settlers at Luneburg, and to reassure the settlement Colonel Evelyn Wood sent from Utrecht a detachment of troops to Luneberg, which had the effect of effectually stopping any further raid in that direction.

Lord Chelmsford himself admitted the effect of the act and wrote that Colonel Wood had "done wonders with the Dutchmen;" and added:

> I am quite sure the High Commissioner will be as much obliged to you from a political point of view as I am from a military one. At the same time Colonel North Crealock, Assistant Military Secretary, forwarded Colonel Wood a Minute from the High Commissioner:
> 'I shall be much obliged if His Excellency the Lieutenant-General will convey my thanks to Colonel Evelyn Wood for the judgment he showed throughout these proceedings.'

In November our hero visited Andries Pretorius, an influential Boer, residing near Laing's Nek, in the Transvaal, to endeavour to induce him to join the British troops in the event of war with the Zulus. Early in December he convened a meeting of Dutch Boers at Utrecht, who promised to accompany him if necessary. On this Sir Bartle Frere wrote to the Home Government:

> I have but little doubt that the firm, conciliatory, and judicious treatment of these gentlemen by Colonel Evelyn Wood will have an excellent effect, not only locally, but generally throughout the south-eastern Transvaal districts.

The frontier of Natal was about 200 miles in length, "divided into two nearly equal faces, forming a re-entering angle in the neighbourhood of Rorke's Drift." On the side of the Transvaal the country is comparatively open, and easily watched, but on the southern side Zululand is "broken and mountainous, and in many places covered with thick forests." These forests evidently furnished a screen behind which the Zulus could choose their rendezvous for a raid into Natal. It was therefore obviously wise to be beforehand with Ketchwayo, and, adopting the advice of the old Roman, "carry the war into Africa." No maps of the country existed, but at length the main routes were ascertained, and General Thesiger divided his force into five columns, with the object of marching on Ulundi, the king's principal *kraal*.

Later on, the number of columns was reduced to three, to advance simultaneously from the Lower Tugela Drift, Rorke's Drift, and Utrecht. The command of the first or right column was given to Colonel Pearson, commanding the second battalion of the "Buffs;" the centre column was confided to Colonel Glyn, commanding the second battalion 24th Regiment; and the left column was given to Colonel Wood, who was already on the spot at Utrecht. Besides these columns there was to be a fourth, composed of friendly natives of Natal, for the most part, which was to move later on between the centre and the right columns.

In the first days of January, Wood's column assembled near Balte Spruit, and consisted of:

> Eight companies first battalion 13th Regiment, and eight of the 90th, four guns 11th battery, 7th Brigade, Royal Artillery, with the Frontier Light Horse, Mounted Boers and Wood's Irregulars, or a total of about 200 mounted men, 1,500 European Infantry, and 300 natives, with four guns and two rocket troughs.

On the 4th January the column advanced to the Blood River. On the same day Sir Bartle Frere, the High Commissioner, handed over to the general—now become Lord Chelmsford, by the death of the fine old gentleman who, having been, like Colonel Wood, a midshipman, had attained the dignity of Lord Chancellor—the task of coercing Ketchwayo, unless he agreed to the British terms by the 11th of the month. On the 6th the Blood River, though in flood, was crossed, and on the 10th, Bemba, the chief of the district, submitted, and was sent with his people to Utrecht. On the same day the concentration of each of the three columns was completed. For the moment it appeared that Wood's column had the best of the country, which was more open than that before the other columns.

But he was not to have a free hand, for danger being supposed to lurk more especially in front of Glyn's centre column, Wood, 35 miles off, was to keep himself in readiness to hold out to him a helping hand. Accordingly, on the 10th, Colonel Wood started down the left of the Blood River, an affluent of the Buffalo, and at once found himself in a very difficult country. He had two guns, six companies 90th, and six companies 13th, with most of his mounted men, and two battalions of friendly Zulus known as Wood's Irregulars. The ground was for the most part marshy, and numerous small streams had to be crossed, their banks being previously cut down.

Nevertheless, in four hours no less than 9 miles had been cov-

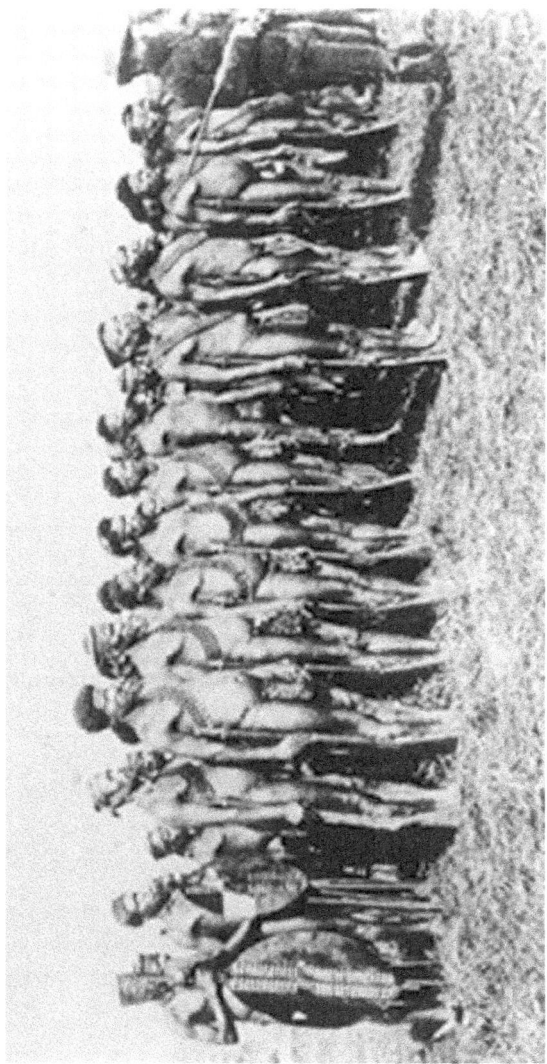

Natal native contingent

ered, and then the column halted for the night, or rather till 2 in the morning of the 11th, when the march was resumed in "darkness and fog." First went a flying column, under the brigadier, composed of the Frontier Light Horse, two guns, 24 marksmen in mule waggons, 600 of Wood's Irregulars. The remainder, under Lieutenant-Colonel Gilbert, went in support at a distance of several miles. The flying column made nine miles and got within twelve of Rorke's Drift by eight o clock, when Lord Chelmsford was met. The general, having seen the centre column safely across the Buffalo without opposition, had ridden out with an escort to meet the left column.

The news he brought rendered the further advance of Colonel Wood unnecessary. He accordingly returned to the camp at Bemba's Kop, but owing to heavy rain did not reach the camp until the morning of the 13th. This operation, though as it turned out useless in a direct sense, had two advantages. It accustomed the troops to the presence of the Zulus, who, though not yet actively hostile, were in the bush in great numbers, and it provisioned the force by the capture of many head of cattle. Of the state of the command Lord Chelmsford wrote on January 14th to the Secretary of State for War:

> I was completely satisfied with the account Colonel Wood had given me of the efficiency of his column, with respect to its transport and commissariat and its ability to move forward at once. I attribute the satisfactory state of the column to Colonel Wood's energy and military knowledge.

And on the same date Colonel Wood was appointed Political Agent in Northern Zululand, while a day or two later he was, in Lord Chelmsford's words:

> Instructed to act altogether independently. . . . He will take up a position covering Utrecht and the adjacent Transvaal frontier wherever he considers his force can be most usefully employed.

Reconnaissances were made on the 15th and 17th by the mounted troops, and on the 18th the column advanced ten miles eastwards to the Sand River, or Insegene, the irregulars, in advance, having a slight skirmish on the eastern side of the White Umvalosi River, which further on runs down three miles to the south of Ulundi. After a day's halt, if not absolute rest, the column moved on the 20th to the White Umvalosi, near the *kraal* of a chief named Tinta, who promptly submitted, and was sent to Utrecht under escort. A reconnaissance

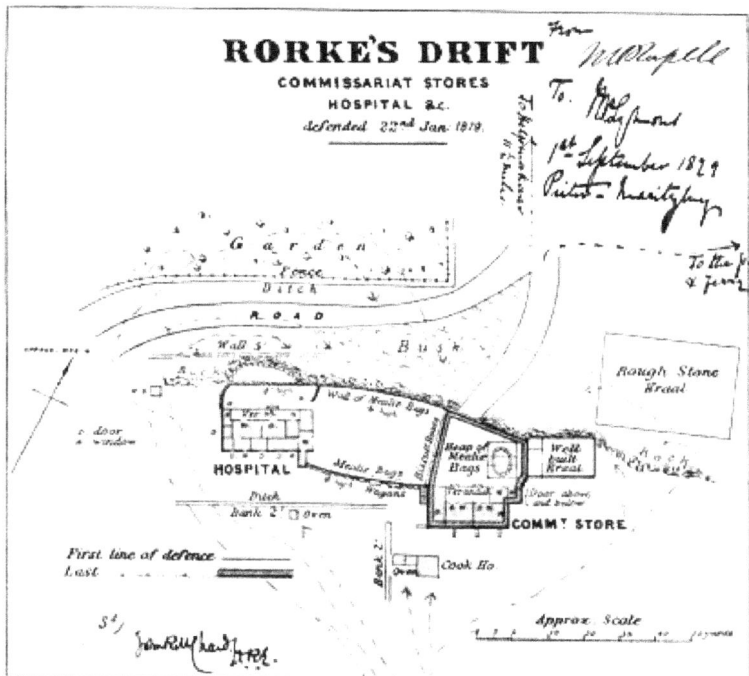

made to the top of a table-mountain in the Zungi range was warmly received by the enemy and had to retire.

On the next day a strong stone *laager* fort was completed and the stores moved into it, under the guard of a company from the 13th and one from the 90th regiments. That midnight a patrol, in three sections, one under the command of Lieutenant-Colonel Buller, and another under Colonel Wood, set out for the Zungi range, and gained the ridge unopposed at 6 a.m. The force united and passed to the eastern end of the range, having on the way discovered the Zulus drilling on the central eminence, called the Inhlobana mountain, to the number of about 4,000 men.

> Their evolutions, which were plainly visible with the aid of a glass, were executed with ease and precision, a circle, a triangle, and a hollow square with a partition across it, being formed rapidly by movements of companies.

Evidently here were foemen, though savages, not unworthy of British steel. The force now descended the mountain, and at 7 p.m. gained a camp which had been formed by Lieutenant-Colonel Gilbert below the south-eastern extremity of the range. A halt on the 23rd was followed on the morning of the next day by an advance, when, at half past 7, a body of Zulus was met and defeated north of the Inhlobana mountain. While this skirmish was in progress the news reached Colonel Wood of the disaster to the centre column at Isandhlwana on the 22nd, when "52 officers, and 806 white non-commissioned officers and men were killed," besides 200 to 300 native troops, and the Zulus "became possessed of two 7-pounder guns with their ammunition, and of about 800 Martini-Henry rifles, with some 400,000 cartridges." In consequence of this reverse Colonel Wood acted prudently and well by at once falling back on his camp on the White Umvolosi at Fort Tinta.

Colonel Wood remained at Fort Tinta the day of the 26th, loading up the burdens of twenty waggons, and on the 26th marched nine miles towards the 'Ngabaka Hawane mountain, twenty miles to the east of Utrecht. But he was in no hurry to fall back faster than was needed, so he halted from the 27th till the 31st on the White Umvalosi, and only then proceeded a short distance further to a good position at Kambula, on the south-eastern side of the mountain, where water and wood were plentiful and where he established a strong entrenched camp.

ISANDHLWANA

Next morning Colonel Buller took about 140 mounted men to the Makulusini Kraal, thirty miles or more to the eastward, this *kraal* being "a centre of resistance and a rallying point" for the most hostile natives. He got there at half-past twelve, having been over eight hours on the road. He had guarded his line of march by leaving thirty men in the pass, and with the rest he advanced into the basin of the hills, and galloped up to the *kraal*, from which the "Zulus fled in all directions." The *kraal* of 250 huts was burnt, some cattle were captured, and the party got back the same evening to Kambula without loss. Such is often the result of happy audacity.

The staff map makes the burning of the *kraal* take place on the 2nd of February, but the *Official History* leaves no doubt it was on the 1st. On the 3rd the fort at Kambula was finished, and armed with two guns; and from the 5th to the 7th two parties went scouting about in search of Zulus, but found none. They returned from their vain search on the 7th, and on the 10th Colonel Buller was out again eastward to his old ground on the Inhlobana mountain, where he got 500 cattle without "any serious resistance."

From considerations of transport for wood, the fort was on the 13th moved two miles nearer the mountain summit, and on the same day Buller went off to punish a chief named Manyanyoba who was raiding the Intombi valley, near Luneberg, and although this chief had been joined by Umbelini, the Zulu who had ordered the Germans away from their farms the previous September, and had in February committed a number of murders in this valley, the Zulus were routed out of the caves in which they took refuge, and slain to the number of thirty-four. Some cattle were taken.

Other raids were made by a force under Colonel Rowlands, V.C., without much result, and on the 26th that officer was despatched to Pretoria in consequence of the attitude of the Boers, so that Colonel Wood remained in sole charge of the district. On the 17th Uhamu, a half-brother of Ketchwayo, offered to surrender, but was unable to do so until the 4th March, when he was brought in with 700 followers. Before he reached Luneberg, a company of the 80th Regiment was sent out under Captain Moriarty, to escort a convoy of waggons with supplies to Luneberg from Derby. It met some of the convoy on the Intombi River, and there, formed *laager*, where it was inspected the night of the 11th by Major Tucker. At four o clock on the morning of the 12th, a sentry was fired at, and the *laager* on the left bank was rushed, with disastrous results, Moriarty and most of his men being *assegaied* as they left their tents.

A party on the right bank, under the command of one Lieutenant Harward, opened fire, but in the face of it 200 Zulus got across the river, whereupon the gallant Harward bolted on horseback, as hard as he could pelt, in the direction of Luneberg, four and a half miles off, to "procure reinforcements," leaving his detachment without an officer. However, there was a plucky sergeant, named Booth, who was equal to the occasion, showed a bold front to the Zulus, and brought his band off without loss. Mr. Harward was court-martialled, but was acquitted, yet did not escape such a "wigging" at the hands of Lord Chelmsford and the commander-in-chief at home, that his combatant career soon came to a close.

Uhamu's surrender was of some value, and much was thought of it at the time by the superior authorities. Sir B. Frere said in a despatch:

> Much credit is due to Colonel Wood and to Captain Macleod, who acted under his orders, for the temper, judgment, and patience they have shown in their dealings with Uhamu. There were at first the gravest suspicions in the minds of persons claiming more than an ordinary knowledge of Zulu affairs as to whether Uhamu was not, in Ketchwayo's interest, devising a scheme to entrap Colonel Wood. There is no doubt but that this defection from Ketchwayo is in every way an event of considerable importance.

And Lord Chelmsford said:

> It will be within your recollection that Colonel Wood for many months past has reported his belief that this important chief would separate himself from the king when opportunity offered, and Colonel Wood has always treated the natives of Uhamu's district, when it was possible to do so, in a manner which would induce them to join, as Uhamu.

Colonel Wood's own report ran:

> Uhamu came in as reported on the 10th inst. and having requested me to get in his wives and family, I sent off on the 12th inst. twenty of his men to endeavour to collect his people. Early on the morning of the 14th a party consisting of 360 rifles under Lieutenant-Colonel Buller, C.B., 30 *burghers* under Piet Uys, and 200 men of Uhamu's under direction of Mr. Lloyd left this camp. Lieutenant-Colonel Buller, C.B., was in com-

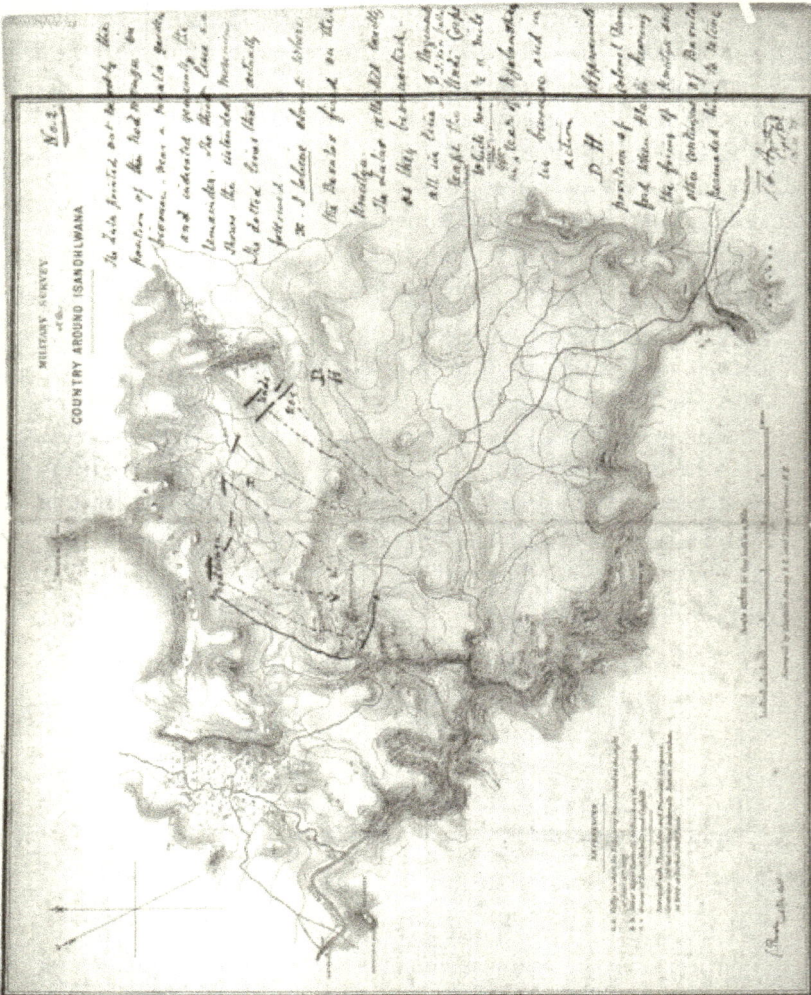

MILITARY SURVEY
of the
COUNTRY AROUND ISANDHLWANA

REFERENCE

mand of the patrol. I accompanied the patrol in order to see the country, and because I considered my presence would be an inducement to Uhamu's men to accompany, as the latter has begged me to look on his men as my "dogs." Leaving the camp at 5 p.m. on the 14th, we reached the caves near Inhlangawine Inambruid, twelve miles to the east of the sources of the M'Kusi River, and about forty-five miles from this camp, at 9.30 p.m. The last seven miles occupied three hours, as we had to cross a very difficult hill. We started back at about 9 a.m., and reached the Zunguin range on the evening of the 15th inst. A few shots were fired at us from the Inhlobane range. The position is stronger and more difficult to take than I anticipated. I have now returned to camp at 1 p.m., bringing with me 958 souls of Uhamu's people.

The Special Border Agent, at Umvoti, reporting on an interview with some Zulus said:

One of them at a private interview told the bishop and myself confidentially that the change in Cetewayo's tone is principally caused by the defection of Uhamu. They perceive plainly it is the beginning of the breakup of the Zulu power.

Sir B. Frere wrote:

I have in other despatches expressed my sense of the importance of Uhamu's defection from Cetewayo, which I entirely concur with his Excellency Lord Chelmsford in thinking is mainly due to the judicious management of Colonel E. Wood and Captain Macleod.

And Lord Chelmsford was not less emphatic:

I congratulate you upon Uhamu's surrender—the whole credit I consider lies with you.

In consequence of this, following upon so much distinguished service, the general asked that the local rank of Brigadier-General might be conferred on Colonel Wood, which request was granted by the high commissioner on the 3rd April, ere a despatch from him reached home with this passage:

Before active operations recommence for further advance in Zululand I wish to bring to the special notice of Her Majesty's Government the great value of the services performed by Colonel Evelyn Wood, in command of the 4th column, and Colonel Pearson, of the 1st column of the forces now in the field.

2. His Excellency Lieutenant-General Lord Chelmsford has, I am sure, very fully reported on the military bearing of their operations in Zululand. What I would now specially bring to the notice of Her Majesty's Government is the political effect of their steady maintenance of positions so far advanced into Zululand as to render an invasion of Natal by the Zulu Army in force an operation of extreme peril. . . . .

But I should place foremost in the list of causes the undaunted bearing of the two columns commanded by Colonels Wood and Pearson, and I beg warmly to recommend the conduct of both officers for the special approbation of Her Majesty's Government.

And the effective instrument of the promotion read thus in General Orders of April 8th:

His Excellency the High Commissioner has been pleased to approve of Lieutenant-Colonel and Brevet Colonel Wood, V.C, C.B., 90th Foot, holding the local rank of Brigadier-General while employed in command of a brigade in South Africa. Dated 3rd April, 1879.

The queen, on the 23rd June, gave effect to the wishes of the High Commissioner by appointing Colonel Wood a Knight Commander of the Bath.

For some time, it had been rumoured that Ketchwayo was bent on throwing his whole army on Wood's column, which a Frenchman named Grandier, who escaped from Ulundi, reported to be the "only commando" the Zulus were afraid of. The Border Agent at Umvoti reported to the same effect and thought Wood might have to encounter as many as 25,000 men. He added:

The Zulus are much impressed with the skill with which this force has been handled and are afraid it may push on for the Inhlazatze and threaten the Royal Kraal. Bishop Colenso heard that the whole army would probably be sent to try and overwhelm Colonel Wood's column.

Even as early as January 28th Lord Chelmsford wrote Wood:

You are now forewarned and must be prepared to have the whole Zulu force on top of you one of these days.

Between the 14th and 18th of March, Colonel Wood accompanied Colonel Buller on an expedition to bring in a number of Uhamu's men who were hiding from the Zulus in caves on the Umkusi River, forty-five miles east of Kambula. As many as 958 were thus brought in, with little opposition, but something else was done; it was found out that the southern side of the Inhlobana mountain was occupied by from 800 to 1000 of the enemy. This led to a reconnaissance, when Lord Chelmsford announced an intention of marching to the relief of Etshowe and asked that a diversion should be attempted on March 28th.

A movement was accordingly made against both ends of the mountain, the eastern under Colonel Buller, the western under Colonel Russell. The former had 300 mounted men and 400 natives, and after a march of thirty miles, bivouacked five miles from the south-east of the mountain. The latter had 250 mounted men, a rocket detachment, a battalion of Wood's Irregulars, and 150 of Uhamu's men. After a march of fifteen miles, he bivouacked four miles west of the mountain.

Colonel Wood with his staff, consisting of Captain the Honourable Ronald Campbell, Mr. Lloyd, political assistant, and Lieutenant Lysons, as orderly officer, reached Russell's bivouac on the night of the 27th, and went eastward at half-past three on the morning of the 28th. Buller left his bivouac at the same time and crept, with the utmost difficulty, though shielded by the morning mist, up a steep path, "hardly passable for mounted men" in a re-entering angle of the mountain, to the summit, which could not have been gained in the face of serious opposition.

Although the Zulus on the top were surprised, they stood to their weapons, killed two officers, and mortally wounded one man. Colonel Wood, who had just received the news that he had been awarded the grant of £100 a year for distinguished service, dismounted, and was leading his horse up the steep slope, with his Staff and a small escort, a little ahead of some men under Colonel Weatherly, when, in the words of the *Official Report*:

At a short distance from the top, a severe and well-directed fire was opened on the party from some holes in the rocks above. By this fire, Mr. Lloyd was mortally wounded, and Colonel Wood's horse was killed, and as these and other casualties appeared to be caused by shots from one cavern in particular, Colonel

Wood ordered Colonel Weatherley to send some of his men to the front to dislodge the Zulus from this hiding-place. As there was some little delay in obeying this order. Captain Ronald Campbell dashed forward, followed by Lieutenant Lysons (known throughout this campaign as 'the boy'), and three men of the 90th, but just as they reached the dark entrance of the cavern, Captain Campbell fell dead, shot through the head by a Zulu lying hidden within. His death was speedily avenged by his companions, and the cavern was cleared.

Colonel Wood saw Campbell and Lloyd buried lower down the slope, while Buller cleared the summit of the mountain, three miles in length by half that distance in width, collecting two thousand head of cattle. Soon afterwards, Buller saw a Zulu Army about six miles off, estimated at 20,000 strong, coming from the south-east. About an hour later, Wood saw the Zulu Army, and ordered Russell to get into position on the Zunguin Nek. There was some difficulty in identifying the spot, and Russell took up a position, six miles from the place intended. Buller went down the west side of the mountain, harassed by natives from the caves, and the Zulus closed with the *assegai* on the scattered members of the party.

> One officer and about sixteen men were lost, and at this spot fell Mr. Piet Uys, the gallant leader of the Boer Contingent, who had rendered such valuable services to Colonel Wood's column.

Buller's troops got greatly disorganised, and would probably have been cut to pieces, had the Zulu main body attacked. As it was, the small loss sustained was mainly at the hands of the inhabitants of the mountain, the modern Troglodytes. The expedition got back to Kambula camp with less loss than might have been expected. But Wood had assuredly created a diversion for the General. He sent Lord Chelmsford this telegram:

> We assaulted the Inhlobane successfully yesterday and took some thousands of cattle; but while on the top, about 20,000 Zulus, coming from Ulundi, attacked us, and we suffered considerable losses, the enemy retaking captured cattle. Nearly all our natives deserted last evening.

Colonel Wood's report of this affair was as follows:

I have the honour to report that the Inhlobane mountain was successfully assaulted and its summit cleared at daylight on the 28th by Lieutenant-Colonel Buller, C.B., with the mounted riflemen and the 2nd battalion Wood's Irregulars, under the command of Second Commandant Roberts, who worked under the general direction of Major Leet, commanding the corps. I joined Colonel Russell's column at dusk on the 27th inst., at his bivouac about five miles west of Inhlobane mountain. I had with me the Hon. R. Campbell, district staff officer of No. 4 column, Mr. Lloyd, my political assistant, Lieutenant Lysons, 90th Light Infantry, orderly officer, and my mounted personal escort, consisting of eight men 90th Infantry, and six natives under Umtonga, one of Panda's sons.

Soon after 3 a.m. I rode eastward with these details, and at daylight got on Colonel Buller's track, which we followed. Colonel Weatherly met me, coming westward, having lost his way the previous night, and I directed him to move on towards the sound of the firing, which was now audible on the north-east face of the mountain, where we could see the rear of Colonel Buller's column near the summit. I followed Colonel Weatherly and commenced the ascent of the mountain immediately behind the Border Horse, leading our horses. It is impossible to describe in adequate terms the difficulty of the ascent which Colonel Buller and his men had successfully made—not without loss, however, for horses killed and wounded helped to keep us on his track where the rocks afforded no evidence of his advance.

We soon came under fire from an unseen enemy. Ascending more rapidly than most of the Border Horse, who had got off the track, with my staff and escort, I passed to the front, and, with half-a-dozen of the Border Horse, when within a hundred feet of the summit, came under a well-directed fire from our front and both flanks, poured in from behind huge boulders of rocks, Mr. Lloyd fell mortally wounded at my side, and as Captain Campbell and one of the escort were carrying him on to a ledge rather lower, my horse was killed, falling on me.

I directed Colonel Weatherly to dislodge one or two Zulus who were causing us most of the loss, but as his men did not advance rapidly, Captain Campbell, Lieutenant Lysons, and three men of the 90th, jumping over a low wall, ran forward and charged into a cave, where Captain Campbell, leading in the most gallant and determined manner, was shot dead.

Lieutenant Lysons and Private Fowler followed closely on his footsteps, and one of them, for each fired, killed one Zulu and dislodged another, who crawled away by a subterraneous passage, reappearing higher up the mountain. At this time, we were assisted by the fire of some of Colonel Buller's men on the summit. Colonel Weatherly asked for permission to move down the hill to rejoin Colonel Buller's track, which he had lost, and by which he later gained the summit without further casualties. At this time, he had lost three dead and about six or seven wounded. Mr. Lloyd was now dead, and we brought his body and that of Captain Campbell halfway down the hill, where we buried them, still being under fire, which, however, did us no damage.

I then moved slowly round under the Inhlobane mountain to the westward to see how Colonel Russell's force had progressed, bringing with the escort a wounded man of the Border Horse and a herd of sheep and goats driven by one of Umtonga's men. We stopped occasionally to give the wounded man stimulants, unconscious of the fact that a very large Zulu force was moving on our left across our front. We were about half-way under the centre of the mountain when Umtonga saw and explained to me by signs that a large Zulu Army was close to us. From an adjacent hill I had a good view of the force. It was marching in five columns with "horns," and dense "chest," the Zulu normal attack formation.

The Ulundi Army being, as I believe, exhausted by its rapid march, did not close on Colonel Buller, who descended after Uhamu's people the western point of the mountain.

We reached camp at 7 p.m., and Colonel Buller, hearing that some of Captain Barton's party were on foot about ten miles distant, at once started in heavy rain with led horses and brought in seven men, as we believe the sole survivors of the Border Horse and Captain Barton's party, who, being cut off when on my track, retreated over the north end of the Ityenteka Range.

During the night of the 28th, all Wood's Irregulars deserted, and early in the morning all the Dutchmen left the camp. Spies brought information that the whole Zulu force was marching on Kambula camp, but as it was short of fuel a party was sent up the mountain. A dense fog enveloped the camp, and when it lifted, at ten o clock, the Zulu army was seen in motion. Without undue haste the wood party was recalled, dinners quietly ordered for half-past twelve, after which the tents were struck. This act appeared to the Zulus as preparatory to a retreat, so they hastened their attack, the advance having previously been deliberate. But the proverb has it that "*more haste makes worse speed.*" And the Zulu hurry enabled Wood to defeat one wing before the other came into action.

There were at least 20,000 of Ketchwayo's lieges, and all the force Wood had to dispose of was the 90th Light Infantry, a battalion of the 13th Light Infantry, and the battery with a few mounted men, the total being 1,998. Thus, there were more than ten Zulus to each man in laager or in the outlying fort two hundred yards to the eastward. This fort at its western end was connected by a palisade sixty yards long with a cattle *laager* lying south on the brow of a steep bluff. The fort was occupied by companies of the 13th and 90th. Dinner being got over—but to avoid repetition, it is better to cite Colonel Wood's report:

> The camp was vigorously attacked by four Zulu regiments from 1.30 to 5.30 p.m. The chief command was exercised by Mnyamane, who did not come under fire, and Tymgwayo. The army left Ulundi on the 24th inst.; four regiments were left near Ekowe and four left at Ulundi. Early in the forenoon Captain Raaff, who was out reconnoitring, sent me one of Oham's men. He told me he was behind with the captured cattle. He put his head badge into his pocket and was recognised by a friend who was ignorant of his having joined us. He marched with the Zulu Army to the Umvolosi. At daybreak he went out drinking and persuaded his companions that they were recalled, ran away to Raaff's men, and told them how the attack would be made at dinner-time.
>
> About 11 a.m. we saw dense masses approaching, moving in file, towards the Inhlobane mountain from near the Umvolosi. Two companies which were out wood-cutting were recalled, the, cattle brought into *laager* with the exception of about 200 which had strayed away from those whose duty it was to herd them, in the direction of the natives. At 1.30 the action commenced. The mounted riflemen under Colonels Buller and Russell engaged an enormous crowd of men on the north side

of the camp. Being unable to check them, the men retired inside the *laager* followed by the Zulus until they were within three hundred yards, when their advance was checked by the accurate firing of the 90th Light Infantry, and the Zulus spread out to front and rear of camp.

The attack on our left had slackened, when, at 2.15 p.m., heavy masses attacked our right front and right rear. The enemy, well supplied with Martini-Henry rifles and ammunition, occupied a hill not seen from the *laager*, and opened such an accurate fire, though at long ranges, that I was obliged to withdraw a company of the 13th Regiment at the right rear of the *laager*. The front, however, of the cattle *laager* was stoutly held by another company of the 13th. They could not see the right rear, and as the Zulus were coming on boldly, I ordered Major Hackett of the 90th Light Infantry with two companies to advance over the slope. The Zulus retired from their immediate front, but the companies being heavily flanked I ordered them back; whilst bringing them in Major Hackett was dangerously, and as I fear, mortally wounded.

The two mule guns were admirably worked by Lieutenant Nicholson, R.A., in redoubt, until he was mortally wounded. The horses of the other four guns, under Lieutenants Bigge and Slade, were sent inside the *laager* when the Zulus came within 1,000 yards of them, but these officers, with their men and Major Tremlett, R.A., to all of whom great credit is due, remained in the open the whole of the engagement. In Major Hackett's counter-attack Lieutenant Bright, 90th Light Infantry, an accomplished draughtsman and a most promising young officer, was wounded, and died here during the night. At 5.30 p.m., seeing the attack slackening, I ordered out a company of the 1-13th Regiment to the right rear of the *laager* to attack some Zulus who had crept into the *laager*, but who had been unable to remove the cattle.

I took Captain Laye's company of the 90th Light Infantry to the edge of the *krantz* on the right front of the cattle *laager*, and they did great execution among a mass of retreating Zulus. Commandant Raaff at the same time ran on with some of the men to the rear of the camp and did similar execution. I ordered out the mounted men, who, under Colonel Buller, pursued for seven miles the flying Zulus retreating on our left front, chiefly companies of the Amaqulosi under Umewayo, killing great numbers, the enemy being too much exhausted to fire in their own defence. From those we have taken, it appears that the column first attacked our left, and then, being repulsed, went round to our front. Rear and right were composed of the Nokeuke and Umbonambi and Unkandampenvu regiments. The Amaqulosi attacked the front, the Ulundi and Umcityu the right front, and the Ngobamokosi the right. We are still burying Zulus, of whom 500 are close to our camp.

This account is clear and precise, save in one point. Colonel Wood characteristically omits the part of Hamlet in the drama. No one would guess from it that it was by Colonel Wood's order Buller and Russell drew the fire of the enemy and compelled the premature attack. The little party of horsemen, some hundred strong, had attacked a body of not less than 2,000 men, and, as the *Official Report* says, Zulu discipline, though good, was not good enough for this sort of thing. So, the right horn of the army was rolled back when it came up to the attack on the north. The left worked round the western face, and the centre came up again at the southern front. A company of the 13th, in the cattle *laager*, had to withdraw, and the attack was evidently about to be pushed on to the main *laager*, when Wood ordered a counter attack by two companies of the 90th, under Major Hackett.

This did good for a while; but the foe was too strong, and the companies fell back within the laager. The Zulus continued to attack for three hours more but were always driven back by the steadiness of the fire from the *laager* and the fort, and the coolness with which the guns of Tremlett's battery were served mainly from a point between the two. At half-past five, when the men were becoming rather weary, it was a question in the mind of more than one spectator which side would tire the sooner. The Zulus began to shake; and then Wood threw a company of the 13th into the cattle *laager*, to retake it, and a company of the 90th, which he accompanied on to the verge of the bluff, where they poured a heavy fire into the mass of foes below.

If there had been any doubt of the issue before, that settled the business, and Buller and Russell and their mounted men, who had been assisting in the defence within the laager, now mounted and turned the retreat into a rout, pursuing for seven miles, and until night fell, the almost unresisting throng, who unlike Englishmen, as history tells us, did know when they were beaten. Moreover, they realised the fact so thoroughly that there was no more Zulu trouble in the Kambula district, though Utrecht, close by, offered to the men of Ketchwayo a tempting object for loot, since, save by a small fort, it was otherwise undefended than by the Kambula camp in advance of it. It almost goes without saying that it turned out afterwards Colonel Wood had underestimated the number of Zulus killed. In a telegram to the general he put it at 1,200. A Zulu who was present afterwards said that:

> The Ngobamokosi could not face the bullets. . . . No one could face them without being struck. . . . . The Umbonambi regiment . . . . were cut to pieces—quite destroyed.

The total loss could not have been less on the Zulu side than 2,000 men.

Reinforcements having arrived from England the distribution of the force on the frontier was altered, and Major-General Newdigate was posted to the command of the Second Division, including the Utrecht District. But the little body that had done such glorious work at Kambula was not broken up. It retained its independence, and a free hand, under the title of "Brigadier-General Wood's Flying Column." These arrangements were promulgated on the 13th April, and on the 14th Wood took up fresh ground for his camp for sanitary reasons, some 600 or 700 yards to the west of that which had seen such good work on the 29th March.

The loss of life on the 28th at Inhlobana (the loss in white men) had been no less than twelve officers and eighty men killed, and seven wounded, out of a strength of 400 under Buller, to say nothing of the native loss, which could not be ascertained owing to the desertion of seven-eighths of the survivors. On the following day the loss was only eighteen non-commissioned officers and men killed, and eight officers and fifty-seven non-commissioned officers and men wounded, but there were many subsequent fatalities among the latter. A *Gazette Extraordinary* was issued at Newcastle, Natal, on March 31st, in which Sir Bartle Frere said:

> The entire defeat of the determined attack made by this large force, after an action of five hours' duration, and the pursuit of the routed Zulus for several miles, cannot fail to have a great effect on the whole Zulu force, and on the future progress of the war. H. E. the High Commissioner begs Lord Chelmsford will convey to Colonel Wood and the officers and men spe-

cially named by him, the High Commissioner's thanks for the effectual services thus rendered by the 4th column.

The Secretary for War thought it sufficient to say that it "seems" the force had acted with a gallantry and determination worthy of great praise. Lord, then Colonel, Stanley is not by any means an old woman, but one cannot avoid thinking, in this connection, of Hamlet's reproof to his mother—"*Seems, Madam, nay it is; I know not seems.*"

After the Kambula fight, as has been said, the Zulu army dispersed, small raiding parties only approaching the Transvaal frontier, mostly in the Pongola Valley; but Wood is not the man to leave much to chance, and he had patrols constantly moving through the district. In May, the patrols pushed in various directions to discover the easiest approaches to Ulundi. On the 8th of the month, the Flying Column left Kambula, and moved, in a south-easterly direction, across the Umvolosi River. On the 20th, with a patrol, the brigadier searched for and buried the remains of some Europeans who had fallen on the 28th March. On the 2nd of June the Flying Column took its place four miles in front of the Second Division, and mostly kept that relative position up to and during the march to Ulundi.

It, indeed, went towards Landtman's Drift on the Buffalo River on the 7th June, and returned on the 15th, escorting 600 waggons, and other vehicles, containing six weeks' supplies, and the following day again went ahead of the Second Division. On the 27th, the brigadier despatched his mounted troops to his left, and destroyed ten military *kraals*, without opposition, the Zulus being concentrated at Ulundi. On July 3rd, he crossed the Umvolosi and reconnoitred over the Ulundi plain. The next was the momentous day, and here Lord Chelmsford may be permitted to speak for himself:

> Umvolosi River, near Ulundi.
> July 4th, 1879.
> This morning a force under my command, consisting of the 2nd division under Major-General Newdigate, numbering 1,870 Europeans, 530 natives, and 8 guns, and the Flying Column under Brigadier-General Wood, numbering 2,192 Europeans and 573 natives, 4 guns and 2 Gatlings, crossed the Umvolosi River at 6.15, and marching in a hollow square, ammunition and entrenching-tool carts and bearer company in its centre, reached an excellent position between Nodwengo and Ulundi about half-past eight a.m. This had been observed by Colonel

Buller the day before.

Soon after half-past seven the Zulu Army was seen leaving its bivouacs and advancing on every side.

The engagement was shortly afterwards commenced by the mounted men.

By nine o clock the attack was fully developed. At half-past nine the enemy wavered; the 17th Lancers, followed by the remainder of the mounted men, attacked them, and a general rout ensued. By noon Ulundi was in flames, and during the day all military *kraals* of the Zulu Army and in the valley of the Umvolosi were destroyed. At two p.m. the return march to the camp of the column commenced.

Lord Chelmsford brought especially to the notice of the Secretary for War the name of Brigadier-General Wood, who had become Sir Evelyn eleven days before. Three days later, Lord Chelmsford wrote again to Colonel Stanley:

> I cannot refrain from bringing again to your special notice the names of Brigadier-General Evelyn Wood, V.C, C.B. . . . . whose service during the advance towards Ulundi from the advanced base, and during the recent successful operations near Ulundi, have been invaluable.
>
> Brigadier-General Wood, although suffering at times severely in bodily health, has never spared himself, but has laboured incessantly night and day to overcome the innumerable difficulties which have had to be encountered during the advance through a country possessing no roads.

Now this was very nice of Lord Chelmsford, for it is evident from the *Official Report* that it was Sir Evelyn Wood's column which really won the victory of Ulundi. This may be seen from the following slight narrative. It was Colonel Buller, with the mounted men of the Flying Column, who on the 3rd July found the nature of the country and the strength and position of the enemy's forces. It was they who crossed the Umvolosi in the morning at 6 o clock. It was they who began the battle, and it was the 13th which bore the brunt of the Zulu attack. When the Zulus broke under the lances of the 17th, it was the mounted men of the Flying Column who completed the rout. They also burnt the *kraals*, which finished the business, except the capture of Ketchwayo.

On the 10th of July, the Flying Column marched towards Kwamag-wasa, and reached that deserted Mission Station the next day, when the construction of a fort was at once commenced. From the 13th to the 15th it marched to St. Pauls. On the day after Ulundi fight, how-ever. Sir Evelyn wrote in his report of the action as follows:

His Excellency has frequently been good enough to speak with approbation of the order, regularity, and celerity of this column. I feel that eighteen months of incessant work in the field, which has not been without anxiety, more or less constant, makes it advisable, both in the interest of the service and for the sake of my own health and efficiency, that I should have a relaxation of work, if only for a short time. I desire, therefore, to place on record that the good service done by this column is due to the cheerful, untiring obedience of soldiers of all ranks, which has rendered my executive duties a source of continued pleasure, and to the efforts of the undermentioned staff, regimental and departmental officers, many of whom have worked day and night to carry out my wishes.

On the next day Lord Chelmsford wrote:

The lieutenant-general commanding desires to place on record his hearty appreciation of the gallantry and steadiness displayed by all ranks of the force under his command during the Battle of Ulundi.

He added:

The two columns being about to separate, the Lieutenant-General begs to tender his best thanks to Brigadier-General E. Wood, V.C., C.B., for the assistance rendered him during the recent operations.

This praise cannot be said to have been overdone. But there was now one at hand whose praise is praise indeed, seeing he well knows how to convey every shade of censure. In a letter of the 9th from Port Durnford, Sir Garnet Wolseley said:

My dear Wood, Just a line to congratulate you on all you have done for the State. You and Buller have been the bright spots in this miserable war, and all through I have felt proud that I num-bered you both amongst my friends and companions-in-arms.

This was followed up, on the 17th, by the following General Order from the same staunch friend:

> In notifying to the army in South Africa that Brigadier-General Wood, V.C., C.B., and Lieutenant-Colonel Buller, C.B., are about to leave Zululand for England, General Sir Garnet Wolseley desires to place on record his high appreciation of the services they have rendered during the war, which their military ability and untiring energy have so very largely contributed to bring to an end. The success which has attended the operations of the Flying Column is largely due to General Wood's genius for war, to the admirable system he has established in his command, and to the zeal and energy with which his ably conceived plans have been carried out by Colonel Buller.

Just a week later, Lord Chelmsford, who had resigned, warmed up a little, and in a speech he made at Maritzburg, he said:

> I never would have believed it possible for any general to receive such assistance and devotion as I have experienced from my men . . . It would be invidious to particularise individuals and services, but, when I look back eighteen months, two names stand out in broad relief, the names of Wood and Buller. I can say that these two have been my right and left supporters during the whole of my time in this country.

The next day he wrote to Wood:

> My hearty congratulations on your promotion to K.C.B.; it ought to have been given to you months ago. As the authorities have apparently woke up and realised the fact that you had not in any way been rewarded for your good work in the old Colony and at the beginning of this war, I hope they will also understand that a good deal is still due to you for Ulundi.

In a *Narrative of the Field Operations connected with the Zulu War of 1879*, published in 1881 by Messrs. Sampson Low and Co., I find some interesting notes on Sir Evelyn Wood. At Keiskamma Hoek, Mr. F. W. Streatfield, the author, says:

> I had never met Colonel Wood before, though I knew him well by reputation. I am thankful to say it was my good fortune to serve under him for two months, and most thoroughly did I appreciate the privilege of having such a soldier as my

commanding-officer and such a man as my friend . . . I feel grateful indeed to him for many an arduous duty and weary march made light by the kindly tone in which the order was given that they should be done; and for the many pleasant and peaceful hours passed in his tent, where he ever ceased to be the commanding officer and became the genial, warm-hearted friend, with never varying kindness and hospitality. Let not the reader imagine that a duty slurred over, or ineffectually carried out, would meet with but a gentle rebuke from Colonel Wood. Far from it. On duty he is to others as to himself, hard as adamant; and woe betide the careless, slovenly soldier who happens to serve under him.

I learn further from Mr. Streatfield's pages that, one night, Colonel Wood had a narrow escape on a patrol at Buffalo Heights:

Through not hearing a soldier's challenge. He was shot at at short range, but luckily missed.

Colonel Wood got fever in May, 1878, but was "as well as ever" by the middle of June, thanks to the care taken of him in "Browns House," as the hospital was called, "near Hudson's Store."

Archibald Forbes, in the famous dispatch he took to the frontier, 110 miles, in fourteen hours, riding through the night, said:

At Ulundi, Evelyn Wood's face was radiant with the rapture of the fray as he rode up and down behind his regiment exposed to a storm of missiles.

On the 5th August, Sir Evelyn left Cape Town for England, and ten days later the following despatch was sent to the Secretary of State for the Colonies by Sir Bartle Frere:

I cannot permit Major-General Sir H. E. Wood, V.C, K.C.B., and Colonel Redvers Buller, V.C., C.B., to leave this colony without venturing to call the attention of Her Majesty's Government to the political services rendered by these officers during the two years and a half they have served in South Africa. It is not my province, nor is it necessary, I should say a word regarding the military services they have performed, and I have already brought to the notice of Her Majesty's Government the important bearing which the position of Sir H. E. Wood's column in Zululand from January to July, had on the safety of

Natal and the Transvaal; but I would beg to call attention to the excellent political effects of the dealings of these two officers with the colonial forces and with the colonists in general.

Up to 1878 there had always been among the colonists somewhat of a dread of the strict discipline which was, as they thought, likely to be enforced by a military officer were they to serve under him, and a great distrust of Her Majesty's officers generally to conduct operations against the Kaffirs. The feeling has now, I believe, disappeared among all who have served under General Wood and Colonel Buller. They have shown the colonists that military officers can deal with volunteers as with their own men and lead them to assured victory without sacrificing or risking more than is necessary in so doing.

To the experience of their treatment of officers and men under them, is largely due the readiness with which officers of the regular army are now appointed to positions in the Colonial forces in the Colony, and the good feeling which obtains at this moment between the Imperial and Colonial troops now in the field in Zululand. I would particularly notice the influence which both officers gained over their Dutch auxiliaries and the Dutch population of the Transvaal districts bordering on Zululand. I believe that whenever Sir E. Wood and his gallant second-in-command may serve again in the Transvaal, they will find all who served under them in Zululand anxious again to join Her Majesty's forces in any capacity that may be desired.

And on the 16th of October Sir A. Horsford, Military Secretary at Army Head-Quarters, informed Sir Evelyn Wood that a communication had been received from the Colonial Office, bringing to notice the very valuable political services rendered by him while in command of a column in Zululand; and informing him that this communication had afforded much gratification to the commander-in-chief, who had caused a record of the same to be made in the records of the Department, where it lies entombed among a vast amount of much more curious matter.

Before Sir Evelyn left South Africa, he received a silver shield from the inhabitants of Cape Colony, and an address with a handsome piece of plate from the people of Natal. But it was when he landed at Plymouth, on August 26th, that he learnt, once more, the people of England are not ungrateful to their heroic servants. At various points he was recognised and heartily greeted; but it was in his own county of Essex that the popular welcome took the warmer tone of personal friendship. When he had paid the necessary visit to the Adjutant-General, Sir Evelyn took train at Fenchurch Street for Rainham, accompanied by his wife. Lord Hatherley, his uncle, and a number of friends. At the little station, which was decked with bright bunting, dank with unintermittent rain, he was met by Sir Thomas Lennard, his brother-in-law.

Nearly every house and every church along the road to Belhus was bright with national flags, and at the entrance to the demesne there was a profuse display of ensigns and devices, while guards of honour of the 2nd Essex Artillery and the 1st and 15th Essex Rifles were in attendance. One device bore the legend "Welcome Home," and another contained illustrations of Sir Evelyn's medals and decorations. He was received with hearty cheers from a large assembly, including many of the leading people of the neighbourhood and indeed the county. The vicar of the parish presented an address conceived in an excellent spirit and prefaced and followed by a speech quite unexceptionable in manner and matter. In his reply Sir Evelyn said:

> One of the most pleasant moments of my life in South Africa was when I saw the way in which my men said 'Goodbye' to me—the men of whom, as it was commonly said, I worked their souls out, the men I worked with day after day and night after night, and whom I had necessarily treated with the sternest discipline—these men in saying 'Goodbye' to me said it in a manner I can never forget. . . . . With the soldiers under me, from the buglers to the colonels, as I was telling the adjutant-general this morning, during the eighteen months I have been in South Africa, I have never had a single disagreement.

A hearty cheer followed the conclusion of the brief speech, and then a procession was formed through the village of Aveley and into the park at the other end, a mile away. The procession was headed by about forty yeoman farmers of the district, followed by the band of the training ship Cornwall and the volunteers with their bands. The general's carriage had the horses detached, and was drawn by some fifty labourers, who dragged it to the fine old mansion where Sir Evelyn's mother was waiting to greet her honoured son. Sir Thomas and Lady Barrett Lennard dispensed liberal hospitality to all comers.

Some days before, at a meeting in Chelmsford, it had been resolved to offer Sir Evelyn a county welcome in the county town, and this decision was ratified by a larger meeting at the Cannon Street Hotel. But other honours were to intervene; he was knighted by the Queen at Balmoral on the 9th September, and was received by the Prime Minister, Lord Beaconsfield, at Hughenden Manor on the 30th of September. He was present at the Livery dinner of the Fishmongers' Company, of which his grandfather and father had been members, where he paid the warmest tribute of admiration to numbers of soldiers, living and departed, who had done their duty in the Gaika, or Kaffir, and in the Zulu campaigns. In rebutting the absurd accusations of inhumanity against the troops, he casually said:

> I can assure you that the only Zulu I personally chastised was one who declined to help us to carry a decrepit woman from a mountain where she must have starved. When I tell you, it was the man's mother, you will pardon this practical effort to induce the heathen to honour his parent.

The county demonstration took place on the 15th October at Chelmsford, where a platform was erected in front of the Shire Hall, enclosing one of the guns captured in the Crimean War. All the notabilities of the county were present, and Sir Evelyn, with his wife and eldest daughter, arrived from Danbury Palace, accompanied by the Bishop of St. Albans. He was received by a guard of honour of the 1st Essex A.B. Volunteers, and a large crowd, for the day was observed as a general holiday, heartily cheered the brilliant Essex soldier, who wore his uniform as Colonel of the 90th Light Infantry. Sir Charles Du Cane presented the sword of honour, as well as the service of plate, and happily cited the confession of Ketchwayo that it was the victory of Kambula which gave the mortal blow to the Zulu power. The sword bore on the blade an inscription to the effect that it was presented to Sir Evelyn:

> In recognition of the eminent services rendered by him to his country during the recent arduous campaign in Zululand, and of the conspicuous zeal, energy, and gallantry, which have distinguished his entire military career.

The speech in reply laid down the principle of action of an English officer:

> Whatever party, whatever policy may direct the wars which are the result of England's Imperial range, the true soldier always fights for home and country. It was well said 'Pro aris et focis'

232

is the life of patriotism. Battles are no longer fought on the hearthstones of these islands, but on the boundaries where our vast rule has extended; and whether it is in Africa or in Afghanistan that the soldier fights, he resembles the spell-bound hero of old legends, who travelled in a circle over hundreds of miles but never got far away from home.

In the evening about 400 gentlemen sat down to a banquet in the Corn Exchange, which was gay with decorations and trophies bearing the names of battles wherein the guest of the day chiefly distinguished himself. Once more he assigned the praise to his comrades, for, as Archibald Forbes had somewhere said:

It is in Evelyn Wood's company that one hears least of Evelyn Wood.

A ball wound up the festivities of the day.

The last of the series of banquets was unique. On November 1st, the Bar of England entertained Sir Evelyn Wood at dinner in the Hall of the Middle Temple, the Attorney-General in the chair, while among the guests were all the judges who were not on circuit. Sir John Holker made an admirable speech in proposing the toast of the evening to the hero of Kambula, who had been for five and a half years entitled to wear wig and gown. Although, three centuries before, Drake had been honoured with a banquet in Middle Temple Hall, yet he was not a lawyer. And although Lord Erskine, like Sir Evelyn, had been both midshipman and soldier before he was lawyer, while the first Lord Chelmsford had served in the navy and fought at Copenhagen before being called to the Bar, yet the fact remains that the banquet of All Saints day, 1879, was, and will probably long remain, like a notable of old time concerning whom Seneca wrote:

Quaeris Alcidae parem?
Nemo est nisi ipse.
(Seek Alcides match?
There is no one but himself.)

In a speech delivered by Sir Evelyn at Grocers' Hall on the 25th November in the following year, I find a passage very characteristic of the man; and this appears to be a convenient connection in which to insert it. Referring to a proposal then in the air for abolishing regimental colours, Sir Evelyn remarked:

It is suggested that they are cumbersome and are the cause of sacrifices. After all they are what?—a coloured rag on a stick, and is it worthwhile to risk men's lives for a piece of tawdry silk? You might as well say that because honour is invisible, and faith impalpable, they do not exist as load-stars for the mind. Colours are potent to check disaster, to rally fugitives, to inspire attack. In the confusion of battle, when formations become disordered and men's nerves are shaken, they act as a sort of movable fortress; a breastwork made up of a determined sense of duty; an ideal round which leading spirits group and form an impregnable reality that snatches victory, and in saving an army preserves the honour of the country. We read how Napoleon at Areola, how Halkett at Waterloo, and many other leaders at critical moments, electrified their soldiers by bearing colours to the front.

Whatever continental armies may do, I hope that we, whose few soldiers have often to withstand the shock of overwhelming numbers of brave savages, will not give up this strong incentive for men to hang together. . . . The chivalry that is shown in the defence of any high ideal, whatever may be its symbol, is surely never wasted. The actors . . . may perish, but the example remains, and their history will serve as an inspiration in the future. Were this a simple and technical question, I would apologise for touching on it, but it is to my mind a moral question interesting to all Britons and involving some of the brightest aspects of the gloom of warfare.

Meanwhile Sir Evelyn had been back to Zululand on one of the saddest missions that was ever confided to any man. I left out of the brief story of his services in the war against Ketchwayo all mention of the death of Prince Louis Napoleon. That most pathetic incident in a campaign full of heroic memoirs deserves a section to itself. The late Prince Imperial of France, who had his "baptism of fire" nine years before in the first fight of the campaign which ended the Third Empire, had frankly given his services to the country that lent him a refuge and had passed, with credit, through the Royal Military Academy at Woolwich.

He had gallantly volunteered for active work in Zululand, though he was "the only son of his mother and she was a widow." Great had been the searchings of heart among some of the highest in England when the request to be allowed to go out was received. Yet how could it be refused? He was a soldier and, as the fates would have it, a British soldier.

The Zulu power was *hostis humani generis*. As no dynastic or international questions were involved in the war, there could be no better opportunity for the young prince to put in practice the lessons he had received on Woolwich Common. So, he went out with the reinforcements, and on the redistribution of the force he was attached to the Staff of the Second Division, under Major-General Newdigate. There, as at Woolwich, he became an universal favourite. His special work was in connection with the quartermaster-general's department, including the selection of routes and camping grounds, under Lieut.-Col., now Major-General, Sir Richard Harrison. He had taken part in more than one of the necessary reconnaissances, and when the division had crossed the Blood River on the 31st of May, and moved onwards to Itelezi Hill on the following day, the country had been thoroughly examined, and not a Zulu had been seen; so it is no wonder that in sending an officer forward to select a camping ground only a small escort should be sent with him, namely six troopers of Bettington's Horse and six of Shepstone's Basutos.

The officer sent was the prince imperial. He was accompanied by Lieutenant Carey of the same department, who obtained permission to join the party, in no sense in command, but merely to obtain some verifications of observations made on a previous reconnaissance. A friendly Zulu was told off as a guide, but the six Basutos did not put in an appearance, and instead of waiting to have them replaced the party started off at a quarter past nine in the morning. At Itelezi Hill at ten o'clock the party was met by Col. Harrison, who spent some time in selecting a good water supply. Then leaving the A.Q.M.G., the party moved on and gained the summit of one of the flat-topped hills with which the region abounds. Here the prince made a sketch of the country, and about half-past two the party descended towards a *kraal* near the Itvotvosi River.

Up to this time no sign of the enemy had been noticed, but in the *kraal* some dogs were prowling about, and some remains of fresh food were found, showing that the *kraal* had been occupied but a short time before. The ground near the *kraal* was covered, save towards the north and northeast, with long coarse grass and Indian corn some five or six feet in height. At three o'clock the prince ordered the escort to "off-saddle" and "knee-halter" for grazing. The men made some coffee, and

235

a rest was enjoyed till ten minutes past four, when the Zulu guide reported that he had seen a Zulu come over the hill. Then the horses were caught and saddled and the prince gave the order "prepare to mount."

As the party was obeying, a volley was fired at them within fifteen yards of the hut by some Zulus, who had crept up through the grass. The troopers were unable to reply, as, by some astounding blunder or carelessness, their Martini–Henry carbines had been allowed to remain unloaded. The volley hit nobody, but it effectually frightened the horses, before the troopers had got control of them. The prince, in the act of giving the word "mount," was unable to get his leg over the saddle of his terrified charger, and he ran alongside it as it followed the plunging horses of the escort, which got completely out of hand. The prince then tried to vault on his horse, not a great feat for one so active as he was, but the saddle wallet he caught tore away, and so the horse escaped.

The Zulus apparently fired after the first lot of the runaways, and brought down one of them, while another trooper and the native guide remained at the *kraal* and were not seen alive afterwards. When Mr. Carey had got across a "*donga*," or dry bed of a storm stream, he learnt that the prince was left behind, and had been noticed running to the *donga* pursued by Zulus. The prince's horse being seen riderless, and it being apparent that the ground was occupied by a goodly number of the enemy, Mr. Carey made no effort to ascertain the fate of the prince, contenting himself with the assumption that he had fallen. So, he and four troopers bolted to the Second Division camp by Itelezi Hill.

In order to get away from the Zulus, Mr. Carey crossed the River Tombokala, and after riding four miles fell in with Sir Evelyn Wood and Colonel Buller, who were looking out for a track for the advance of the Flying Column the next day. By this time, it was all but dark, the 1st June in the Southern Hemisphere having as brief daylight as the 1st December in England. Nothing could be done but wait till the dawn, and that had scarcely shown itself when strong parties were sent out from both camps to examine the ground.

There was no long delay in ascertaining the worst. One trooper lay where he had been shot, the other nearer the *kraal*; and not far from the first one, in the bed of the *donga*, lay all that was mortal of the hope of the Imperialist party in France, and the death of him had been worthy of the illustrious race from which he sprung. He had turned and faced the savage horde and had emptied his revolver into them. Then his sword was useless against the *assegais*, and he fell where he stood, with sixteen wounds, all in front, like "the noblest Roman of them all."

A bier was formed with some lances and a blanket, and the body was carried to an ambulance, and so taken to the Second Division camp. The doctors used such preservative measures as were possible, and the body was dispatched to Pietermaritzburg the same evening, under an escort of the 17th Lancers. It reached the capital of Natal just a week later and was received in solemn state by the townsfolk. In due course it was taken to Durban and there embarked on H.M.S. *Boadicea*, which at Simon's Bay transferred it to H.M.S. *Orontes* for conveyance to England, where it was interred for a time in the chapel at Chiselhurst, and now rests in the Mausoleum at Farnborough.

The bereaved mother made up her mind soon after peace was restored by the capture of Ketchwayo, to visit the scene of her son's glorious death, and it was only natural that Sir Evelyn Wood, who had been the first to arrive on the scene, should be selected to accompany the Empress, who was—Oh, the pity of it!—left without a throne, a husband, or a child. This was in March, 1880.

In the previous December he had been appointed to the command of the Belfast District, with the rank of Brigadier-General, but he was only in charge of the Ulster headquarters seventeen days, when he was transferred, with a similar rank, to Chatham, and here he assumed command on the 12th January. His mission in March was obviously one requiring the utmost tact and delicacy. It occupied three months; and when the mournful visit had been paid, and the Empress returned to England, it was said, by a high official at court, of her cicerone, that "well as Evelyn Wood had done whatever he had put his hand to, he had never achieved a greater success" than as guide and companion to the august lady who had been left so conspicuously alone in the world.

LEONAUR

ALSO FROM LEONAUR
AVAILABLE IN SOFTCOVER OR HARDCOVER WITH DUST JACKET

ZULU:1879 *by D.C.F. Moodie & the Leonaur Editors*—The Anglo-Zulu War of 1879 from contemporary sources: First Hand Accounts, Interviews, Dispatches, Official Documents & Newspaper Reports.

THE RED DRAGOON *by W.J. Adams*—With the 7th Dragoon Guards in the Cape of Good Hope against the Boers & the Kaffir tribes during the 'war of the axe' 1843-48'.

THE RECOLLECTIONS OF SKINNER OF SKINNER'S HORSE *by James Skinner*—James Skinner and his 'Yellow Boys' Irregular cavalry in the wars of India between the British, Mahratta, Rajput, Mogul, Sikh & Pindarree Forces.

A CAVALRY OFFICER DURING THE SEPOY REVOLT *by A. R. D. Mackenzie*—Experiences with the 3rd Bengal Light Cavalry, the Guides and Sikh Irregular Cavalry from the outbreak to Delhi and Lucknow.

A NORFOLK SOLDIER IN THE FIRST SIKH WAR *by J W Baldwin*—Experiences of a private of H.M. 9th Regiment of Foot in the battles for the Punjab, India 1845-6.

TOMMY ATKINS' WAR STORIES: 14 FIRST HAND ACCOUNTS—Fourteen first hand accounts from the ranks of the British Army during Queen Victoria's Empire.

THE WATERLOO LETTERS *by H. T. Siborne*—Accounts of the Battle by British Officers for its Foremost Historian.

NEY: GENERAL OF CAVALRY VOLUME 1—1769-1799 *by Antoine Bulos*—The Early Career of a Marshal of the First Empire.

NEY: MARSHAL OF FRANCE VOLUME 2—1799-1805 *by Antoine Bulos*—The Early Career of a Marshal of the First Empire.

AIDE-DE-CAMP TO NAPOLEON *by Philippe-Paul de Ségur*—For anyone interested in the Napoleonic Wars this book, written by one who was intimate with the strategies and machinations of the Emperor, will be essential reading.

TWILIGHT OF EMPIRE *by Sir Thomas Ussher & Sir George Cockburn*—Two accounts of Napoleon's Journeys in Exile to Elba and St. Helena: Narrative of Events by Sir Thomas Ussher & Napoleon's Last Voyage: Extract of a diary by Sir George Cockburn.

PRIVATE WHEELER *by William Wheeler*—The letters of a soldier of the 51st Light Infantry during the Peninsular War & at Waterloo.

www.ingramcontent.com/pod-product-compliance
Lightning Source LLC
Chambersburg PA
CBHW032045080426
42733CB00006B/194